Weird and Tragic Shores

The Story of Charles Francis Hall, Explorer

Alfred A. Knopf   New York   1971

Chauncey C. Loomis

Weird and Tragic Shores

The Story of Charles Francis Hall, Explorer

to my father

No; there are no more sunny continents—no more islands of the blest—hidden under the far horizon, tempting the dreamer over the undiscovered sea; nothing but those weird and tragic shores, those cliffs of everlasting ice and mainlands of frozen snow, which have never produced anything to us but a late and sad discovery of the depths of human heroism, patience, and bravery, such as imagination could scarcely dream of.

—*Blackwood's Edinburgh Magazine,*
November 1855

acknowledgments

When I first began to consider Charles Francis Hall as a possible subject of a biography, I was encouraged by Alan Cooke, an Arctic historian and bibliographer presently at the Scott Polar Research Institute in Cambridge, England, and by his wife, Jane. Without their encouragement and help, I probably would not have even started to write this book. In the early stages of research, I also received encouragement and help from the late Paul Fenimore Cooper, who generously gave me the materials on Hall that he had gathered while he was writing his excellent book on King William Island, *Island of the Lost* (New York, 1961).

In the various phases of my research and writing, I was assisted by many institutions, many individuals—by the Cincinnati Historical Society, the Stefansson Collection at Dartmouth College, the Scott Polar Research Institute, the American Geographical Society, the Danish Ministry for Greenland, the Centre for Forensic Sciences, the Explorers Club, the United States Navy Observatory, the Arctic Institute of North America—by Evelyn Stefansson Neff, Erica Parmi, Louis Tucker, Dorothy Powers, Philip Lundeberg, Edward Towle, Howard Chapelle, Melvin Jackson, Herman Friis, John Teal, Eigel Knuth, Peter Dawes, William Davies, W. W. Phipps, Dr. Philip Nice, Dr. A. K. Perkons, D. M. Lucas, Donald Jackson, Darrel Mansell, Noel Perrin, James Epperson, Michael Rewa, Robert Hunter, Kenneth Paul. Such a cold list does not indicate the warmth of my appreciation.

I owe my particular gratitude to three institutions: to the Smithsonian Institution for giving me a postdoctoral research fellowship and access to the extraordinary Hall Collection; to the Center for Polar Archives at the National Archives for assistance in other archival research; to Dartmouth College for allowing me to pursue my eccentric interests without recrimination.

And I am particularly grateful to four individuals who have devoted much time to the book: to Barbara Cunningham, who typed in adversity; to Herbert Weinstock of Alfred A. Knopf, Inc., who edited with acumen; to Alison Wilson of the Center for Polar Archives, who displayed a genius for finding things of value in obscure corners of archives; and to Mrs. Wilson Follett, who followed the preparation of the book from beginning to end and gave it a final ruthless reading before it went to press.

Finally, I am grateful to those men who accompanied me on my own trips to the North: Job Potter, Bryan Pearson, Thomas Gignoux, William Barrett, Dr. Franklin Paddock.

contents

illustrations

Weird and Tragic Shores

The Story of Charles Francis Hall, Explorer

prologue

In the nineteenth century, Arctic exploration captured man's imagination just as space exploration has captured it today. The coldness and indifference of the Arctic, its beauty and terror, the unknown riches and dangers that lay in its unexplored vastness—all these appealed to man's capacity for wonder and his desire for challenge. The Victorian reading public followed the preparations of an expedition to the North with the same avid attention modern television viewers give to a space flight. Newspaper readers learned of iron sheathing on ships, experimental screw propellers, and ingenious methods of heating cabins, just as today we learn of nose cones, solid fuels, and oxygen support systems. Increasingly in the nineteenth century, the expeditions became a matter of national enterprise. The controversies aroused and the questions asked are familiar: Could not money and energy be better spent in more practical and humane ways? Was this purely a national enterprise, or was it the culmination of the work of many nations? Was science perhaps becoming too arrogant? Should such exploration be under military control, or was it best kept in the "private sector"?

Despite the growing questions and doubts, however, Arctic exploration continued to appeal to the popular imagination. The Arctic was a playground for man's mind, and many nineteenth-century books about the Far North were science fiction, imagining lost civilizations and strange creatures there. Jules Verne wrote some of his best nonfiction and most imaginative fantasy about the region; in both, he saw its exploration as a manifestation of man's Faustian yearning and unconquerable will. History seemed to confirm his interpretation.

In the first half of the nineteenth century, the British concentrated their attention on the search for a northwest passage, a search that had begun early in the sixteenth century

when John Cabot came on unknown land masses blocking
his course to the Orient. Cabot was looking for a short trade
route to Cathay, and for several centuries after his inadvertent
discovery of subarctic America expeditions in search of a
westward passage to the Orient remained business enterprises,
backed by hardnosed merchants whose motives were primarily
financial. The names of the explorers themselves—Frobisher,
Davis, Hudson, Bylot, Button, Baffin—may now be enveloped
in a romantic haze, but the purpose of their expeditions was
as clear and practical as the numbers in an Elizabethan account book. When those numbers began to show a massive
deficit, the first phase in the search ended; private merchants
could no longer afford to pour money into enterprises that
always ended in failure, and sometimes in disaster.

In the eighteenth century the British government played
an increasing role in the search, and the motives for it
changed. Early in the century there were still hopes that a
practical trade route might be found, but by late in the century it was evident that even if a passage were found it would
be of little mercantile value. As hopes for a trade route faded,
new motives for the quest emerged; it became a matter of
scientific curiosity and national prestige. Encouraged by the
Royal Society and impelled by a desire for British discovery,
the government dispatched naval expeditions, offered a reward of twenty thousand pounds for the discovery of a passage, and put constant pressure on the Hudson's Bay Company to prosecute the search while it plied its fur trade in
inland Canada.

The first two and a half centuries of exploration had been
an agonizing process of elimination. For almost two centuries
the mercantile nations of Europe hoped that a waterway
existed through temperate America, but their hope was
diminished by inland expeditions of fur traders and was
finally killed by the meticulous explorations of George Van-
couver up the west coast of the continent. For more than one

hundred years, other expeditions futilely probed the western
shores of Hudson's Bay, at the cost of much money and many
lives. By the end of the eighteenth century, the English recognized that if there was a passage, it lay far north—somewhere
in the unknown maritime Arctic above the Canadian mainland. Only two explorers had seen the shores of this supposed
polar sea: Samuel Hearne, in 1771, working for the Hudson's
Bay Company, reached the mouth of the Coppermine River,
and Alexander Mackenzie, in 1789, working for the North
West Company, descended the Mackenzie River to tidewater.
Neither Hearne nor Mackenzie carried his explorations much
beyond the mouth of the river.

With the onset of the Napoleonic wars Arctic exploration
temporarily ceased, and early in the nineteenth century, after
nearly three hundred years of exploration, the complexities
of Canada's Arctic Archipelago remained a mystery. The
reasons for its longstanding impenetrability are not hard to
find: any map of northern Canada speaks for itself. The
Archipelago and its outer defenses are an exploded jigsaw
puzzle: gulfs, bays, sounds, inlets, straits, islands, peninsulas
form a maze that was a nightmare to early navigators, a nightmare intensified by the eccentricities of magnetism so close
to the magnetic pole. For the bold and the optimistic, every
bay was a strait leading to the riches of the East; for the
timorous and the pessimistic, every strait was a bay that might
trap them forever. The history of the search for a northwest
passage is a history of mistaken identifications. John Cabot
thought that Newfoundland was the Asiatic mainland. Henry
Hudson, after groping through Hudson's Strait, sailed his
Discovery southward in Hudson's Bay toward disillusionment,
mutiny, and death, confident that he was in the Pacific.
Martin Frobisher thought that a bay in Baffin Island was a
strait leading to Asia. Luke Foxe thought that Roe's Welcome
Sound was a gulf. William Baffin and Sir John Ross, two
centuries apart, made a similar error: each in his time thought

that Lancaster Sound, the true entrance to the northwest passage, was a bay or an inlet.

The complex configurations of land and sea were bad enough in themselves, but added to them was another element, even another dimension: sea ice. For navigators the terror of the ice was its dual nature, its solidity and fluidity. It could pierce and crush, yet it was also ghostly and protean, appearing and disappearing in innumerable consistencies, shapes, and sizes. The ice made the geography of the maritime Arctic unstable and constantly shifting. A passage clear one year might be clogged with floe ice or solid pack the next. In one day a ship might be led by an open water lane, or "lead," into a trap that could close overnight and immobilize her for years. One afternoon in the fall of 1831, in minutes John Ross was able to walk on the ice from where the *Victory* was then frozen in to the place where she had been frozen in during the preceding winter; in a year the *Victory* had traveled only a few miles, and ultimately she had to be abandoned to the ice. Ross was a frequent victim of ice. When he peered down Lancaster Sound and thought he saw mountains closing it off into a bay, he was probably tricked by an Arctic looming —a mirage caused partly by the ice.

The Archipelago also had its secondary defenses: cold, darkness, starvation, and scurvy. The cold pierced even a ship well battened-down against the siege of winter; it made day-by-day life difficult, and it restricted movement outside the ship. For week after week, crews had to remain close to their iced-in ships, while all around them were bleak stretches of ice, bitter cold, and the depressing continuous darkness of the long Arctic winter. The psychological ordeal was as damaging as the physical.

In such a region starvation was always a threat, but an even greater threat was scurvy. Naval ships were usually well-enough stocked with foodstuffs to prevent starvation, but preserved foods were ineffective against scurvy. It could be held off with such an antiscorbutic as lime juice, but explorers had begun to discover that the best defense was fresh meat, and fresh meat was not easily available to men unfamiliar with the hunting techniques of the Eskimos. Scurvy was treacherous and debilitating, its effects showing only gradually: gums began to bleed, old sores to ache (a scurvy-ridden American sailor suffering severe pains in his knuckles remembered that twenty-five years before a schoolmaster had injured those knuckles with a ruler). The victim would become logy, depressed, irritable, and, most serious, prey to such a killing disease as pneumonia. Unchecked, scurvy inevitably led to a slow and miserable death.

The complexity of geography in Arctic Canada, the crushing power and protean nature of sea ice, the cold and the long night of Arctic winters, the dangers of starvation and scurvy, the history of failure and disaster in Arctic exploration—these all contributed to making nineteenth-century British expeditions carefully planned, magnificently mounted operations. Following the Napoleonic wars, British Arctic exploration was financed mainly by the government and was usually under the direct control of the Admiralty, which had gained in power, wealth and prestige during the wars; in the peace that followed them, exploration became a major outlet for the British navy's resources and energies, and the techniques of exploration took on a decidedly military cast.

The Second Secretary of the Admiralty, Sir John Barrow, was fascinated by the North, and when the famous whaling captain William Scoresby reported favorable ice conditions in 1817, Sir John immediately persuaded the navy to dispatch a series of expeditions to the north and northwest. In the three decades that followed, William Edward Parry, John and James Ross, George Back, and Sir John Franklin led explorations that gained more knowledge of the inner waters of the Arctic Archipelago than had been accumulated in the preceding two centuries, but there still was no discovery and navigation of a northwest passage. The expeditions of Parry, Ross, Back, and Franklin had simply proved that a northwest passage could no longer be considered a feasible trade route, and its discovery was no longer a way to instant profit. In 1844 Sir John Barrow could argue that knowledge was power, pointing to the Hudson's Bay Company as an example of how geographical exploration could generate power and, in turn, profit, but most Arctic experts knew that the sub-Arctic Canadian mainland was one thing, the high-Arctic Canadian islands another. It would be a long, long time before such barren land and water would yield a return on the investment of expensive and dangerous exploration.

But Sir John, intent on continuing the search, had another and more compelling argument than possible profits: national pride required it. He noted proudly that the British, in their various expeditions, had discovered the "doors of the northwest passage," and that they "would be laughed at by all the world for having hesitated to cross the threshold."[1] Sir John and others in the government, uncomfortably aware of Russian and French activities in the Arctic, feared that one of their rivals might navigate through the Archipelago before them. In a private letter to Lord Haddington, First Lord of the Admiralty, Sir John appealed to the pride of the Admiralty itself: "The Admiralty having done so much, it would be most mortifying and not very creditable to let another Naval Power complete what we have begun."[2]

The Admiralty was not alone in seeing exploration as a worthy national enterprise: the public press was chauvinistically enthusiastic about most expeditions that left Britain's shores. *Blackwood's Edinburgh Magazine,* always interested in the Arctic, compared British exploration to great battles fought by British armies and maintained that in spite of the luxuries of civilization, the British were still tough, and showed it in their Arctic explorations. "The Saxon Briton is no coward," it announced, but it went on to attribute English zeal in exploration particularly to "the Danish element of the British nation—the spirit of the religion of Odin still animates it." As for the French, *Blackwood's* allowed them to be "as brave as lions," but suggested that, unlike the British, "few of them could stand the intolerable ennui, sufferings, and darkness of two or three Arctic winters."[3] Patriotism, expressed as a competitive sense of national power and glory manifesting themselves in geographical discovery, played a large part in nineteenth-century exploration; as the century progressed, Englishmen, Russians, Americans, Danes, Norwegians, and Frenchmen planted their flags with patriotic fervor in Arctic wastes as if the prestige of their countries depended on it. Arctic exploration often involved cooperation between nations and undoubtedly was serious business, but at times it appeared to be an international game, with the top of the globe the playing field, the northwest passage and the North Pole the goals.

There were other motives, more supranational, ostensibly more idealistic. The quest for scientific knowledge, immediately useful or not, had become important, and such organizations as the Royal Society, the Geographical Society of London, and the British Association for the Advancement of Science acted as powerful pressure groups in favor of government support of costly expeditions. Even more persuasive to government than the special motives of the scientists themselves was the vast popularity of scientific activity. The researches in meteorology, magnetism, and hydrography carried out by Arctic expeditions were of little interest to laymen or to politicians, but during the early part of the nineteenth century a romantic image of science had captured the minds of the public—a popularized, idealized vision of science created by non-scientific imaginations and related only remotely to the painstaking processes of actual scientific investigation. To its many enthusiasts it was "the forefront of civilization"; its beneficent possibilities seemed endless. In 1845 the sophisticated George Henry Lewes wrote, "Science finds itself year by year, and almost day by day, advancing step by step, each accumulation of power adding to the momentum of its progress . . . Onward and forever onward, mightier and forever

mightier, rolls this wondrous tide of discovery."⁴ Exploration,
if not a pure science itself, was a form of discovery and an
exciting analogue to science: like science, at least in the popular mind, it involved man investigating the secrets of his
world—or, in the militant rhetoric of the period, "conquering
Nature."

Arctic exploration thus was partly a manifestation of nineteenth-century optimism. Many Victorians saw a challenge
around every corner and considered it axiomatic that all
challenges would be met and overcome by the zealous spirit
of nineteenth-century Western man. The great globe itself
offered one of the biggest challenges in its unexplored wastes,
and many expeditions were viewed as responses to that challenge. *Blackwood's* attributed unexplored regions to Providence, seeing them as "a reward and a stimulant to the
growing progress of mankind." It went on to speculate that
"the evident design of Providence in placing difficulties before
man is to sharpen his faculties for their mastery."⁵ The writer
simply assumed that mastery would come. Behind much nineteenth-century exploration lies the Victorian need "to strive,
to seek, to find, and not to yield." It was not by chance that
Tennyson expressed Ulysses' spiritual yearnings in terms of
physical exploration; Tennyson was fascinated by it and in
many of his poems related it to spiritual or intellectual quest.
Nor was he alone in doing so: the strenuous, the assertive,
the optimistic aspects of nineteenth-century thought took
clear and vivid form in the rigors of exploration, and the
men who found their way in ice or jungle, mountain or
desert, were often symbolized by the popular imagination
as heroic figures representing Man facing and overcoming
Nature.

Therefore, when an expedition sailed into unknown Arctic
waters, it bore the emotional involvement of many persons—
indeed, of the whole nation. By brains, brawn, and naval
efficiency, such an expedition was supposed to overcome

Nature at her most brutal and indifferent; it was supposed to make good the belief that man will prevail on his earth.

   In the summer of 1845, HMS *Erebus* and *Terror,* under the command of Sir John Franklin, sailed through Lancaster Sound into the labyrinth of Canada's Arctic Archipelago. The two ships, with one hundred and twenty-nine men aboard, had set out from England in May. On July 4, after a stormy Atlantic crossing, the expedition had arrived at the Whalefish Islands, off Greenland's west coast; there supplies were transferred from a tender, and final preparations were made for the voyage ahead. The tender returned to England bearing letters. "You have no conception how happy we are," one sailor wrote, and another exclaimed, "Sir John is such a good old fellow—we all have perfect confidence in him!"[6] After leaving the Whalefish Islands, the *Erebus* and *Terror* sailed to northern Baffin Bay in order to avoid its treacherous Middle Pack, a shifting mass of ice infamous to Arctic navigators. Finally, they reached Lancaster Sound, from which Franklin hoped to navigate through the complexities of the Arctic Archipelago to the Beaufort and Bering Seas. He was in search of a northwest passage.

   The last white men to see the *Erebus* and *Terror* were the crewmen of a whaling ship, the *Enterprise.* While cruising Baffin Bay late in July, Captain Martin of the *Enterprise* sighted the *Erebus* and *Terror* moored to an iceberg at latitude 75° 12', longitude 61° 6'. Captain Martin sailed his whaler close to the *Erebus* and hove to. From Ice-Master James Reid, and then from Sir John himself, Martin learned of the purpose of the expedition and something of its plans. The two ships were moored waiting for an ice barrier to break so that they could make for Lancaster Sound.

   For a week following this meeting, the *Enterprise* remained in the vicinity of the *Erebus* and *Terror,* and one day some of

Franklin's officers paid a visit to Captain Martin; in his statement later to the Admiralty, Martin did not name the officers,
but one was perhaps the captain of the *Terror,* Francis Rawdon Moira Crozier. The officers gave Martin details of the
expedition. Its commander, Sir John Franklin, was an experienced naval officer and a famous explorer. As a midshipman
in 1801, he had participated in an exploration of the Austral-
ian coastline; in 1818 he was second-in-command in an abor-
tive attempt to reach the North Pole; in 1819–22 and in
1825–7 he had commanded two overland expeditions through
the Canadian barrens to the shores of the Polar Sea and had
surveyed part of its complex coastline. Franklin was experienced and respected, but he was old for exploration—almost
sixty—and it had been eighteen years since he had last
been in the Arctic. In spite of his age, the Admiralty considered him one of the best candidates to lead its latest expedition in search of a northwest passage, and he was eager to take
the command. His good friend and fellow explorer William
Edward Parry wrote to the Admiralty, "He is a fitter man to
go than any I know, and if you don't let him go, the man will
die of disappointment."[7] Serious, pious, responsible, and
experienced in Arctic travel, Sir John Franklin was finally
put in command of the greatest Arctic expedition that any
nation had yet mounted.

During their visit to Captain Martin, Franklin's officers
boasted about their supplies and equipment. Martin later
testified that they told him they were equipped to remain
in the Arctic for six years. Either Martin was mistaken or the
officers were trying to impress the whaling captain with the
munificence of the Navy: the expedition was actually equipped
for only three years. Nevertheless, the quantity of supplies
was impressive; aboard the two ships were 136,656 pounds of
flour, 64,224 pounds of beef and pork, 1,008 pounds of raisins,
1,000 pounds of mustard, 7,088 pounds of tobacco, 3,600
pounds of soap, and a plentitude of other necessities and
luxuries, including 2 organs, 200 pens, massive quantities of

ink and paper, bound volumes of *Punch,* and 100 Bibles. The ships had already sailed in Arctic and Antarctic waters, and just before Franklin's departure they had been further equipped for polar navigation. Their bows had been sheathed in sheet iron; devices for warming the cabins by hot water had been installed; and, most important, each had been furnished with auxiliary engines and screw propellers, the first such propellers to be used in Arctic navigation. So sure was the Admiralty of the success of its splendidly mounted expedition that it had not made any prearrangements for relief and rescue in the event of unforeseen emergency; once Sir John left his tender behind him, he was on his own. The Admiralty, the government, and the English people had only to wait with confidence for the reappearance of the expedition at the western end of the northwest passage after a year or two—at the most, three.

Shortly after the visit of Franklin's officers, Captain Martin received an invitation from Sir John himself to dine with him aboard the *Erebus,* but Martin, busy with whaling, was forced to decline. A few days later he sailed the *Enterprise* away from the vicinity of the *Erebus* and *Terror.* When he last saw the two ships, they were still moored to the iceberg, waiting for a break in the ice that blocked their course to Lancaster Sound.

For some time after the last sighting of Franklin in Baffin Bay, the Admiralty and the English people waited placidly— after all, it would take at least one year, probably more, for Sir John and his expedition to make their way through the maze of the Arctic Archipelago to the Bering Sea. In the spring of 1847 there was some agitation for the formation of relief parties, but the Admiralty decided to wait out the summer. When summer and autumn passed with no word from Franklin, however, it decided to dispatch three relief expeditions in the following spring and summer. There was still no sense of urgency, but no longer was there complete optimism. The first relief expedition that left, however, optimistically went to the Bering Sea, hoping to intercept Frank-

lin on the western side of the northwest passage. It found no
sign of him. A second expedition, led by Sir John Richardson,
who had accompanied Franklin on both of his overland expeditions in the eighteen-twenties, and by Dr. John Rae, an
officer in the Hudson's Bay Company, descended the Mackenzie River to examine the northern Canadian coastline.
No sign of Franklin was found, and Richardson returned to
England, leaving Rae to continue the search. A third expedition, the most ambitious, was commanded by Sir James Ross
and consisted of two ships, the *Enterprise* and *Investigator*.
Ross sailed his ships through Lancaster Sound into the inner
Archipelago. He dispatched exploratory parties in different
directions: he himself, accompanied by a young lieutenant,
Francis Leopold McClintock, who later became famous, investigated the northern and western shores of North Somerset
Island. Again, no sign of Franklin was found. Ross returned
to England to report nothing and to hand back to Lady Franklin the letter that she had hopefully asked him to give to Sir
John if he were found. It was the first of many such letters
she was to write: "My dearest love,—May it be the will of
God if you are not restored to us earlier that you should open
this letter & that it may give you comfort in all your
trials. . . ."[8]

By the time that this letter was returned to Lady Franklin
in November 1849, she had reason to worry about her husband. All three relief parties had returned empty-handed, and
the Franklin expedition had been out of contact with the
civilized world for more than four years. The Admiralty and
the nation as a whole joined in her concern. The Admiralty
offered a reward of twenty thousand pounds to any ship that
found and helped Franklin and his men, and it prepared a
series of expeditions to be sent north in 1850. There was
enough public concern to arouse the eager attention of commercial interests: books about the Arctic sold well, and Arctic
exhibits began to appear in places of public amusement. As
happens so often in *causes célèbres*, supernaturalism played

its part. "Zadkiel," a well-known astrologer, peered into a crystal ball that he had purchased at Lady Blessington's auction and saw Franklin's men on pack ice; he prognosticated that Franklin and most of his crew would be saved. A more sensational incident involved the ghost of one Weasey Coppin, a little girl who had died of gastric fever. Shortly after her death, Weasey appeared before her family and projected on the floor of the Coppin living room a complete Arctic landscape, including two ships surrounded by ice. Then, in ghostly handwriting on the wall, appeared the words *"Erebus* and *Terror.* Sir John Franklin, Lancaster Sound, Prince Regent Inlet, Point Victory, Victoria Channel."[9] Lady Franklin for one did not scoff at Weasey's revelation. In her grief she had already had recourse to a clairvoyant. Moreover, she agreed with the implications of Weasey's vision. From the beginning, she had insisted that her husband would follow orders, and Franklin had been ordered to turn southward and westward from Cape Walker, a direction that would bring him into the area suggested by Weasey's vision. She believed that the Admiralty, for all its good intentions, was concentrating on the wrong region of the Archipelago, to the north instead of to the south of Cape Walker. In 1850 the Admiralty dispatched two separate expeditions, the Hudson's Bay Company another, and the United States still another. In all, twelve ships were sent out after Franklin during the spring of 1850, but not one was going to go to what Lady Franklin considered the right place.

Her solution was to create an expedition of her own, financed and organized mainly by herself and a few friends. Under the command of Charles Forsythe, the *Prince Albert* sailed from Aberdeen on July 5, 1850. It was headed in the right direction: Forsythe was to sail down Prince Regent Inlet, cross North Somerset Island close to where Ross and McClintock had been the year before, and head southward toward King William Island and the south of the Great Fish River (now known as the Back River). The *Prince Albert* got

only as far as Prince Regent Inlet, where it was forced back
by ice. The Archipelago was teeming with search ships, however, and on the way out to Baffin Bay, the *Prince Albert* encountered one of them that had news: shortly before, one of
the British ships had found signs that Franklin had wintered
on Beechey Island—the ruins of some shacks, the remains of
foodstuffs, and three graves. There was, however, no written
record, no message. It was only a straw, but it was the first sign
of Franklin that had been discovered, and the *Prince Albert*
returned to England bearing the straw to Lady Franklin.

Many other ships remained in the north for the winter. By
then American ships had entered the search. Newspapers
throughout the United States had carried stories on Franklin's
disappearance; the interest of the American public had been
further aroused when Lady Franklin visited the United States
and sent a letter requesting help to President Zachary Taylor.
The government had been hesitant about sending expeditions,
but when a shipping magnate, Henry Grinnell, offered two
vessels and some financial backing, the United States joined
in the search. Under the command of Navy lieutenant Edwin
de Haven, the *Advance* and *Rescue* sailed north in the summer of 1850. The expedition had aboard as surgeon and
scientist Dr. Elisha Kent Kane.

In the winter of 1850-1 the Arctic Archipelago was the
setting of many strange scenes as various expeditions tried to
make contact with Franklin. They flew kites and balloons.
They shot rockets. They left large caches of coal and other
supplies. They trapped foxes, tagged them with messages, and
let them loose. Some of the men, Francis Leopold McClintock
in particular, experimented with sledging techniques; slowly,
civilized man was beginning to learn from the Eskimos the
art of travel and survival in the Arctic. But all attempts to
contact Franklin failed, and the evidence that he had wintered
on Beechey Island was not particularly significant: that had
been during the winter of 1845-6, too early in the voyage to
suggest anything of importance about his later fate. Neverthe-

less, Lady Franklin, encouraged, dispatched the *Prince Albert* again.

And so the search continued. Ship after ship, English and American, converged on the Archipelago from the east and the west. Between 1848 and 1853 more than thirty expeditions, almost forty ships, went north after Sir John. At first their purpose was relief and rescue; then, as time went by, all they hoped for was solution of the mystery, and all they could hope to find were relics and graves. The beginning of the Crimean War in 1853 seemed to make further search by the British impossible. In 1854, in spite of Lady Franklin's impassioned protests, the names of Sir John Franklin and his one hundred and twenty-eight men were struck from the Admiralty lists, and what the *Daily Telegraph* called "the iron-studded doors of the Admiralty"[10] were shut to all appeals. Lady Franklin's further appeals to the United States also were futile; by that time its citizens were becoming a little bored with the subject of the lost expedition. In the concluding chapter of *Walden* Thoreau could use the tragedy in one of his tropes without feeling callous or tasteless: "Is it the source of the Nile, or the Niger, or the Mississippi, or a North-West Passage around this continent that we would find? Are these the problems which most concern mankind? Is Franklin the only man who is lost, that his wife should be so earnest to find him? Does Mr. Grinnell know where he himself is?"

Just as all hope seemed gone, the first extensive evidence of what had happened to the Franklin expedition was discovered. The discovery was by chance: Dr. John Rae, not searching for Franklin but surveying the coastline near Boothia for the Hudson's Bay Company, happened on a group of Eskimos who reported that, four years before, an Eskimo hunting party had seen forty white men headed south on the ice near King William Island. The men had been sick and emaciated, and they had purchased seal from the Eskimo hunters. Later that season, Rae was told, the Eskimos found bodies along the shores of southern King William Island and on the mainland near the Great Fish River.

Rae reported something else that he had heard from the Eskimos, something about the bodies near the Great Fish River, that shocked the nation. "Some of the bodies were in a tent or tents; others under the boat which had been turned over to form a shelter, and several lay scattered about in different directions," his report read, and it went on: "From the mutilated state of many of the bodies, and the contents of the kettles, it is evident that our wretched Countrymen had been driven to the last dread alternative as a means of sustaining life."[11] Rae was immediately accused of angling for the reward that had been offered for evidence of Franklin's fate. His report was doubted because it depended on the word of "false savages" who, it was hypothesized, probably had murdered the white men themselves. The idea of cannibalism among the elite of the British Navy was so shocking that many persons simply could not accept it.

But much of Rae's report was backed by evidence: from the Eskimos he had purchased relics, mainly silver forks and spoons, that had beyond doubt come from Franklin's ships. Obviously, his report had to be followed up with another expedition, but the government balked. The Crimean War was still being waged, and the cost of the search was already astronomical. *The Times,* which had always been a little skeptical about Britain's Arctic endeavors, applauded: "We rejoiced in the recent determination of the Admiralty not to throw away good lives after bad."[12] Lady Franklin, however, still had the sympathy of the public—and of Charles Dickens, who called the Admiralty "churlish" in *Household Words* and went on: "No government, no parliament priding itself on jealousy for the honour of England, can leave such a duty as this unperformed."[13] The government decided to send a small overland party, and Lady Franklin again organized a private expedition, putting Francis Leopold McClintock in command.

On July 1, 1857, eleven years after the disappearance of the Franklin expedition, the *Fox* sailed from Aberdeen. After wintering in the ice of Baffin Bay, McClintock navigated the ship to Boothia Peninsula, then dispatched an overland party to the west coast of King William Island. There, deposited in a cairn on a point ironically named Victory, was the first and only written record of the Franklin expedition ever found. Further investigation uncovered further evidence of what had happened to the expedition. Much of the evidence was pathetic and suggestive: silver forks and spoons bearing the crests of Franklin and some of his officers; a stone jug marked "R Wheatly, Wine and Spirit Merchant, Greenhithe, Kent"; a clothes brush belonging to Private Henry Wilkes; a single stocking labeled "W. Orren" (an able seaman on the *Erebus*); a sextant bearing the name of Hornby, mate of the *Terror;* bits and pieces of a mahogany gun case; canteens; a shovel and pickaxes; rope; blankets; these and other utensils of civilized man. Some of the objects were necessities, but McClintock wondered why men in desperate straits would burden themselves with clothes brushes, silver plate, and heavy gun cases.

The search party also found skeletons—only a few, but those few gave measure of the ordeal undergone by the Franklin expedition. McClintock's men found two skeletons in a ship's boat that was on a sledge; apparently one party from the *Erebus* and *Terror* had hauled the boat on the ice almost sixty-five miles before giving up in exhaustion and leaving behind them the boat, the sledge, and two of their companions. McClintock himself found one other skeleton on its face near a rock. By examining the fragments of clothing around the skeleton, he ascertained that it was the remains of Petty Officer Harry Peglar: Peglar apparently had sat down on the rock to rest, then pitched forward on his face to die.

The written record found on Point Victory was brief, but it established the essential facts. The first part was written on a standard form carried by all naval expeditions. It was dated

May 28, 1847, and fixed the location of the *Erebus* and *Terror* as northwest of King William Island. It stated that the expedition had spent its first year on Beechey Island after having explored the waters of Wellington Channel and the west side of Cornwallis Island. It went on:

> Sir John Franklin commanding the expedition.
> All well.
>
> Party consisting of 2 officers and 6 men left the ships on Monday 24th May 1847

It was signed by Lieutenant Graham Gore and Mate Charles Des Voeux, both of the *Erebus;* after filling out the form, they had deposited it in a cairn. Although they had written that all was well, the end was beginning as they wrote.

The next part of the record was written on the margins of the same form almost a year later. The marginal message was written by Captain Fitzjames of the *Erebus.* He wrote that the two ships had been beset by ice on September 12, 1846 (so they had already been iced in when Gore and Des Voeux wrote their message, but at the time they did not know how deadly the besetment was to be). According to Fitzjames, the ships had been abandoned on April 22, 1848, by the one hundred and five survivors of the expedition, who had come across the ice to King William Island under the command of F. R. M. Crozier. Sir John Franklin himself had died on June 11, 1847; Fitzjames did not give the cause of his death. Below Fitzjames's signature Captain Crozier had added: "start on tomorrow 26th for Back's Fish River."

The stone jug, the clothes brush, the silver plate were clues to what happened next. The men rid themselves of some nonessentials and headed south along the shores of the island. The skeletons tell the next phase: as Crozier led the desperate march southward to where he hoped there would be game, his ranks were steadily depleted by scurvy and starvation.

McClintock and his men traced the terrible route down the

coast of King William Island to the estuary of the Great
Fish River before they decided to turn back and return to
England with their news. The final fate of Francis Crozier
and what survivors remained with him was left a mystery, but
McClintock felt that he already had enough to tell. It was
grim news, but by this time, twelve years after the disappearance, it was almost inevitable. For Lady Franklin there was
the slight consolation that her husband had died before the
worst of the ordeal began; for the other bereaved there was
at least virtual certainty where before there had been a nightmare of ignorance. For the English people there was a shock:
the romantic and heroic idea of the British Navy in all its
power overcoming Nature at her harshest had suddenly been
reduced to the pathetic image of Francis Crozier leading the
gaunt and diminishing remnants of a great expedition along
the barren shores of an Arctic island. Scurvy, with its bleeding gums and running sores, is not the stuff of heroic romance.

So ended another phase of Arctic exploration, "the search
for Franklin." It had covered a decade of intense exploration,
involving fleets of ships, hundreds of men, and millions of
pounds and dollars. Discoveries had been made. The complexities of the Arctic Archipelago were at last understood,
and all but its northernmost portions had been found and
charted. A northwest passage had been discovered and trav-
ersed. It can be argued that Franklin himself discovered a
passage, although he tragically failed to navigate it, but it is
certain that Captain Robert McClure and some of his men
made their way by ship and foot from the Bering Sea to the
Atlantic Ocean. McClure, searching for Franklin, had been
forced to abandon his ship to the ice near Banks Island. He
and his men went over the ice on foot to Melville Island.
There, by greatest good chance, they were rescued by another search expedition and carried eastward to the Atlantic.
The first traverse of a northwest passage was from the west
to the east and was made partly through error, near disaster,
and luck.

Much had been learned about the behavior of sea ice and Arctic tides; considerable contributions had been made to the studies of magnetism, meteorology, zoology, botany, and geology. Even commerce had gained a little something: the expeditions opened up new waters for fisheries. But the price paid for these gains had been high, and the loss of the Franklin expedition took some of the bloom off the romance of science. It was traumatic not just for England but also for Europe and the United States; some part of their faith in themselves and their destiny had gone with Sir John and had disappeared with him. Even *Blackwood's* changed its attitude; it spoke for a large part of the public in an article on Franklin in which it deplored science as "a placid Juggernaut, a Moloch with benevolent pretensions":

> We confess we have not heart enough in the grand enterprise of knowledge, to view such a sacrifice as that of Franklin and his crew without a chill of horror: there is something frightful, inexorable, inhuman, in prosecuting researches, which are mere researches, after such a costly fashion.[14]

And the question remained: Why? Why did one hundred and twenty-nine of the British Navy's best men die so miserably? Vilhjalmur Stefansson posed the question in a way that implied his answer to it:

> One of the most baffling problems of Canadian exploration is how Sir John Franklin and his party of more than a hundred contrived to die to the last man, apparently from hunger and malnutrition, in a district where several hundred Eskimos had been living for generations, bringing up their children, and taking care of their aged. . . . The Eskimos lived by hunting with weapons of the Stone Age; the British were armed with shotguns and muskets, not quite so good as ours today but certainly a lot more effective than the bows of the Eskimos. They must have had

both hooks and nets for fish where the Eskimos had only hooks. They could have made for themselves harpoons from the wood and metal of their ships better than the ones which the Eskimos possessed, made of driftwood and native copper or bone.[15]

Stefansson's answer is partly that the British did not hunt enough in the Arctic. Actually, they did do some hunting: Captain Martin, the whaling man who saw the expedition in Baffin Bay, said that the men were shooting sea birds in their free time. But Stefansson believed that hunting in the Arctic was not something to be done in spare time; he believed that it had to be a way of life, the major concern of anyone who wanted to survive in the Arctic in the period before the airplane and the icebreaking ship. He noted that the English often depended on French Canadian guides or Indians to do their hunting for them; "meat hunting" by officers or even enlisted men did not fit into the pattern of military behavior that prevailed in most British Arctic expeditions of the period. Hunting was viewed too much as a sport, not enough as the absolutely crucial business of survival. Indeed, Captain George Nares referred to the men who hunted during his polar expedition as "sportsmen."

Stefansson believed that nineteenth-century naval custom and discipline, in which the British took such pride, lessened the chances for survival on Arctic expeditions. Naval-issue clothing had to be worn, rather than the warm garments that the Eskimos had perfected over the centuries; there are prints from early in the century showing British officers with high hats and braided uniforms against the background of ice fields. Officers' messes were maintained even in the most dire circumstances. Enlisted men had to carry disproportionate burdens on overland expeditions, and there are recorded cases of officers sitting in sledges pulled by enlisted men. The size of most expeditions was swelled by the presence of personal servants. Such military custom might have its advantages in a civilized environment, but in a region where the permissible margin for error is so slight, it was too cumbersome and inflexible.

The greatest failure of English Arctic exploration in the nineteenth century, according to Stefansson, was the failure to observe and learn from the Eskimos. Many of the expeditions ignored or distrusted them, and relations with them were at best uneasy. Even McClintock, who adopted their sledging techniques, referred to them as "the ruthless Esquimaux." On Franklin's second overland expedition his men had threatened to fire their guns at Eskimos in the Mackenzie delta who began to seem aggressive. Perhaps an event that occurred in the area of the Great Fish River in 1834 contributed to what happened in 1847: in that year, unknown to George Back himself, three members of Back's expedition shot and killed three Eskimos who, the men said, had fired arrows at them. News spreads rapidly among Eskimo groups and, as many explorers have discovered, the Eskimos have extraordinarily tenacious memories. The Eskimos of the King William Island and Great Fish River region would not have forgotten what happened in 1834 and would have hesitated to help white men in 1847.

Some explorers, both English and American, did profit from observing the Eskimos. George Back learned something of the language and the customs; Francis Leopold McClintock became an expert on sledging partly by watching Eskimos; Elisha Kent Kane experimented with Eskimo food and clothing; Dr. John Rae traveled with Eskimos and, more than any other white man before him, recognized that they knew the secrets of survival in the Arctic. But in the eyes of many explorers, the Eskimos remained exotic, either primitive and childish or treacherous and untrustworthy; even those men who admired their ingenuity in survival did so with reservations. The feeling prevailed that Europeans and Americans should raise the Eskimos to a civilized level rather than descend to their level by imitating them. Rae was severely criticized for his adaptation to Eskimo ways, and Kane, for all his curiosity about the Eskimo way of life, saw it only as a temptation to be resisted when he and his men were in trouble; it was better to die a civilized man than to imitate the brutish savage.

The brunt of Stefansson's argument is that white men in the mid-nineteenth century attempted to insulate themselves from the Arctic environment and its natives instead of adapting themselves to the environment by imitating the natives. Rather than live off the Arctic, they tried to live in spite of it. Moving in large, cumbersome groups and hampered by the inevitable logistical problems, attempting to remain independent of the very environment that could have supported them, they became easy prey for starvation and scurvy. They were men of great courage and pride, and many of them died unnecessarily, including the members of the Franklin expedition. Of course, Stefansson had an ax to grind. He was one of the Arctic's greatest propagandists, creating in one famous phrase, "the friendly Arctic," an image of the north dramatically in contrast to our usual image of it. He often overstated his case. "Friendly" as the Arctic may be on occasion, it is also hostile: many Eskimos, for all their experience, have died there by drowning, freezing, or starving (Eskimo stories about cannibalism among themselves are not infrequent).

With the return of Francis Leopold McClintock in 1859, further search for Franklin seemed unnecessary, even cruel. To many persons, knowledge of the bare outline of what had happened was enough; additional detail would only bring additional horror and raise again the specter of cannibalism. Even Lady Franklin seemed to accept the end of the great search. The Admiralty and the Navy, the British and Ameri-

can governments, powerful commercial interests and wealthy
private citizens, all had done their best; now it was time to
cease and let the whole terrible affair be ennobled by history.
Tennyson wrote the epitaph of Franklin (who was his distant relative) that was placed on Franklin's cenotaph in West-
minster Abbey:

> Not here! the white North has thy bones; and thou
>   Heroic sailor-soul,
> Art passing on thine happier voyage now
>   Toward no earthly pole.

At the very time when McClintock was returning from his
final voyage to the Arctic, however, an obscure businessman
in Cincinnati, Ohio, was preparing to go north. He had received a call from Heaven, and he hoped to do by himself
what governments and navies had failed to do: to locate and
rescue survivors of the Franklin expedition. Just as the cur-
tain was coming down on the Franklin tragedy, Charles
Francis Hall elbowed his way on stage—bearded, squat, and
only half educated, seeming rather vulgar after all the aristo-
crats and naval officers, statesmen and tycoons who had been
on stage before him. Impelled by a sense of personal destiny
and of religious and patriotic mission, Hall was to become
an explorer; he was to work virtually on his own and to display energy, will power, and independence remarkable even
in a nineteenth-century American. His obsession with the
Arctic was to drive him to its weird and tragic shores on three
expeditions, until at last he would die and be buried so far
north of the magnetic pole that the needle of a compass put
on his grave points southwest.

chapter one

Cincinnati, New London, and New York

C harles Francis Hall was twenty-seven years old when he arrived in Cincinnati in 1849 with very little money, few possessions, and a young wife named Mary. Where he had come from and why, whether he intended to remain in Cincinnati or only to pass through it on his way farther west, is now unknown; like many other restless Americans of his time, he left no tracks until he finally paused in one place long enough for his name to appear in community records. What is known about his early life comes mainly from biographical sketches written after his death, and they are at least partly inaccurate: they all agree that he was born in Rochester, New Hampshire, in 1821, but his wife once mentioned in a letter that he was born in Vermont and moved to Rochester with his family when he was still a child.

The sketches all emphasize the rural simplicity of Hall's boyhood. His formal education was slight; after a few years at a local common school, he was apparently apprenticed to a blacksmith. Several of the sketches insist that he read assiduously on his own, and they evoke the image of a young Lincoln, a youth in homespun reading by firelight. "And thus he plodded his way along," one sketch elaborates, "like many another dreamy lad whose heart and aim is all beyond, and outside of, his daily occupations." The author of that sketch sees some advantage in Hall's early days as a blacksmith, however: "Though not much to his taste, this heavy work assisted him materially in developing his muscles and hardening his constitution, thus indirectly helping to fit him for the arduous adventures of his later years."[1]

At this phase of Hall's life, his early youth, all the sketches become vague. Even the most detailed contains only two sentences covering the next five or six years: "While yet a young man, he left his native place, and with it the blacksmith's trade. Setting his face westward, after some experiments elsewhere, he settled in Cincinnati."[2] What and where were those "experiments elsewhere"? Did Hall go to New York or Boston (a C. F. Hall appeared in the Boston City Directory of 1843 and 1844) to experience city life and learn a new trade, or did he set out west immediately, moving slowly toward Cincinnati, "experimenting" along the way? Whatever he did, he left no evidence behind him; he was an obscure wanderer, one of the thousands of nameless digits in statistics on population shifts. So far as documentary history is concerned, Hall did not exist until his name appeared in the Cincinnati city directory of 1849: "Hall Charles F., southside 5th, between Park and Mill."

Considering Hall's later career as an explorer, it is tempting to see him at this stage in his life as a young frontiersman who moved west to challenge the great wilderness, but if he had intended to become a frontiersman, Cincinnati at midcentury would have been a disappointment. It was a booming city. If its suburbs across the Ohio are included in the count, its population was almost two hundred thousand. On the site of the old Fort Washington, which had defended the early settlement against Indians, sprawled a gaudy symbol of Cincinnati's growth, the pseudo-Oriental Bazaar built by Mrs. Frances Trollope in 1829 to supply Cincinnatians with the frippery that she thought they needed to become civilized.

The store had failed, embittering the already caustic Mrs. Trollope against the city, but the building remained as a monument to her personal failure at commerce in a city rich with commercial success. In spite of Mrs. Trollope's criticism of the city's crudity, even in her time Cincinnati had outgrown the austere frontier stages of its development, and by mid-century it could afford all the luxuries of civilization. It was booming enough to support both the sacred (almost one hundred churches and several theological seminaries, including the famous Lane) and the profane (twenty-eight whiskey distilleries and twenty-one breweries). In education it was in advance of many eastern cities: not only did it have thirty primary and secondary schools, it also had three colleges, four medical schools, and a law school. Perhaps educational institutions, churches, and whiskey distilleries are necessities and do not indicate an advanced civilization. Clearly not a necessity are artificial flowers, and Cincinnati had three manufactories of artificial flowers, employing forty persons who were devoted to gracing the rooms of Cincinnati Society with their products. By mid-century Cincinnati had a rich and elegant, if not an old, Society. As early as 1834, Charles Fenno Hoffman, visiting from New York, wrote to a friend: "What would most strike you in the streets of Cincinnati would be the number of pretty faces and stylish figures one meets in the morning. I have had more than one opportunity of seeing these western beauties by candle-light, and the evening display brought no disappointment to the morning promise."[3] The ladies organized receptions and masquerades, sometimes held in their spacious houses, sometimes in the ballroom on the third floor of the Bazaar, or, after 1850, in the newly built Burnet House.

    Someone, of course, had to pay the piper: the ladies' industrious husbands. Above all else, Cincinnati was a commercial and industrial city. Its residents were never allowed to forget that its schools, churches, mansions, and hotels, its elegance and dawning intellectuality, were dependent on

its economic expansion. The pigs that were driven through
its streets to be slaughtered in its abattoirs were a constant reminder of one of its nicknames: "Porkopolis." A
British woman wrote, "Cincinnati is, literally speaking, a
city of pigs. Alive and dead, whole and divided into portions,
their outsides and their insides, their grunts and their squeals,
meet you at every moment."[4] By mid-century its meat-
packing business had become the largest in the world. The
stench from its tanneries, the smoke from its foundries, the
din from its steamboat factories—these, too, were reminders
of where the schools and the artificial flowers came from.
Cincinnati had banks, investment houses, insurance companies, and even a business school, but pure finance was
secondary to manufacturing. Here William Procter met
James Gamble, in 1837 amalgamating their small candle
and soap factories; here John Brunswick began to make
billiard tables, Charles and Maximilian Fleischmann yeast,
and Dietrich Gruen watches. It was a city of makers, de-
lighting in the technological revolution that was changing
America, fascinated by the machines that were making it
rich. In 1850 Cincinnati was a frontier only in a new, meta-
phorical sense of the word, a frontier of business and technology.

In our national myth, western migration is pictured as
rural, but in fact such cities as Cincinnati, St. Louis, and San
Francisco attracted many more migrants than did the open
land. If Charles Francis Hall had come west to blaze trails or
to hack farmland out of wilderness, he had come to the wrong
place. But there is no reason to think that he had intended to
become a frontier scout or a pioneer farmer. Hall probably
was tired of country life when he left the infertile hills of
New England, and a growing western city would have offered
him more excitement and opportunity than the wilderness.
For ten years he not only accepted Cincinnati as his domicile,
he actually seemed to revel in its enterprising spirit.

His career there began modestly enough. He and his wife

settled in a boardinghouse on the city's west side. Somewhere he had picked up the semiskill of seal-die molding (a molder cast the work of engravers into the metal dies that were used in seal presses), and soon he was working with a highly skilled engraver, Benjamin C. True. For three years Hall worked in True's seal-engraving shop, learning a business that was far more important in the nineteenth century than it is today. Nowadays we see embossed seals only when we go to a notary, but in the last century they were used not only by notaries but also by businesses, both as official stamps and as advertising devices. Beautifully embossed seals on stationery and envelopes were the equivalent of today's engraving in establishing the tone of a company. Cincinnati, with its multitude of new companies, supported five seal-engraving businesses in 1850.

As Hall's later career shows, he was not a man to work for (or indeed, with) anyone else: independence was for him a way of life that became an obsession. After three years with True, he went into business on his own. He found a sizable workshop on Fourth Street, in the center of Cincinnati's business district, and there with considerable fanfare set up "Hall's Engraving Rooms." It is improbable that Hall had learned much about the fine craft of seal- and line-engraving during his three years with True, skilled as that artisan was. Hall admired both craftsmanship and technology, but he lacked the long training and the skill to succeed in either; undoubtedly he was capable of engraving simple seals, but he was essentially an entrepreneur during his years in Cincinnati, a dealer in other men's skills. On the finest "Hall" seal now in the Smithsonian Institution are carved the tiny initials "B.C.T." and "True F [ecit]." Teacher apparently worked for ex-pupil. Pupil, in time, would honor teacher by giving his name to a small cape far to the north of Cincinnati.

Hall had the shrewdness to raise the capital necessary to start his business, and the energy to expand it as time passed. He was a promoter, the only engraver in the city to take full-page advertisements in the city directory year after year. These advertisements, gorgeously printed in various typefaces and illustrated with samples of Hall's seals (sometimes actually embossed on the page), indicate the sort of work that his shop did as he enlarged his business. "SEAL ENGRAVING IN ALL ITS VARIETY," one announces:

> Particular attention given to designing, engraving and blazoning appropriate Coats of Arms, for corporate bodies, civil and ecclesiastic; Crests and Arms of ancient families sought and engraved; Copperplate Engraving and Printing, such as Marriage, Business and Address Cards, Notes, Drafts, &c. ENVELOPE DIES, PLAIN AND ELABORATE. Self-sealing advertising envelopes [self-sealing envelopes were a novelty at the time], colored Embossed cards, Book Titles, Boot and Hat-tip stamps, Steel Stamps for silversmiths, boiler manufacturers, carpenters, &c. Bankers, Post Office and Steamboat Stamps, with complete inking apparatus for the same; Hall's Improved Percussion and Lever Seal Presses; a complete assortment of English, French and German plain and fancy Billet Paper Envelopes, suitable for weddings, balls, parties, &c.&c.; Cake Boxes, and every description of Wedding Stationery; Jewelry and Silver plate marking for the trade.

Behind the "Hall's Improved Percussion Press" mentioned in this advertisement lay a story that revealed something of Hall's character: the man was combative. In this case, his ire was roused by a patent. Most seal presses of the time were either lever- or screw-driven; the operator placed the document to be embossed between the dies, and then pressed down on a lever or turned a screw to squeeze them together. Such machines, likely to weigh ten pounds or more, were cumbersome, expensive, and, in the case of the screw press, slow. In the late 1840's two Cincinnati inventors, E. P. Cranch and James Foster, designed a small percussion press that could be worked with a light blow of the hand, rather like a stapler. Although considerable ingenuity was displayed in the design, the Patent Office turned down Foster's first application for a patent because the mechanical devices involved were not original. Foster reapplied a few years later, arguing persuasively that although the devices were not new, they were being used for a new purpose. Although Foster filed the application himself, he had by then sold the rights to the device to one Platt Evens; Evens's attorney immediately wrote to the Patent Office to make it clear that Evens had been assigned the rights even though Foster was making the application. Foster did not contest Evens's claim. At this point, just as the Patent Office was about to award the patent to Evens, it received an angrily scrawled letter from Charles Francis Hall. "I am deeply interested in this matter," Hall wrote, "as I have now been engaged over two years in the Manufacture and Sale of Percussion Presses & Seals. In fact to my efforts is to be attributed the extensive notoriety the article enjoys." Hall went on to claim that Evens had worked with him in his engraving business for a year, during which time he had "taken money from my hands" to purchase the rights to Foster's device and had agreed to give Hall one-half ownership. Moreover, by "flattering promises" he had induced Hall to put money into manufacturing and selling the device under the name of "Evens' Percussion Press." Evens had left Hall's establishment in the previous year and now was in business on his own, selling his press as "Evens' Patented Press." Did Evens actually have a patent, Hall asked, or was the name simply an advertising gimmick?[5]

The Patent Office replied that Evens did not yet have a patent, and Hall immediately began a campaign against Evens, using the facilities of his printing shop. A broadside flyer appeared from Hall's Engraving Rooms, boasting of the new "Hall's Improved Percussion Press" and accusing Evens of "acts little short of perjury":

> This invention was not introduced to the public until
> the year 1851, when its many virtues becoming known,

C. F. Hall, Seal Engraver of Cincinnati, believing its adap-
tion complete to the wants of the business community,
immediately took it up and gave it notoriety under the
name and title of "Evens' Percussion." Although Evens
never invented even an improvement on the Percussion
Press, yet C. F. Hall was INDUCED to call it "Evens" from
this, his only reason—TO SILENCE THE CONSTANT IMPORTUNI-
TIES of one, whose insatiate desire was to become FAMOUS
on the strength of other men's inventions at C. F. HALL'S
OWN ENTIRE EXPENSE. There never was a PATENT GRANTED
on any Percussion Press, notwithstanding BOLD efforts are
being made by certain or UNCERTAIN parties to DECEIVE the
public in the matter. Vindictive feeling, coupled with a
strong love of gain and fame sometimes carries people
beyond reason and law—both have been outraged by a
RUSE notice [Evens's advertisement claiming that his press
was patented] and in DECEIVING U.S. Government Offices by
acts little short of perjury.

Clearly Hall was not a man to meddle with; aroused, he was
capable of intemperate words and, as his later career showed,
intemperate action.

Evens was awarded his patent soon after Hall's broadside
appeared, but Hall immediately sued, claiming one-half
ownership. Early in 1855 the Cincinnati Superior Court decided in Hall's favor, and so he won his battle. It is doubtful
that half ownership in a percussion seal press patent was
worth all the trouble, but the Hotspur in Hall might well
have said, ". . . in the way of bargain, mark ye me, I'll cavil
on the ninth part of a hair." Hall often seemed to enjoy combat for combat's sake.

By 1855 Hall's interest in his seal-engraving business had
begun to flag, but he soon found another outlet for his energy:
he decided to publish a newspaper. In the beginning it was
an unpretentious effort, appropriately called the *Cincinnati
Occasional.* The first issue was a small, single-page, single-
column sheet dated August 5, 1858. It announced the success-

ful completion of the Atlantic Cable, and several issues thereafter were devoted entirely to that subject. Possibly Hall was subsidized by Cyrus Field's company, but more likely he was simply carried away by his enthusiasm for this latest example of technological progress; one way or the other, his rhetoric was rather strident as he exhorted the city fathers to celebrate the event:

> Let there be beacon lights upon every hill top around the city and bonfires at every street crossing. Let cannon answer cannon, and rocket answer rocket from every point that can be seen from the city. Send illuminated balloons to the upper air, vibrated with the tones of every bell from every tower, and then tremble the wires through Land and Sea, with our congratulations to the rest of mankind. The Old World and the New are now *one—forever one!* Let the hills, vallies, and the mountains clap their hands—*rejoice*—for GOD IS GREAT.[6]

Hall's writing is often self-consciously fine and stilted, but energy erupts in his capitals, italics, and exclamation points.

The *Occasional* began as a neighborhood paper, with advertisements entirely from businesses near Hall's own shop on Fourth Street, but the list of advertisers soon lengthened and Hall became more ambitious. The little paper, at first a single sheet and very occasional, was enlarged to several pages and appeared almost every day. The *Occasional*, however, was not a proper newspaper; Hall printed only a few news items in each issue, filling most of the remaining space with his enthusiastic editorializing; the *Occasional* was a hobbyhorse, a mouthpiece for his quirks and special interests. Balloons, for example: something about balloons excited Hall's imagination, and in the autumn of 1858 the pages of the *Occasional* were filled with pictures of balloons and with stories about balloon experiments, balloon races, balloon disasters. Apparently this series was triggered by a race between "Professors" Steiner and Godard, the former representing the

United States, the latter France. These two gentlemen ascended in their balloons from Cincinnati on the afternoon of
October 18; that night Godard descended in Monroeville,
Ohio, Steiner in Sandusky. (The United States therefore won
the race, much to Hall's satisfaction; he was a competitive
patriot in all things.) Before and after this race, Hall discussed balloons in detail in the *Occasional*. He outlined the
history of ballooning, telling sensational stories about it—
the story of Madame Blanchard, for example, who ascended
one night from Paris amid a fireworks display set off in her
honor. Unfortunately, her balloon was hit by an inaccurately
aimed rocket. "Her lifeless body," Hall wrote, "was found in
one of the public highways of the metropolis."[7] He discussed
the technical problems faced by balloonists: the gas of Cincinnati, although excellent for the purposes of illumination,
was too heavy for effective ballooning. As a matter of historical curiosity he noted, not altogether humorously, the
solution to the problem of balloon navigation offered by the
ancient who had suggested harnessing a dozen eagles to a
balloon, along with a hundred pigeons, just out of reach of
the eagles. Hall called on the mechanics of Cincinnati to work
on the problem of air navigation: "Will not some of our
mechanical geniuses produce something new—some device
by which we can navigate the air? IT CAN BE DONE! Now do it.
The time is coming when the great life element will yield
carriage service to mankind. Cincinnatians, hasten the day!"

Hall apparently considered balloons to be good press, but
his interest in them was not entirely commercial. He once had
a thousand copies of the *Occasional* scattered over the city
from Professor Godard's balloon *Leviathan*. It was nothing
more than a spectacular publicity stunt, but Hall's article in
the special "Balloon Edition" showed his fascination with
balloons as an aspect of technological progress. He pointed
out that the stunt combined "three triumphs of man's adaptation of the wonderful powers of nature to his use": the news
in the paper had come via the telegraph and "the incom-

prehensible electric fluid"; the paper had been printed on presses driven by steam, "the useful worker of the age"; the edition had been distributed from a balloon lifted by "the expansive power of subtile gas." To Hall, balloons were a symbol of human enterprise. "The embarking of an Aeronaut on a trip to the skies has lost none of its interest by its frequency," he wrote in his Balloon Edition. "Every new essay of man to sail away from the Earth, his abiding place, awakes our wonder at his daring and our curiosity as to what new triumphs skill and enterprise will win."[8]

By winter, Hall was printing five thousand copies of some editions of the *Occasional*. Made ambitious by his success, he decided to publish a daily newspaper. The last issue of the *Occasional* appeared on December 17, 1858, the first issue of the *Daily Press* on February 22, 1859. Hall hired an editor for his new paper, and as a result the *Daily Press* was at first more professional than its predecessor, but also duller, lacking in the eccentricities of form and content that had enlivened the *Occasional*. After three months the editor either resigned or was fired; thereafter the pages of the *Daily Press* blossomed with capitals, italics, and exclamation points, and balloons began to play a prominent part in its news coverage.

Proud of his new paper, Hall was also proud of the press that printed it. Instead of being driven by steam, his press was driven by dry heat; Hall had found a new hobbyhorse, the caloric engine. He announced in an editorial that his Ericsson Caloric Engine was "the first and only one of the kind put in operation west of the Alleghanies" and that it was based on the principles used by John Ericsson in his "celebrated but unfortunate caloric ship."[9] The story of John Ericsson's caloric ship is one of the byways of American technology in the age of steam. Ericsson was an engineer of considerable ability (he was a pioneer in adapting the screw propeller to ships, and was the builder of the *Monitor*), but he was misled into serious error when he built his caloric engine. Like many others of his time, Ericsson believed in an

elastic, indestructible, "caloric" fluid, supposedly the essence
of heat, and he further believed that this fluid could be con-
served, regenerated, and reused with no loss of energy. The
key to his caloric piston engine was his "regenerator," a wire
mesh intended to save up the caloric from a spent charge of
hot air; the caloric was then picked up by another charge of
air, to be used in driving the next phase in the engine's cycle.
Although he did not know it, he was contending with the
Second Law of Thermodynamics, but he had enough faith in
his invention to build a 250-foot ship, in which he placed a
huge caloric engine. Ericsson's ship died not with a bang
but with a whimper. It did not explode—it simply was not
efficient. Some optimists continued to have faith in the idea,
and for many years after Ericsson's ship failed there continued
to be supporters of his theory, a little splinter group of hot-
airists in the age of steam.[10]

Hall was one of them. On the masthead of the *Daily Press*,
in large letters, he put the words "BY CALORIC," and he made
the engine a subject of frequent editorials. In one he gave
a set of statistics: the iron and brass machine filled six feet by
two feet of space and weighed one and a half tons. This
monster generated only five horsepower, an inefficiency remarkable even in the age before light metals, but Hall apparently was boasting about the weight and size of his machine
rather than apologizing for it. He believed that he was
saving three dollars a day by using dry heat instead of steam,
and he remarked that the engine "took care of itself" (he did
not say how). "We believe the day is fast approaching," he
concluded, "when locomotives on our railroads, boats on our
rivers, will be propelled by Ericsson's Caloric Engines. What
a blessing to the world!" Hall was so enthusiastic about his
toy that friends converted his initials C. F. into "Caloric
Fool."

While Hall busied himself with his enterprises, hustling
around Cincinnati drumming up advertisers, fighting legal
jousts, investigating new inventions, and hatching plans to

further his career, his domestic life apparently went on placidly. During these years of obscurity, and in the years of fame that followed, Mary Hall remained a mute figure in the background of Hall's life; she probably was patient, and she certainly was long-suffering. Ambitious, moody, irascible, restless, Hall must have made a difficult husband. Throughout the eighteen-fifties they lived together on the premises of Hall's Engraving Rooms, and there, in 1855, she bore Hall his first child, a daughter named Anna. By the time that his second child was born, five years later, Hall was on his way to the Arctic, to all intents and purposes having deserted his wife and children.

When, why, and how Hall became interested in the Arctic is a mystery. In later years he claimed that he had been interested in it all during the eighteen-fifties and that he had read about it ever since his arrival in Cincinnati. Possibly he had done desultory reading on the subject for a long time, but his intense interest developed only in the late eighteen-fifties, not long before he actually decided to go north. Perhaps it was roused by the death of Elisha Kent Kane.

Kane died in Havana on February 16, 1857, at thirty-six years of age. As a boy of eighteen he had been stricken with rheumatic fever, and his heart thereafter had been weak, but he had transcended his illness to lead a short life of adventure and travel such as most healthy men only dream of. He had become most famous as an Arctic explorer, although he had also traveled in South America, Africa, Europe, and Asia. Born into a wealthy and distinguished Philadelphia family, he had not wasted his privilege: by academic education at the Universities of Virginia and Pennsylvania he had become a medical doctor; by wide, informal reading he had become a "scientist" in a broad sense of the word that exists no longer: he was a man who felt at home in chemistry, physics, geology, botany, and zoology; who observed, measured, and noted all natural phenomena almost by reflex action, without any sense of stigma as a dilettante.

Kane had participated in two Arctic expeditions, the First (1850–1) and the Second (1853–5) United States Grinnell Expeditions in search of Sir John Franklin, as, respectively, medical officer and commander. The Second Grinnell Expedition in particular had been an ordeal. Although its ostensible purpose was a search for Franklin, its members hoped also to prove the existence of an Open Polar Sea—a huge body of open water hypothetically located north of the ice packs that had blocked the course of so many expeditions. Proponents of the Open Polar Sea maintained that the packs would disappear at about latitude eighty degrees north. Kane and others hypothesized that the Franklin Expedition was somewhere in the Polar Sea, unable to break through the ice that ringed it. The theory of the Open Polar Sea is an example of how theoretical geography often led explorers into traps that were sometimes fatal: the men of the Second Grinnell Expedition probed up into the ice-clogged waters between Ellesmere Island and Greenland, but, abandoning their ship to the ice that they had been so certain would disappear, they were forced to retreat southward by sledge and boat. That only three of the party died was a tribute to the leadership of Kane, and to his skill in adapting Eskimo methods of survival.

Kane's two books about his Arctic experience became best sellers and made him famous. This small, sickly man became a beau ideal, an image of breeding and courage, of manliness and learning combined in graceful measure, and his death was bewailed throughout the country. The obsequies that embellished the transportation of his body from Havana to Philadelphia can be compared only with those that accompanied Lincoln's funeral train. With great ceremony the body was placed on a ship from Havana to New Orleans, where it was greeted by a band and by city dignitaries, who escorted it to a riverboat. As the paddle-wheeler passed settlements along the Mississippi and Ohio, bells tolled and mourners stood along the banks. On March 7 the boat reached Cincinnati. If Hall was in Cincinnati that day, he must have joined the throngs watching the solemn procession that accompanied the body from the steamboat to the special train that was to carry it on the next stage of its long journey to Philadelphia. In his later writings, Hall referred to Kane constantly, always with adulation; in his own way he imitated the Philadelphia aristocrat. Quite possibly the events of March 7, 1857, were crucial in starting Hall on his career as an explorer.

Whether or not it was Kane's death that set Hall off, in 1857–8 he was absorbed in an intensive program of reading about the Arctic. For several years he had been in the habit of taking notes on whatever reading he was doing, and of jotting down random thoughts, quotations, and statistics in innumerable little notebooks. These notebooks are a fantastic hodgepodge. On a few pages of one are the following items: a letter to a newspaper from Baron Humboldt on slavery (he was against it); a quotation of Lord John Russell on prose style (advising imitation of Defoe's simplicity); a fact recorded apparently for its own sake ("85,000,000£ national debt of Grt. Britain after Russian War"); a list of articles Hall intended to read; several scriptural quotations, Latin tags, and newspaper "fillers" ("IMPORTANT EXPERIMENT —On Saturday Drs. Contaret, practical chemists from France, succeeded in deodorizing the contents of a privy under the direction of the New York City Inspector. The sink contained 312 cubic feet of fecal matter."). Hall's notebooks are relics of an unfocused but energetic effort in self-education.

In 1857 the notebooks began to take on focus, becoming less haphazard as Hall concerned himself with the Arctic. In the past he had read about the Arctic with casual interest, but now he began to study with intensity of purpose. He went regularly to the Young Men's Mercantile Association Library to comb the latest magazines and newspapers for articles about recent Arctic activities and to study back files of periodicals.

He purchased and borrowed all the books he could find that in any way concerned the North; he read Humboldt, Scoresby, Barrow, Parry, Ross, Franklin, Richardson, Beechey, Back, McClure, and, of course, Kane. He wanted to inform himself about Arctic history, Arctic navigation, Arctic geography, Arctic flora and fauna. Painstakingly he read; painstakingly he recorded and remembered what he read. The notebooks reveal a particular concern with the problems of Arctic survival. Hall recorded Kane's opinion that fresh meat was the "only specific" for scurvy, and he listed the food supplies of several expeditions. He clipped articles about diet: one was a chemist's report that fat is "more solid" than lean, another a story about an old woman who lived for a month on half a pound of sugar. He carefully noted advice on clothing and shelter given by such experts as Kane, and he even clipped a newspaper list of things to do and not to do during the Ohio winter. (The list is comic, considering what Hall was soon to endure. It suggests that one should "never sleep with the head in the draft of an open window, . . . never wear India-rubbers in cold, dry weather, . . . avoid sitting against the cushions in the backs of pews in churches.")

Something of Hall's personal thought also emerges from the notebooks of this period; whenever he was not jotting down facts and statistics about the Arctic, he was quoting little messages of moral uplift. He espoused the positive and the assertive, possibly because he was stiffening his sinews to make a decision that would change the course of his life. From the 1857 *Annual of Scientific Discovery* he quoted, "All obstacles yield to a resolute man." He clipped a filler from his own newspaper: "TRUE COURAGE—I love the man that can smile in trouble, that can gather strength from distress, and grow brave by reflection. It is the business of little minds to shrink, but he who is firm will pursue his principles unto death." He quoted, at their most assertive, Carlyle ("Every noble work is at first impossible") and Goethe ("The longer I live the more certain I am that the great difference between men is energy, invincible determination"). When he read a biography of Christopher Columbus, he was impressed by Columbus's obsessive drive; in large handwriting, underscored and with a pointing hand in the margin, he copied a passage from the book:

WHAT POVERTY, NEGLECT, RIDICULE, CONTUMELY & DISAPPOINT-
MENT HAD HE NOT SUFFERED! HIS EXAMPLE SHOULD ENCOURAGE
THE ENTERPRISING NEVER TO DESPAIR.

Clearly Hall believed, or wanted to believe, in the efficacy of energy and will power. He had to—they were almost the only assets that he could bring to the endeavor that was gradually taking shape in his mind.

In the spring of 1859, Hall's previously private concern with the North became public when stories and editorials about the Arctic began to appear in the *Daily Press*. On May 25, fourteen years after Franklin's disappearance, he printed an editorial under the heading of a question: "Does Sir John Franklin Still Live?" The meaning of the editorial, which was full of bombast and snippets of poetry ("How sleep the brave who sink to rest / By all their country's wishes blest?"), is at best fuzzy, but apparently Hall intended to say that Franklin might still be alive: "In the chronicles of the ocean, when the wrecked mariner has been cast among its raging billows, an unseen hand has often guided him to a happy shore; and in the annals of mortal suffering, when hearts have sunk and hands have failed, a meteor ray has often flashed upon the soul, and an arm of strength been commissioned to deliver."

A week later, in an editorial entitled simply "Lady Franklin," Hall quoted a monologue, "Lady Franklin's Appeal to the North," which began "Oh, where my long-lost one! art thou, / 'Mid Arctic seas and wintry skies?" He went on to express deep sympathy for Lady Franklin in her ordeal, and commented that "all men must feel a lively interest in the fate of these bold men, and be most desirous to contribute toward their restoration to their country and their homes." The implication was that Franklin's men were still alive to be restored. On June 18 he began a series about four Russian sailors who had been marooned on Spitzbergen for six years with virtually no equipment. At first they had suffered greatly, but gradually they had become inured to the harsh environment and had adapted to it. When they were rescued, all were alive and healthy. Hall drew the obvious conclusion: so might Franklin and his men have survived and be waiting for rescue.

During that spring, Dr. Isaac Hayes, who had been surgeon on Kane's second expedition, was preparing to go north again to prove the existence of the Open Polar Sea and to reach the North Pole. On June 30 Hall printed a long editorial entitled "Arctic Exploration," which concluded:

> The United States should contribute liberally toward the advancement of Arctic discoveries. In no direction does the eye of wonderment turn more readily than to the unknown North. There, around the Northern axis, are millions of square miles of open Polar Sea, ice-ribs, and land yet undiscovered. Let the United States Government be the first to plant her flag upon the North Pole. Americans can do it—and *will*. Dr. Hayes, count us one of the American Arctic Expedition now fitting out.

Hall's offer to join the Hayes expedition was apparently only rhetorical, but he soon reached the moment of decision. Two weeks after writing this editorial, he sold his newspaper and set to work organizing an expedition of his own. He intended to find and to rescue survivors of the Franklin Expedition.

During the ten years that Hall had lived in Cincinnati he had achieved at least moderate success. He had arrived a migrant, semiskilled workman; by the end of the decade he was a moderately successful, if not precisely substantial, businessman. He apparently had enjoyed his career; he had showed enthusiasm for Cincinnati's technological and financial enterprise, sharing in its expansion, reveling in its spirit. During the decade, he had educated himself far above the level that he had reached when he first arrived in the city; even his handwriting had improved in the course of the ten years. He had a wife and a daughter, and was soon to have a son. Although he had a reputation for eccentricity, he apparently was liked by his friends and neighbors.

Yet suddenly, at the age of thirty-eight, Hall decided to scuttle his career and set out on an endeavor for which he had no training, a venture that promised only hardship. Several years later, after he had returned from his first expedition, he wrote, "It seemed to me as if I had been called."[11] The voice that called him, he firmly believed, came from without. Even allowing for the rhetoric of the time and for Hall's own overheated prose, his journal makes it evident that he indeed had a sense of religious mission: Hall was devout, and he believed that God had destined him to find Franklin survivors or at least to solve the mystery of the expedition's fate. But the voice that called him obviously came also from within and was the voice of his own self; in making his decision, Hall was impelled by inner needs and desires that he did not understand and that we can discern only dimly. Perhaps the world was too much with him and he yearned after the image of the wilderness that haunted so many American romantics during the period when the wilderness itself was rapidly disappearing. Although Hall had enjoyed his life in Cincinnati, perhaps his little enterprises, his seal-press patent, his engraving business, his newspapers, and his publicity stunts had begun to weigh him down. In ten years he had inevitably become enmeshed in the myriad responsibilities and dependences that are a part of civilized life. He had gained much, but only at the expense of his independence. He could have gone farther west to an agrarian frontier, but he was not a farmer by inclination; besides, the west was already spawning communities of its own, and it was possibly community life

that Hall wanted to escape. One place where he could escape
it was the Far North.

The word "escape" can be misleading. It comes too easily to
the mouths of those who wish to condemn a nonconformist,
and it usually implies that what is being escaped *from* is somehow real, what is being escaped *to* somehow unreal. Hall
would not find a land of romance or heroics in the Arctic; he
would encounter realities different in kind from the realities
of life in Cincinnati, perhaps simpler, but harsher in their
simplicity, and he would discover that primitive life has responsibilities and dependences more stringent if less complex
than those of civilization. When he returned a second time
and a third to the fierce world he experienced on his first
expedition, he was not "escaping" in any pejorative sense of
the word. Before he left on the first expedition, however,
escape surely was one of his motives, and in his ignorance he
idealized the world that lay in the Canadian north.

Whatever his motives, Hall immediately set to work trying
to promote his expedition. His first step was to call on as many
prominent Cincinnatians as he could, in the hope of persuading them to sign a petition asking the British government for
the loan of a ship, the *Resolute,* which had been abandoned to
the ice by the British fleet in search of Franklin in 1853, found
adrift by an American whaler two years later, then refitted
and returned to England by the United States government.
Hall wrote his petition and had it signed by several important
men, including Governor Salmon Chase and Senator George
Pugh. He was in the process of obtaining other signatories
when word reached Cincinnati that Francis Leopold McClintock and the *Fox* had arrived in Portsmouth, England, on
September 24, bearing news of Franklin's death, evidence of
the subsequent loss of the ships, and relics of Crozier's terrible
march down the shores of King William Island.

Most men would have been discouraged: McClintock's
success seemed to eliminate the need for any further search
expeditions. But Hall was determined to go ahead with his

plans, reasoning (or rationalizing) that many questions remained unanswered and that McClintock had not been able to talk at length with the King William Island Eskimos, who, Hall was certain, had all the answers. "Moreover," he wrote several years later, "I felt convinced that survivors might yet be found." He could not resist a burst of competitive patriotism and went on: "I said to myself, since England has abandoned the field, let me, an humble citizen of the United States, try to give to the Stars and Stripes the glory of still continuing it, and perchance succeed in accomplishing the work."[12] So certain was he that he would reach the Arctic that he began to train for the expedition—in a way that did nothing to diminish his reputation for eccentricity. He took to camping on a hill behind Cincinnati's observatory. He pitched a tent, carried up a Spartan supply of food and water, and spent several cool autumn nights in what passed for the wilds. The only hardship he had to endure, however, was caused by the curiosity of the local citizens: one night two drunken Irishmen paid him a visit and insisted that he give them some of the whiskey that they assumed he must have; when he denied having any spirits with him, they fired a shotgun in his direction, and he was forced to flee barefoot and almost naked. The newspaper reports of this incident aroused the mirth of the entire city.

But men of importance—Governor Chase, Senator Pugh, Mayor Bishop, industrialist Miles Greenwood, future governor William Dennison—took Hall and his project seriously. They were impressed by his intensity of purpose and swayed by his conviction that more could be done than had been done by McClintock. Perhaps they, and others like them who helped Hall, hoped to experience adventure vicariously through this energetic man.

For some reason Hall gave up the idea of petitioning the British for the loan of the *Resolute,* but he did write a circular describing his project; it was signed by twenty-eight city leaders:

THIS IS TO MEMORIALIZE ALL lovers of Man and of Geography, History and Science, to cooperate, by all methods and means in their power to facilitate and assist our fellow countryman, Charles Francis Hall, of Cincinnati, Ohio, in the formation of, and fitting out an American Expedition, in search of Survivors of Sir John Franklin's Exploring Party (consisting of 138 persons [the number is inaccurate]; only 27 of whom are known to be dead.) Secondly, for satisfactorily settling and completing the history of the last Franklin Expedition; and Thirdly, to promote and benefit the cause of Geography, Navigation, Natural History and Science.*

At this stage, Hall hoped that he could create a full-scale expedition. The plan he outlined in his circular was ambitious:

Such an Expedition, with proper vessel or vessels, with competent and experienced Commander, Officers, and Crew, with a complete outfit and provision for from two to three years cruise; to embark from an Eastern port of the United States of America, on or about the first day of June, A.D. 1860; and proceed via Davis' Straits, Baffin's Bay, Lancaster Sound, Barrow's Strait, Prince Regent's Inlet to Bellot Strait; thence from the North coast to Boothia to commence the search—extending it to King William's Land, and the adjacent regions, until a thorough and satisfactory investigation shall have been made of all that portion of the Arctic world, and the humanitarian object attained of discovering some survivor of the lost companions of Sir John Franklin or ascertaining the ultimate fate of the members of that Expedition, who up to this day remain unaccounted for, being no less than one hundred and eleven souls, whose history the loud voice of mankind, from all generous natures, demands shall not remain forever shrouded in obliv-

* Original spelling, punctuation, and word use of source materials have been preserved throughout.—C. L.

ion, while energetic intelligence and American enterprize can hope to rescue a single survivor, or furnish the solution of their ultimate history.

In the beginning, then, Hall hoped to command a large expedition with possibly two ships at his disposition, and he intended to follow the familiar route through Lancaster Sound into the Archipelago. In time his grandiose plans were diminished.

By January 1860 Hall had realized that there was a limit to what he could accomplish in Cincinnati; there he could solicit the attention of wealthy men and gather some funds, but on the East Coast were the explorers who knew the Arctic, the whalers who could supply ships, the men of financial and political power who could help him shape his plans into an actual expedition. He busied himself writing letters to such men as Isaac Hayes, Henry Grinnell, and Cyrus Field, making good use of letters of introduction given to him by his more prominent backers in Cincinnati. By early February the groundwork was laid, and on February 7 he left Cincinnati to return to the East for the first time since he had left it as a young man. On that day Hall began to keep a journal. His notebooks had been a collection of random thoughts and facts rather than a journal, but now he began to jot down a day-by-day account of his activities. At first the daily entries were spare and factual, but as Hall's enthusiasm mounted he wrote longer entries, and through the purple prose and stock rhetoric of his style the man himself would occasionally emerge, looking out at the world with a diffidence that only partly concealed his driving energy and ambition.

After spending a few hours in Columbus talking to Governor Dennison, Hall took a train to Philadelphia, where he stayed for two days before leaving for New York. In Philadelphia he met Isaac Hayes and Robert Kane, Elisha's brother, and spent hours talking about his own plans and about Hayes's projected North Polar expedition. Before he left for

New York he was drawn irresistibly to the wharfs, where he was pleased by a chance encounter with a schooner captain who had been on a northern whaling voyage in 1853 and had seen some of the Franklin search ships that had crowded the Arctic that year.

Hall remained in New York only one day; he planned to return for a long stay, but he wanted to go to New London immediately in order to begin negotiations with whaling firms for a ship. He did not waste the day, however, because he met the man who was to forward his career as an explorer more than any other person. When Hall met him, Henry Grinnell was the United States manager of the Liverpool and London Insurance Company, but the position was only a latter-day occupation for a man who had made a fortune many years before. Grinnell had been born in the great whaling port of New Bedford; before he was twenty he had moved to New York and become a clerk in a commission house, then a partner with his brothers in the firm of Fish, Grinnell & Company, which before Henry joined it had already expanded from a small whale-oil business into a large shipping firm. Under the leadership of the Grinnell brothers and Henry's brother-in-law, Robert Minturn, the firm grew even larger, and soon was one of the strongest mercantile houses in New York. Henry had retired in 1850, not to relax, but to devote more time to his other interests. He was one of the founders and the first president of the American Geographical and Statistical Society (now the American Geographical Society), and he was patron saint of American activities in the Arctic. When, in 1849, the United States government balked at sending out rescue expeditions after Franklin, it was Grinnell who organized and financed the First Grinnell Expedition. Three years later, he did the same for the Second Grinnell Expedition, commanded by Kane. Although he was still involved in whale oil and shipping, and therefore perhaps desired knowledge of the northern seas, his motives were essentially unselfish, a combination of the humanitarian and the scientific: Grinnell was a merchant, but he was also a philanthropist.

Hall dined with Grinnell on the evening of February 13, and was pleased at the great interest shown in what Hall was calling "The New Franklin Research Expedition." They arranged to meet again when Hall returned to New York, and Grinnell gave him the names of several men to see in New London. The next afternoon Hall left for that port on the Norwich and Worcester Railroad. After Hall explained his mission, the N. & W. agent in New York gave him free passage on the train. Hall's persuasiveness counted even in small things, for his funds were very limited.

Knowing that his week in New London would probably make or break the expedition, Hall acted rapidly. On the morning after his arrival he called on the whaling firm of Williams and Haven, and was excited when the partners offered him a small (91-ton) schooner, the *Amaret,* for a mere two thousand dollars. He was excited less because he considered the ship a bargain than because the *Amaret,* when she had been named the *Rescue,* had been the tender for the *Advance* on the First Grinnell Expedition. Hall took it as a good omen that he was offered a ship that had been on Elisha Kent Kane's first Arctic voyage, and always referred to her as the *Rescue.* He could not commit himself to the purchase until his plans were settled and he had the necessary funds, but he assured Williams and Haven that he probably would accept their offer in the near future.

Hall spent much of the week engrossed by the tales of New London and Groton whalers who had been on Arctic cruises and who were to play a large part in his own career. He was willing to listen for hours as the tough, experienced men reminisced about their experiences on the Baffin Bay and Davis Strait whaling grounds. Captain Christopher Chapel told Hall of his winters in Northumberland Inlet (now known as Cumberland Sound); Captain George Tyson described

the Eskimo seal-hunting techniques that he had seen used
during his several years in the north; William Sterry, a
nautical jack-of-all-trades who was a favorite crewman of many
whaling captains, told stories about the long periods of time
when he had actually lived with Eskimos; Mr. Haven of Williams and Haven shocked Hall by telling him, as Hall wrote
in his journal, "of the disgraceful conduct of a well-known
Commander (not unknown to history) who during a winter
in the Arctic Regions turned his vessel into a ————!" (Hall,
although leaving a blank, clarifies what the commander
turned his ship into with his comment, "What was it that
brought destruction upon Sodom & G? This was damnable to
thus treat the untutored Esquimaux. The males were indignant at the outrages committed upon their wives and daughters by CIVILIZED (?) WHITE MAN: O, my countrymen! Instead
of lifting that poor benighted people by teaching virtue and
civilization, you carry devils and damnation to them.")

Although Hall obviously enjoyed listening to the whalers,
he also had a practical purpose in mind as he listened; he
had to find a captain and crew for his proposed voyage. Early
in his stay in New London, he met his first choice for captain,
John Quayle. Not only was Quayle an experienced Arctic
navigator, he also had commanded the *Rescue* on her last
three voyages and therefore had the advantage of being
familiar with the ship that Hall hoped to obtain. Although he
was impressed by Quayle, and although Quayle had volunteered to command his ship for him, Hall took care, as it
turned out wisely, to look for other possibilities. Both Captain
Christopher Chapel and Captain B. F. Brown, who were
planning cruises to Baffin Bay in the summer, offered Hall
passage if he failed to find a ship of his own. More attractive
to him was the offer of Captain Sidney O. Budington. He, too,
could offer only passage, but he had an advantage in Hall's
eyes: living with him was an Eskimo, Kudlago, whom he had
brought back from Baffin Island on his last cruise, and if Hall
went north with Budington, he would be able to use Kudlago

as an interpreter and guide. Hall wrote after meeting him that "he was as fine a speciman of that strange people as was ever seen." (Of course Hall had no standard of comparison at this time; not long after, he accosted a Chinese on the streets of New York and asked him if he was an Eskimo.) Hall was immediately biased in Kudlago's favor when he heard that Yankee sailors called him "Yankee John" because he preferred American to English whalers. Mrs. Budington had instructed Kudlago in civilized ways and had tutored him in English. She told Hall that he was quick to learn but always remained impassive: the first time he saw the most impressive of man's creations, the locomotive, his face remained calm as it roared past him. "He looked upon the works of civilization with interest," Hall wrote in his journal, "but never with wonder."

Hall's trip to New London stimulated and pleased him. At long last he had met men who knew the Arctic—and every one of them had assured him that some of Franklin's men might still be alive. He had located a ship that would suit his purpose, and in John Quayle he had found an experienced ship's captain. If by some chance he was not able to buy the *Rescue*, he could fall back on one of the offers of passage on a whaler, which would at least get him to Baffin Island. His optimism is indicated by his reaction to the foul weather that battered New London during much of his stay. "I believe it sacrilege to say that the Elements war," he wrote. "The Elements never war. As the snow came driving into my face— into my clothes—down into my busom, I said 'how beautiful you are. Thou wert created by the same hand that made the stars—Worlds—SYSTEMS! The same power doth rule thee now that ruleth the Heavens.' God be praised. The Elements are always at Peace." It was a dangerous attitude for a man about to go into the Arctic.

Hall returned to New York by steamer. Again he had free passage thanks to the kindness of the ticket agent: "There is good feeling among all whom I approach for the proposed

Expedition," Hall remarked when noting this contribution. He arrived in New York on the afternoon of February 23 and spent much of that evening closeted with Henry Grinnell, reporting his progress in New London to the man who he hoped would be his patron. Grinnell offered Hall the use of his library, and the next day took him to the library of the American Geographical and Statistical Society. There Hall spent many hours during the weeks that followed, absorbed in reading works about the Arctic that he had not been able to obtain in Cincinnati.

He was a devout observer of the Sabbath, whenever possible spending his Sundays quietly by himself. On the first Sunday after his return to New York he sat in his hotel room, counting his blessings and enumerating them carefully in his journal:

1. A vessel of great historical interest—properly strengthened for the ices of the North—is all ready for this expedition.
2. A Commander, of tried experience, having perfect command of the Esquimaux Language—in ability to control dogs for sledge travelling even surpassing the Esquimaux —awaits an engagement. [Hall had just received a letter from Quayle repeating his offer to command the ship.]
3. The Kane family has offered assistance in the enterprise.
4. Childs and Peterson [a Philadelphia firm] as represented by Mr. Childs, has also offered assistance.
5. But last, tho' the greatest of all—Henry Grinnell, the one to whom the world owes a debt of gratitude for his spirit in sending forth two Expeditions to recover those who had gone into the unknown North for the purpose of doing GOOD TO MANKIND. Yes, Henry Grinnell is with me. This, I say, is the greatest of all. He believes, with me, that there are survivors of the Franklin Expedition—that no PROPER search has yet been made to determine the great fact.
6. I should not forget to write of those in my dear city, Cincinnati—of Senator Chase, Gov. Dennison of Colum-

bus—all of whom feel to do all they can to assist in this work.

Clearly item six is an afterthought and an anticlimax: his weeks in the East had erased almost all thoughts of his "dear city" from Hall's mind. If the truth be known, he was a bit dazzled by his experiences in the East, in particular by his meetings with the Great. He was taken to the Athenaeum Club and there introduced to what he called "many of the 1st Class men." He was dined if not wined (Hall was a tee-totaler) by Cyrus Field in his mansion, and he bowled tenpins in the private gymnasium on the top floor. (After that glorious evening, Hall, made somewhat incoherent by the experience, scrawled in his journal: "The 20th Century man—The-Atlantic-Cable-genius that linked two worlds into one—Cyrus W. Field—the AMERICAN! Yes 20th Century man! One hundred years ahead of the common people. He's the man for my model.") Above all it was Henry Grinnell who aroused Hall's awe. One morning (Hall noted precisely that it was at "9 O'clock 45 Min.") he was in his hotel room when he heard footsteps in the corridor: "I heard footsteps which instantly conveyed to me the thought: perhaps they are Mr. Grinnell's —A rap!—I opened the door & indeed there he was before me. Can it be possible that so poor a creature as I can be worthy the consideration of so worthy a man as he?"

If there is a whiff of snobbery and sycophancy in Hall's reactions to the Great World, why not? It was indeed remark-able that Henry Grinnell sought out Charles Francis Hall in his dingy hotel room and spent many hours with him, intro-ducing him to his friends, guiding him around New York, listening to his plans, giving him advice and help. The reason, of course, was that Grinnell and others had been impressed by the man and his mission. If Hall was occasionally a sycophant, more often he was too concerned with what he was doing to be bothered about his social inferiority. He attached himself to the rich and the powerful because that was the only way that he could further his project; if he was sometimes over-impressed by their grandeur and his inferiority, no harm was done: it was of only minor and occasional concern to him. They, in turn, were impressed not by his sycophancy but by his earnestness and intensity. This awkward, sometimes boorish man had the ability to convince others with his own conviction.

The organization of his expedition was rapidly coming to a head. After receiving the letter from Captain Quayle repeating his offer to command the expedition ship, Hall wired a reply and asked him to come to New York at his earliest convenience, adding that his fare would be paid. Hall wanted to have Grinnell meet Quayle, because much depended on Grinnell's approval; Hall still had no firm commitment from Grinnell of funds or anything else. For almost a week he waited nervously for Quayle's arrival. Williams and Haven had asked him to decide by March 8 about the purchase of the *Rescue;* on March 6, Hall wrote to them asking that the deadline be put off for ten days. Until he had Quayle under contract and, more important, until he knew that he had the money, he did not want to commit himself to such an expense.

When Captain Quayle finally arrived from New London, Hall immediately took him to Henry Grinnell's office for a conference. To Hall's distress, Quayle demurred about accepting the command. He modestly said that others were better qualified, citing Captain Christopher Chapel. He said that if Chapel accepted the command, he, Quayle, would gladly serve as First Officer—a proposition that Hall found "generous and full of the love for man." Naïvely, Hall did not even consider the possibility that Quayle was stalling for time. He immediately wired Chapel, asking him to come to New York. That night Hall, Quayle, and Grinnell met at Grinnell's mansion for dinner and further discussed the expedition. It was agreed that the route to be taken to King William Island was through Hudson's Strait, Foxe Channel, and Fury and Hecla Strait, rather than the usual northern one through Lancaster Sound. All looked upon it as a good omen that when Quayle accidentally tipped a glass on their chart, the spilled wine followed the proposed route.

The next two days proved to be momentous. Grinnell had asked Hall to address a meeting of the American Geographical and Statistical Society on the evening of March 8. The featured speaker was Dr. Isaac Hayes, whom Hall had seen several times during his stay in New York. Hayes had come up from Philadelphia to work on the final stages of preparation for his North Polar expedition, and he was to discuss it at the meeting. Another attraction was Captain Sidney Budington and the Eskimo Kudlago: at the request of the Society, Hall had wired an invitation to Budington.

Captain Chapel arrived in New York early that morning with his wife, and Grinnell and Hall called on them at their hotel. Mrs. Chapel quietly but firmly said that she could not permit her aging husband to sail into Arctic waters again, and Captain Chapel did not argue with her. Hall's disappointment was tempered only by his mounting excitement at the prospect of the meeting to be held that night.

He did not describe the meeting in his journal; instead he pasted into its pages three newspaper clippings that described the event. Dr. Hayes had spoken at some length, tracing his proposed route to the Open Polar Sea and the North Pole on a large map. Hall had spoken only briefly, outlining his plans and stressing the fact that McClintock had accounted for only a small number of Franklin's men. Kudlago had been the biggest attraction for the newspapermen at the meeting, although they had some difficulty with his name (two spelled it "Cudlockdchue" and the third "Cudlouchdchdue"). Hall's faith in Quayle's ability seemed well founded when the Captain spoke fluent Eskimo with Kudlago, translating his comments about the civilized world for the benefit of the press.

Unfortunately, these public affairs helped to conceal something that was going on in private. During the course of the

evening, Hall noticed Isaac Hayes and Captain Quayle con-
versing quietly in a corner, but he did not think about it at
the time. The entry in his journal on the following day reveals the subject of the conversation:

> I dare not put upon paper the double dealing—the rank
> inhumanity of Dr. I. I. Hays—& of Capt. P. T. Quayle—
> Here I am, life devoted to the rescuing of some lone sur-
> vivor of Sir John Franklin's men—& yet I met with these
> parties who appear to be friends & yet within their hearts
> must lurk deep damnation! Why? Capt. Quayle had been
> recommended to me by the various citizens of New London
> as being the proper party to command the New Franklin
> Research Expedition—I was introduced to him—he. ap-
> peared anxious for the adventure. Hays, learning of his
> excellent qualities as a navigator, through certain means
> got an interview with him—has in fact upset all my work—
> This damnable work has been communicated to me by
> Capt. S. O. Buddington of New London. Let the Cur-
> tain drop—I will go on, God willing, with my work.

Hayes had stolen Hall's captain for his own expedition. Hall
later added that he had proof that Hayes and Quayle had met
previously, and that they had only pretended to meet for the
first time that night.

Although the loss of Quayle was a serious blow, Hall had
other possibilities to fall back on. Budington, even as he told
Hall of Hayes's "damnable work," repeated the offer to transport him to Baffin Island aboard the *George Henry,* which
Budington was to command on his next cruise; he assured
Hall that with the aid of Kudlago a crew of Eskimos could be
hired in Baffin Island, and that a small party could make its
way from Cumberland Sound or Frobisher Strait to King
William Island by boat. Budington even offered to oversee
the construction of an expedition boat. The next day Captain
and Mrs. Chapel called to apologize for the behavior of their
friend Quayle; they told Hall that Chapel's brother would be

cruising to Repulse Bay in the summer and probably could take Hall with him; at Repulse Bay Hall could employ Eskimos to guide him through Fury and Hecla Strait to King William Island. Hall apparently also had another plan of his own, about which he is very vague in his journal. All he wrote was that on Saturday, March 10, two days after the Geographical Society meeting, he handed Henry Grinnell "an outline of a proposition." Grinnell asked him to return on the following Monday for his opinion of it.

Hayes's treachery still rankled. Hall spent that Sabbath in his hotel room brooding about it. "I pity him," he wrote, obviously not meaning it. "I pity his cowardice & weakness," he went on, getting warm. "I spurn his TRICKERY!—his DEVILTRY!!"

Blow followed blow. On Monday, he went to see Henry Grinnell, as arranged: "At 4 o'clock P.M. I called on Mr. Grinnell—he had concluded it would be an injudicious step for me to go as proposed—My heart is———Well, I will do as God sees best———" Hall was resilient, however, and he was convinced that energy and will power would overcome any obstacle. He had started a course in navigation with "an old gentleman" as tutor; all during this troubled week he continued to go to his lessons, for, as he wrote in his journal, "Navigation I must understand, or else how shall I lead forth from the wilderness of the North the poor survivors of the Franklin Expedition?" The image of himself as a guide so appealed to him, apparently, that he did not bother to consider the possibility that some of the "poor survivors" might know more navigation than he could ever hope to learn. Not only did he continue his lessons in navigation after Grinnell had criticized his proposition, he also soon jotted down another proposition on the back pages of his journal:

> The undersigned, C. F. Hall of Cincinnati, O., will leave the United States, on the last Tuesday of May next (D. V.) on board the good ship "George Henry," S. O. Buddington,

Master, the owner of said vessel, Messrs Williams &
Haven of New London, having generously extended to me
conveyance to Northumberland Inlet.

My object is to acquire personal knowledge of the language
& life of the Esquimaux, with a view thereafter to visit the
Lands of King William, Boothia & Victoria—to endeavor
by my personal investigation to determine more satisfactorily the fate of the 105 companions of Sir John Franklin,
now known to have been living on the 25th day of Apr. 1848
[Hall here is referring to the message found by McClintock
in the cairn at Point Victory].

Hall went on to sketch his plan: he and a crew of Eskimos
would leave the *George Henry* and sail a small boat up an
arm of "Northumberland Inlet" (Cumberland Sound), then
make a short portage "to a lake said to be by the natives
within a short distance of said western extremity of said Inlet.
Having arrived at said lake, our voyage will be continued
westward to the outlet, which by Esquimaux report, is a
navigable river emptying into Foxe Channel." From Foxe
Basin, the party would sail to Igloolik, near Fury and Hecla
Strait, and there hire more Eskimos to guide it to King
William Island. As it turned out, Hall was not to use this
route; indeed, for some unknown reason the *George Henry*
did not even put into Cumberland Sound, but the plan is remarkable for one thing: it is based entirely on what might be
called the "hearsay geography" of Eskimos; no white man had
been all the way to the head of Cumberland Sound, let alone
into the interior of Baffin Island. It is an example of the
Eskimo skill in the oral depiction of terrain, a skill with
which Hall was soon to become familiar: the lake west of
Cumberland Sound is Nettilling Lake, the navigable river
is the Koukjuak.

Hall concluded his proposal with a ringing statement of
motive ("The proposed Voyage is one I make for the cause of
science—for the cause of Geographical Discoveries—WITH

THE SOLE VIEW TO ACCOMPLISH GOOD TO MANKIND") and with
an estimate of expense:

Salary for 2½ years of a Companion $600	$1,500
Provision—mostly Pemmican for long journies	$ 250
Instruments, Chronometers, Ammunition & Guns	$ 350
Boat with rigging (to be specially made)	$ 100
General outfit, Articles for Barter with the Esquimaux	$ 300
	$2,500
Additional Pemmican &c	$ 500
	$3,000

He hoped to persuade Henry Grinnell not only to contribute
toward this modest sum, but also to act as treasurer of the
fund when it was collected. On the day after he wrote the
proposal, he read it aloud to Grinnell; much to his relief,
Grinnell approved of it and said that he would contribute
to and oversee the fund. He even gave Hall a letter to this
effect. "HE IS THE FRIEND OF ALL MEN," Hall exclaimed in his
journal. "He has blessed the World—the World will bless him
& his memory forever." That night he wrote to Williams and
Haven, requesting passage on the *George Henry*.

Feeling that his plans were definite, Hall decided to return
to Cincinnati. He stayed in New York only long enough to see
Horace Greeley in the offices of the *Tribune*. As Hall had
hoped, the publisher said that he would pay well for any com-
munications that might be sent from the Arctic during the
expedition, although Greeley admitted that he was skeptical
about there being any Franklin survivors. Hall also paid a
last visit to Grinnell just before he took the train to Philadelphia. That day Grinnell had received a letter from his son
Cornelius, in England. At a party given by Lady Franklin,
the boy had met Francis Leopold McClintock, who had

severely criticized the reported behavior of Isaac Hayes on the Second Grinnell Expedition. When the expedition had seemed doomed in Kane Basin, Hayes had tried to make a desperate sledge journey to Upernavik but had been forced to return; McClintock told Cornelius Grinnell that in his opinion, although the sledge journey had been made with Kane's permission, it had been an act of desertion. Hall, obviously delighted to hear that his new enemy had been criticized by the most famous living Arctic explorer, left New York with the sweet taste of righteousness in his mouth— perhaps even enough to sweeten the sour fact that he had to borrow twenty-five dollars from one J. B. Kitchen (whose name appears in the journal only in this connection) to get home to Cincinnati.

He paused for a few days in Philadelphia and Pittsburgh on his return trip, arriving in Cincinnati on March 20. He immediately went to bed with a severe cold, and there he stayed for a week. For the following month and a half his journal entries are skimpy. He continued his navigation lessons, using a textbook; he wrote and received letters to and from the East; he read more books about the Arctic and pored through newspapers for Arctic items. (He noted a report from New York that Henry Grinnell was to be treasurer for the Isaac Hayes expedition, but he wrote nothing about his reaction to the fact that he and Hayes were to share Grinnell's favor and services.) He made arrangements for the preparation of more than a ton of pemmican; he hired a carpenter to make a sledge, which was to be a copy of Kane's; he negotiated for the purchase of such necessities as firearms and gunpowder. Presumably, he spent some time with his pregnant wife and his daughter, but he does not mention them in his journal.

His main problem, of course, was money. One day he drew up a list of thirty eminent prospective contributors, each of whom was to donate one hundred dollars: the list was topped by the President and Vice President of the United States and included senators, congressmen, judges, and businessmen.

Nothing ever came of the scheme, although he did get donations from some of the individuals on the list (not from the President and Vice President). Miles Greenwood, a philanthropic industrialist, was the first Cincinnatian to volunteer a contribution, and he also acted as Cincinnati manager for the fund, arranging meetings at which Hall spoke to publicize his venture, including one gala affair at Burnet House.

It is not difficult to disentangle the finances of the "New Franklin Research Expedition," as Hall insistently called his venture in spite of its reduced scale. Apparently he received not cash contributions but guarantees of specific amounts of money for the payment of bills: in other words, his expedition was underwritten up to an amount that is now unknown (we do not know, for example, if he reached his desired total of $3,000 in guarantees). The only financial statement available is contained in an appendix to Hall's book *Arctic Researches and Life Among the Esquimaux,* and that is a budget, an itemized breakdown of expenses and contributions. This budget is startlingly small: $980. In the expense column are such items as:

James Green, of New York, 2 self-registering thermometers	$ 3.00
Anson Baker & Co., of New York, 6 guns, 1 rifle, duplicating locks, etc.	$159.00
John H. Brower & Co., New York, 232 lbs. Borden's meat-biscuit	$ 30.00
J. & G. W. Crandall, New London, woolen shirts	$ 7.00
Harris, Williams & Co., New London, pipes, tobacco	$ 20.00

The two largest single items were the expedition boat, which cost only $105, and the pemmican, which cost $240. In the donations column are a few moderately large donations, including Henry Grinnell's $343, but most are very small; Mrs. Hall's sad little $27 was by no means the smallest.

Services and equipment were also donated and duly noted in the appendix. The most important single donor was the firm of Williams and Haven: they gave Hall and his meager equipment free transportation into and out of the Arctic. So small was the expedition that Hall was able to account for such items donated as "Z. B. Coffin, Cincinnati, O., 1 lb. tea," "Hamlen & Smith, Cincinnati, O., 1 dirk and tooth extractor," and "Thomas H. Bates & Co., New York, fishhooks, 9 m. needles, and 2 dozen sewing cushions." Such was the equipment of the New Franklin Research Expedition.

"Thursday, May 10—Bid farewell to home—started on my journey East preparatory to embarking on the 29th from New London, Ct." Traveling as usual on free passes, Hall, after spending one day in Philadelphia, arrived in New York on May 13. For several days thereafter he happily worked on the final arrangements for the expedition and spent many hours with Henry Grinnell anticipating the venture. All seemed to be going well. Then his past caught up with him and momentarily threatened to blast the fruition of the months of hard work. On May 17 he was in Grinnell's office when "a gentleman called enquiring for me." The gentleman was a deputy sheriff, who informed Hall that his equipment and supplies had been attached at the request of one William C. Pomroy; he handed Hall a summons to appear before the Court of Common Pleas within twenty days. Pomroy claimed that in Cincinnati on December 16, 1859, Hall had signed a promissory note for $438.70, to be paid in three months, and that the sum had never been paid. What happened in this case can be reconstructed only from a few crumpled documents that Hall angrily shoved into an envelope after the affair was finished, and they leave many questions unanswered: Who was Pomroy? Had Hall borrowed money from him, or was the note signed for some service or goods? Had Hall actually signed the note? Was Pomroy's claim legitimate, or was he cheating in some way? Finally, how was the case settled? It was settled out of court, but how?

Two days after Hall received the summons, he strode into the office of Benjamin Franklin Sawyer, Pomroy's lawyer. Pomroy was there at the time (was he in the East simply to prosecute this matter, or had he left Cincinnati for good?), and Hall, as he wrote in his journal, "gave him such a lecture as my soul & the occasion bid me." A lecture, of course, was no solution, but somehow a solution was found: within a few days, Hall and Grinnell were threatening a counter-suit, and shortly thereafter Hall's goods were released. Among the papers that Hall shoved into the envelope was a smaller, yellow envelope scored over with his handwriting: "History will bring to some actors in this scene shame and repentance! The hardened heart of the first named below will be exception—how can shame & repentance be brought to a heart of stone?—Wm. C. Pomroy, J. Allen Wells, B. Franklin Sawyer." Then he used some scriptural rhetoric, which, rather shockingly, he seemed to find pertinent: "My persecutors shall stumble & they shall not prevail; they shall be greatly ashamed; for they shall not prosper." Across the top of the envelope he wrote, "A PRECIOUS DOCUMENT WITHIN." Apparently, the envelope once contained material that explained how the case was settled, but now it is empty, and the whole affair remains in fog.

Pomroy had created the last obstacle to the New Franklin Research Expedition, and when that obstacle was removed, Hall was ready to leave. Several years later, in the introduction to his book about the expedition, he looked back over the long months of preparation that he had been forced to endure. There is a note of pride in his reminiscence:

> Courage and resolution were all that I needed; and though some persons might not concur in the wisdom or prudence of my effort, still, as my mind was upon it, try it I would, and try it I did. I need not enter upon all the many difficulties I encountered. These fall to the lot of every man who essays to try his hand at something new, and especially so if he starts on a path trodden without success before

him. But difficulties sharpen the wit and strengthen the
mind. The experience of my native land was before me in
proof of what man could accomplish; and I can now safely
say that, though the obstacles in my way were many and
great, I finally succeeded in overcoming them.

Just before Hall left New York for New London, Grinnell
gave him some good news: the *Rescue* was to sail with the
George Henry as a tender. Although the little schooner was
going along to assist in the whaling operations, not as a part
of Hall's expedition, Hall was warmed by the idea that one of
Elisha Kent Kane's ships was to be with him for at least part
of his journey.

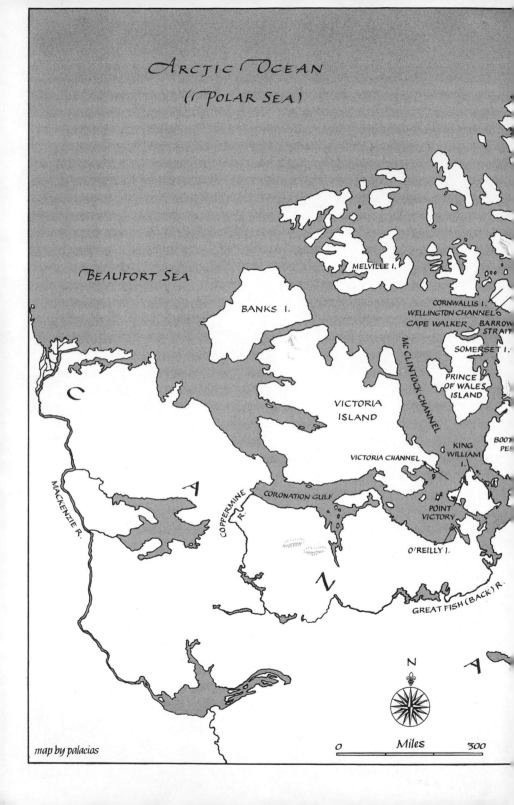

ARCTIC OCEAN
(POLAR SEA)

BEAUFORT SEA

MELVILLE I.

BANKS I.

CORNWALLIS I.
WELLINGTON CHANNEL
CAPE WALKER   BARROW
                   STRAIT

SOMERSET I.

Mc CLINTOCK CHANNEL

PRINCE
OF WALES
ISLAND

VICTORIA
ISLAND

C

A

VICTORIA CHANNEL

KING
WILLIAM
I.

BOOT
PEN

MACKENZIE R.

COPPERMINE R.

CORONATION GULF

POINT
VICTORY

O'REILLY I.

N

GREAT FISH (BACK) R.

N

map by palacios

0   Miles   300

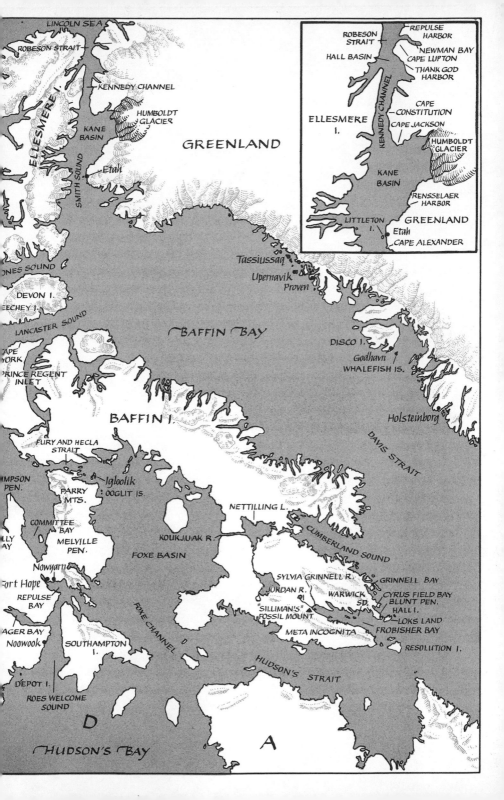

chapter two

Baffin Island—
Initiation

The *George Henry* and the *Rescue* sailed from New London on May 20, 1860, with thirty-one persons aboard, only one of whom was directly involved in the New Franklin Research Expedition: Charles Francis Hall himself. The *George Henry*, after all, was on a routine whaling cruise, and the expedition was only a side issue for her officers and crew; once Hall was put ashore on Baffin Island, with his sledge, boat, and meager equipment, the *George Henry* would go whaling. Enough had been written in the newspapers about the expedition, however, so that there was a small group of spectators on the wharf to watch Hall sail out to the *George Henry* in a harbor boat, accompanied by the mayor of New London and by Henry Grinnell. Grinnell had some last words as a steam tug towed the barque out to sea. He spoke to Hall of explorers of old, who, he said, relied not only on their own strength but also on the strength of God. Hall later wrote, "He bade me ever do the same; and, commending me to that MIGHTY BEING, he once more, with moistened eye, said 'Farewell!' and hastily embarked on the tug that was to convey the visitors on shore."[1]

Hall's elevated emotions at the departure were soon overwhelmed by other sensations. No sooner had the ship passed Montauk Point than he became violently seasick. He was miserable for several weeks, but as the ship sailed into more northern waters he recovered, to feel the excitement of a

landsman on his first sea voyage. The ocean stimulated Hall's
enthusiastic piety. He saw God in everything around him—
in petrels that sheared the air inches above the waves, in
whales and porpoises that breached near the ship every day,
in storms that he watched while clinging to a mast, in weird
refractions of Arctic light. Many travelers to the North have
thrilled at seeing their first iceberg; Hall went into a religious trance. He felt the berg's presence in the lowering
temperature before he actually saw it, and as the ship approached it, "it appeared a mountain of alabaster resting
calmly upon the busom of the dark blue sea." Hall called it
his "idol," and it evoked the usual burst of capitals, exclamation points, and underscoring in his journal: "I stood in the
presence of God's work! Its fashioning was that of the Great
Architect! He who hath builded such monuments, and casteth
them forth upon the waters of the sea, is God, and there can be
none other!" The farther north the *George Henry* sailed, the
more exalted Hall became:

> June 20th, Lat. 53°—07′ N, Long. 51°—16′ W. Approach-
> ing the North Axis of the Earth! Aye, nearing the goal of
> my fondest wishes. Everything relating to the Arctic Zone
> is deeply interesting to me. I love the snows, the ices—
> Icebergs—the Fauna and the Flora of the North! I love the
> circling sun, the long day, the Arctic night, when the Soul
> can commune with God in silent and reverential awe! I am
> on a mission of love. I feel to be in performance of a duty
> I owe to mankind, myself, God! Thus feeling, I am strong
> at heart, full of faith, ready to do or die in the cause I have
> espoused.

He was only at latitude 53° 7′, yet he felt that he was
approaching the north axis of the earth—he still knew the
Arctic only through his reading, but was convinced that
he loved it. Time and experience were to strain Hall's faith
in God and his love of the Arctic as God's handiwork. In the
North he was to see some ungodly things, ugly and brutish

rather than beautiful and sublime, but at the beginning of his first voyage he had a novice's enthusiasm, and could write on his thirtieth day out:

> The day is rainy and chilly—but what of this to a determined soul? Oh, to be strong from circumstance; to be excited by the powers of the mind; to be inspired, as it were, by the divine Spirit, that I may continue to the end of life in my studies of Nature and her laws! May I be strong in the day of battle; may I not forget that I am a child of Deity—a humble instrument created for Work!

Hall spent much of his time at sea reading and writing, but he also watched the officers and crew at their work and talked to them about the Arctic in their free moments. One of the crewmen was the old Arctic hand William Sterry, whom he had met in New London; "Sterry the cooper—Sterry the Ship's carpenter—Sterry the Ship's blacksmith—Sterry the mill-wright—Sterry the horse-jockey—Sterry the genius—the I-M-M-O-R-T-A-L Sterry," Hall called him in his journal. Sterry kept Hall constantly amused with his antics and his chatter, but he also knew Eskimos as well as anyone, having lived with them alone for months at a time, and he told the eager Hall much about their ways. Budington, whom Hall respected more each day (most pages of his journal contain the phrase "Capt. B. says . . . ," or "Budington reports that . . ."), was also willing to talk about Eskimos. He told Hall a story about Ugarng, an Eskimo whom he had brought south some years before, as he had brought Kudlago south. One day, he said, Ugarng earnestly asked why his dogs, who pulled his sledge and helped him hunt seal, were always dying off, whereas his aged mother, who was worthless to him, persisted in living. Hall was not amused.

Kudlago was aboard, but he had caught a cold in the fogs off Newfoundland and been seriously ill ever since, so Hall had little opportunity to talk to him. Kudlago was nursed and given special care. At his request a tent was put on deck

for him, and eider ducks were shot so that he might eat their
hearts and livers raw, as he was wont, but his condition
worsened. He probably had pneumonia; Eskimos, so hardy in
some ways, are strangely delicate in others and are very vulnerable to some viruses. By late June Kudlago was so sick
that they moved him out of his tent and back to his bunk. On
July 1, just as Greenland came into sight, he died. In the end
he talked of his home, and, according to Hall, his last words
were "*Teik-ko se-ko? Teik-ko se-ko?*" ("Do you see ice? Do
you see ice?") Hall presided over his burial at sea just off the
coast of Greenland. Kudlago was a loss, for Hall needed an
Eskimo guide and interpreter, and Kudlago would have been
the obvious choice. Nevertheless, Hall seemed to take morbid
pleasure in his role as minister in the burial, making "such
remarks as were deemed proper for the occasion" and "reading portions of appropriate exhortations from the 'Masonic
Manual.' "[2]

The *George Henry* put into Holsteinborg, Greenland, on
July 7. There she laid over for several weeks. Already excited because the sun had not set the previous night, and because of their kayak escort into the harbor, Hall could
hardly wait to get ashore and put his feet on Arctic soil at
last. According to his book on the expedition, on landing he
reached down, grabbed a handful of rocky earth, pressed it
to his lips, and apostrophized his surroundings: "Greenland's
mountains, I greet you!"[3] It was one of many operatic moments in Hall's written work. Perhaps they were pure fiction,
poses struck for the reading public, but more likely they actually occurred: it was an era of emotion-charged gesture.

Hall whiled away the time in Holsteinborg by indulging in
the favorite activity of Victorian travelers, the gathering of
statistics and specimens. He filled pages of his journal with
statistics on Holsteinborg: the district contained 187 Eskimos
and 10 Danes; of the 29 buildings in the village, 24 had stoves;
during the previous year the villagers had secured 5,000 lbs.
of seal blubber and 2,000 lbs. of shark liver; the 12 teach-

ers in the area were paid anything from $125 (Danish) to $6
per annum, etc. When Hall was not gathering statistics, he was
roaming the village and countryside with his sextant, telescope, measuring tape, and geological hammer. He was not a
trained scientist like Elisha Kent Kane, but he had educated
himself in botany and geology, and he shared the nineteenth-
century compulsion to weigh, measure, and collect.

On one of these excursions Hall was accompanied by an
Eskimo in whom he was particularly interested, Adam Beck,
who had been implicated in one shadowy, grim episode of the
search for Franklin, an episode that had led to Beck's ruina-
tion. During a stopover at Cape York on Ross's voyage to the
Archipelago, Beck, an interpreter for Sir John Ross aboard
the *Felix* in 1850–1 (the years of the most intense search for
Franklin), had talked to some Eskimos who apparently told
him a story that he repeated to his British officers. The Cape
York Eskimos, Beck said, reported that in 1846 two ships had
been destroyed by ice somewhere in the area, and their crews,
taking to the land, had been massacred by Eskimos. The
officers, horrified at the idea that this might have been the
fate of the Franklin expedition, questioned Beck harshly. Sir
John Ross believed his interpreter, but others branded him
a liar. A party was sent back to Cape York, led by Danish interpreter Carl Petersen, who asked the Eskimos about Beck's
tale. Petersen returned to the *Felix* to report that the Eskimos
did not confirm the story. Beck insisted that he had truthfully
told what he had heard, but few believed him; it was an un-
spoken assumption that he had made up his appalling yarn
in hopes of gaining some sort of reward. Beck became a pariah
to Arctic explorers, a man with a taint of horror about him.

In their climb up the mountains behind Holsteinborg, Hall
and Beck talked about the incident of ten years before. Beck
was ruined, poor and broken, but he continued to insist that
he had told the truth. "Carl Petersen no speak Husky
[Eskimo] quick—not good Husky speak—small speak Husky!"
he repeatedly told Hall; then, in rage: "Petersen speak Adam

Beck, lie! Carl Petersen plenty lie—damned lie!" Hall felt
sorry for Beck and believed that he had reported truthfully
what he had heard from the Cape York Eskimos; according
to Hall, he was simply "the instrument of communicating
fabrications of Cape York Esquimaux." This talk with Beck
was Hall's first encounter with a problem that was to become
crucial in his travels: How is one to separate fiction from fact
in the many stories told by Eskimos? Or, if accepting the essential truth of a story, how is one to know if the story
concerns the right persons? Perhaps the Cape York Eskimos
indeed had told a story based on fact, but perhaps it had concerned an event in the distant past, having nothing to do with
Franklin. As Hall was to discover, Eskimos tended to confuse
various stories about "kadloonas" (white men).

  Although he felt sorry for Beck and believed his story, Hall
did not ask him to be guide and interpreter for his expedition,
but he did ask another Eskimo, Lars Kleijt, a pilot in the
Holsteinborg harbor. Lars refused. His wife had died recently,
and he did not wish to leave his children in the dubious care
of his aged mother. "My mother old man," he explained.
"She no get dinner—my little ones die." Hall had to be content with acquiring only dogs in Holsteinborg; he purchased
six fine Huskies, hoping that he would find an Eskimo on
Baffin Island to teach him how to handle them.

  The *George Henry* and the *Rescue* left Holsteinborg for
Baffin Island on July 24. Holsteinborg had given Hall his first
taste of the Arctic; there he had seen Arctic flora and fauna
and Eskimos living in their own environment. The Eskimos
had impressed him greatly. "God has certainly blessed this
people with most noble VIRTUES," he wrote in his journal.
But a first taste could be misleading—Danish Greenland was
one thing, the Canadian North another. Greenland was civilized; Danish missionaries had been active there since the eighteenth century, and the Greenland Eskimos proudly called
themselves "Greenlanders." The natives, many of whom had
Danish blood in their veins, lived in houses and were at least

partly educated. In sailing from Greenland, Hall was heading toward the uncivilized, unexplored North—the Arctic wilderness.

Captain Budington had decided to head for Frobisher Strait rather than Northumberland Inlet. This suited Hall, as he believed, along with most white men of that time, that Frobisher Strait was indeed a strait, through which he could navigate to Foxe Channel. During the two-week crossing he came again under the spell of the maritime Arctic. He was awed, as so many other explorers have been, by the strange and often beautiful optical illusions created by refraction in northern seas. Mountains appeared and disappeared on the horizon; the sun, surrounded by a corona, was duplicated so that there were two suns and two coronas; the moon rose swollen to immense size and distorted into strange shapes; indescribable forms moved with miraculous fluidity between water and sky. As usual, Hall thought of God:

> A thousand youthful forms of the fairest outline seemed to be dancing to and fro, their white arms intertwined—bodies incessantly varying, intermixing, falling, rising, jumping, skipping, hopping, whirling, waltzing, resting, and again rushing to the mazy dance—never tired—ever playful—ever light and airy, graceful and soft to the eye. Who could view such wondrous scenes of divine enchantment and not exclaim, "O Lord, how manifold are thy works! In wisdom hast Thou made them all; the earth is full of Thy riches!"

A few days after this display of refraction, the *George Henry* was befogged off the coast of Baffin Island, and Budington had to hold his ship clear of the land for several days. When the fog cleared Hall was dazzled by his first clear sight of Baffin Island's mountains, not high, but rugged and snow-covered. As the ship sailed south down the coast toward

Frobisher Bay, he spent hours gazing at the land through his telescope, and one day he saw a strange sight: a small open boat, and in it white men. The Baffin Island coast from Cumberland Sound to Frobisher Bay was one of the major Arctic whaling grounds, but there was no whaling ship in sight.

> Capt. B. hailed them: "Who are you?"
> The steersman answered officer-like, "Crew from the *Ansell Gibbs* of New Bedford."
> "Where from?"
> "The north."
> "Where bound?"
> "South."
> As the Capt. & I stepped to the gangway, with a knowing nod he said in a low tone, "They are run-aways!"

In the boat were nine sailors, and they were indeed runaways, most of them from the *Ansell Gibbs*, one of a fleet of whalers in Cumberland Sound. Deciding that they could not endure the privations of northern whaling, they foolishly had stolen a boat and headed south, hoping to reach Nova Scotia. They had left Cumberland Sound only four days before, but already they suffered from hunger and exposure. Nevertheless, they stayed aboard the *George Henry* only a few hours; then, obviously fearing detention, they set out again. As Hall watched them leave, he drew hope from their harebrained endeavor and wrote in his journal: "If 9 men have undertaken such a journey—such a voyage of near 2000 miles, with so little preparation, what heart should I have to prosecute my undertakings!"*

---

* The deserters from the *Ansell Gibbs* were hardly a good example, although Hall did not know it at the time; not until his return to the United States did he learn their fate. As they sailed south after leaving the *George Henry*, their meager supplies gave out. They shot a bear and ate its meat for a short time; then two of them ran off with what was left of it and with the one compass aboard. Then one of the remaining men died, and the others, led by one Samuel Fisher, ate the corpse. Not long after, Fisher tried to murder one of his companions, but he was killed by his intended victim and was himself eaten. Two

Two days after the deserters from the *Ansell Gibbs* appeared and disappeared, the *George Henry* found anchorage in a bay that the Eskimos called Ookoolear, which Hall renamed Cornelius Grinnell Bay, after Henry Grinnell's son. He was often thus to take the prerogative of an explorer; in the years that followed he scattered the names of his friends and patrons around the Arctic landscape with largesse, although most of them seem somehow out of place: there is a Pugh Island (U.S. Senator), a Bishop Island (Mayor of Cincinnati), a Greenwood's Land (industrialist), a Hamlin's Bay (dentist); there is even one bleak stretch of water bearing the improbable name of Cincinnati Press Channel. Hall was only acting in a tradition of European explorers begun long before his time; ever since John Cabot and Martin Frobisher, explorers had replaced Eskimo names with the names of the British royal family, American politicians, tycoons, poets, novelists, naval officers, ships, wives, and girl friends. It is as if the explorers thought that they could transform the strange, grim land around them—tame the wild country by the magic of a name.

When the *George Henry* dropped anchor in Grinnell Bay, the whaler *Black Eagle* was already there, and its captain soon came aboard the *George Henry*, bringing with him Ugarng, the Eskimo whom Captain Budington had taken south with him some years before. Ugarng, a great hunter and the husband of many wives, was a leader of the Nugumiuts, a tribe that led its wandering existence in the area of Frobisher Bay. Like most Eskimo tribes, the Nugumiuts made local migrations according to the seasons: in the winter they lived in Frobisher Bay, hunting seal on the bay ice and walrus at the edges of floes; in the spring they

---

months after their ordeal began, the weak and demented survivors were rescued by Eskimos off the Labrador coast. The deserters from the *Ansell Gibbs* were an example not of will power and hardihood, as Hall thought, but of the stupidity of underestimating the Arctic.

traveled northwest, pursuing basking seals to the very head of the bay; and in the summer they continued the northwest migration to Lake Amadjuak, where they hunted deer and musk ox. In the late summer they moved southeast to Grinnell Bay, where the women spent the early fall processing the skins of the deer that had been killed at Amadjuak, a chore that, according to Nugumiut religious beliefs, had to be done before the beginning of winter hunting. It was at this stage of their yearly cycle that Hall first met the Eskimos who were to be his companions and tutors for the next two years: they were living in their skin tupics (tents) in their summer encampment, finishing one season, preparing for the next.

As soon as possible, Hall went ashore with Ugarng to see the Eskimos in their camp. He took along the dogs that he had purchased in Greenland; they bounded ecstatically around the camp and rolled in the snow while he met the men and women he was to come to know well. There was Kokerjabin, Kudlago's widow, grief-stricken at the news of her husband's death. There was Paulooyer, called Blind George by the American whalemen because he had been blinded by an illness ten years before, and Nikujar, Ugarng's principal or "family" wife, who had been the wife of Blind George until he had lost his sight and had become incapable of providing for her. There were Nukertou, Kunniu, Kimmiloo, Shimerarchu, and others, most of whom were related to one another either by blood or by ever-shifting marital alliances. Hall's first reactions foreshadowed his future relations with them. He was pleased to see signs of their honesty: the whalemen could leave equipment on the beach without fear that it would be stolen. On the other hand, he was horrified to see at the edge of the camp the skeleton of an Eskimo woman who had died three years before. Beside the skeleton were her rotting tent and possessions; her friends and relatives had simply let her die where she had last lain down.

During the brief stop at Grinnell Bay, Hall roamed the

countryside near the Eskimo camp, and one day an incident occurred that left a deep impression on him. The entry in his journal begins: "Monday, Aug 13th, 1860—THANKS BE TO GOD, I STILL LIVE! I have just escaped with my life! PROVI-DENTIALLY escaped! No other arm but the Almighty's could have shielded me from so imminent danger as that to which I have just been exposed." He had been leaning over, digging quartz crystals from rocks, when his revolver fell from its holster, hit a stone, and discharged. The bullet had not touched him, but for a terrible moment the powder burns on his face and hands had made him think that he was mor-tally wounded. When he realized that he was uninjured, his reaction was almost hysterical: he could interpret the event only as a miracle, and immediately he "erected a monument of stone over the spot in commemoration of the event and of the goodness of God in thus preserving me." In many later entries of his journal he referred to the accident as proof that God was protecting him so that he could complete his mission.

Captain Budington had decided to whale just south of Grinnell Bay, at a place called Nugummiuke by the Eskimos and renamed Cyrus Field Bay by Hall. On August 16 the *George Henry* and the *Rescue* sailed south, taking with them many of the Grinnell Bay Eskimos, whom Budington had hired to assist him during the season's whaling. During the sail Hall furthered his acquaintance with Ugarng, and when they arrived at Grinnell Bay he presented the Eskimo with a fine knife. The two men, very pleased with one another, arranged to go on a week's tuktoo (caribou) hunt together, beginning that very afternoon. Hall quickly outfitted him-self with knife, ammunition, sextant, nautical almanac, and food. Then he waited and waited—until he was told that Ugarng had left without him. He rushed to his journal and wrote: "It is evident that Ugarng is a devil & one of the big ones at that! What trials I am subjected to—death of Kudlago, fogs, headwinds, calms & storms, lateness of arrival here! Now

Ugarng's treachery." It was only his first experience with
Eskimo undependability.

Hall was given the opportunity to travel with Eskimos a
few days later when Captain Budington went out in the
Rescue with an Eskimo crew to scout possible whaling sta-
tions. Hall accompanied them across Cyrus Field Bay to
Blunt Peninsula, which separates Cyrus Field Bay from
Frobisher Bay. The *Rescue* sailed up an inlet that cut deep
into the peninsula; on either side of the inlet steep hills
rose, but at the end a flat, narrow neck of land blocked the
inlet from Frobisher Bay. The *Rescue* dropped anchor and
her crew went ashore in a boat. Hall crossed the neck of land
by himself, climbed a ridge of rocks, and gazed out at the so-
called Frobisher Strait, which (although he did not know it
at the time) was to be the site of his explorations and discoveries during the next two years. Across the shimmering
expanse of the waterway he could see the mountains of the
land called Meta Incognita. He also saw, so fleetingly that at
the time he thought it was the result of refraction, a white
line of ice and snow laid out across the tops of the mountain
ridges: a glacier. When he looked northwest with his telescope, he thought that he saw mountains closing off the
"strait" into a bay, but he rightly attributed them to refraction; what he saw refracted was probably a cluster of
islands fifty miles up the bay. Frobisher "Strait" indeed was
closed off into a bay, not by mountains, but by the flats that
Hall a year later called Greenwood's Land—flats that Hall
could not possibly see from more than one hundred miles
down the bay.

The view from his little mound of rocks was splendid, and
Hall was also excited by a sense of history. If geographers
were correct, he was looking at what was the location of some
of the earliest English Arctic exploration. In preparation for
his trip he had read about the voyages of Martin Frobisher,
and he knew that almost three hundred years before, Frobisher had probably sailed the waters on which he was gazing.

Since that time only a few whalers had sailed them; when Hall stood looking out from his mound of rocks, he was virtually rediscovering Frobisher Strait and Meta Incognita.

Hall returned to the *George Henry* elated and optimistic about his expedition—he would find an Eskimo guide and crew and they would get into the expedition boat, sail through the strait to Foxe Channel, and be on their way to King William Island. In anticipation he took his boat for a trial run and was pleased at the way she handled. Budington soon added to his optimism by offering Sterry's services; if Sterry wished, he could go with Hall to King William Island. Hall had often talked to Sterry about his plans, and he knew that the old Arctic hand wanted nothing more than to accompany him. A few days later a new group of Nugumiuts came aboard the *George Henry*, led by a young hunter named Koojesse. Hall, who no longer trusted Ugarng, decided at first sight that Koojesse was his man for an Eskimo guide and offered him the job; Koojesse said that he would be pleased to guide him, but that it was already too late in the season. He told Hall that the voyage should be put off until the following summer. Budington had hinted the same thing, but Hall had resisted the idea. He was getting restless and could not stomach further delay.

The next day, however, Koojesse and Ugarng both told Hall something that, if true, would force him to change all his plans. He met with the two Eskimos in his cabin and laid out a chart of the entire area, on which he illustrated the route that he wished to take through Frobisher Strait to Foxe Channel:

> As I ran my pen along the chart in Frobisher Strait, showing them the track I intend to follow, when I got up to about Longitude 72°, they stopt me, crying "ar-gi! ar-gi!" (No, No)—They then took hold of my hand, moving it around till it connected with Meta Incognita then following S. Easterly the north coast of this land till arriving to the

channel leading into Hudson Strait, about longitude 66°,
thence up Hudson Strait to Kings Cape. This makes Frobisher Strait a BAY!

If indeed Frobisher Strait was a bay, then obviously Hall
would not be able to sail through it to Foxe Channel; he
would have to find some other route, possibly south and west
through Hudson's Strait. For a time he was skeptical of Koojesse's and Ugarng's geography, but when other Eskimos also
insisted that the strait was a bay, he was convinced: in mid-
September he decided that thereafter in his journal he would
refer to the body of water as Frobisher Bay. Another Eskimo
gave him an additional piece of intelligence: he said that
the inlet named Jackman Sound, which cut deep into Meta
Incognita, actually went all the way through that land and
opened out at Hudson's Strait. This small throughway would
offer a shortcut to Hudson's Strait if Hall decided to go that
way. In his later explorations, Hall did not get to Jackman
Sound; if he had reached it, he would have discovered that,
for once, an Eskimo was wrong about geography—Jackman
Sound is a bay, not a strait or throughway.

Any hope that Hall still had of going to King William
Island that year was destroyed on the night of September 26.
Several days before, the George Henry and the Rescue had
been joined by another Williams and Haven whaler, the
Georgiana, commanded by Captain George Tyson, whom
Hall had met in New London. On September 26 snow began
to fall, and by noon the three ships were rocked by an increasing wind. The whaleboats were called in, and preparations were made for foul weather. By late afternoon the
winds had reached gale force, and by evening it was evident
that the Rescue's anchors would not hold. Peering through
the murk, Hall and Budington watched helplessly as the
schooner lunged toward the rocky coast. To Hall's horror, his
expedition boat also broke free from its anchor and followed

the *Rescue* in toward shore. The storm lasted two days. When it abated, the *Rescue* and Hall's boat were found smashed beyond repair on the rocks. "I need not say how much I grieved at the loss of my boat," Hall wrote. "To me it was irreparable, and for a time I was nearly overcome by the blow; but I reasoned that all things were best in the hands of a good Providence, and I therefore bent submissively to His will." It was not Hall's nature to bend altogether submissively, however, and even as he watched his boat driving ashore, he persuaded Captain Budington to lend him a whaleboat for his expedition.

The storm forced Hall to recognize the dangers of the autumn season: boat or no boat, he finally admitted that it would be foolish to set out for King William Island before the next summer. Not long after the storm, Budington, who was disappointed by having secured only one whale, decided that he would sail for home, although the cruise had been planned to last for eighteen months. For a short time Hall was faced with a major decision: should he return to the United States with the *George Henry* or remain behind with the Eskimos? The decision was made for him when Budington discovered that, although the ice was slow in forming in Cyrus Field Bay, heavy pack already blocked Davis Strait. The *George Henry* would have to winter in the North. Hall, now with an entire winter and spring in the Arctic before him, decided to use the *George Henry* as a headquarters and base, but to spend as much time as possible with the Eskimos. His life aboard the ship was pleasant and restful. He continued to admire Budington, and he enjoyed the crew. Only once was there strain. On Christmas day Hall allowed himself to be persuaded by Sterry and others to give the crew some of the alcohol that he had brought as emergency fuel. He was horrified when the men mixed it with tea and celebrated the holy day with a drunken binge. He was angry at the men, but angrier at himself: "Let it stand as a record against me—

against a poor weak creature of the Earth. May High Heaven forgive me. I will live to see the day when the stain—the shame—I have incurred by this act will be wiped out."

During the fall he spent increasing time away from the ship, with the Eskimos in their camp, learning what he could about their way of life. The arrival of a remarkable Eskimo couple made his education easier. They were Ebierbing, called Joe by whalemen, and Tookoolito, called Hannah, and Hall's meeting with them was an occasion of moment in his life. One day he was writing in his cabin aboard the *George Henry* when he heard a soft, sweet voice behind him say, "Good morning, sir." In the instant before he turned, he thought that he was dreaming. The voice was that of a refined woman, and he hardly expected to meet a refined woman on Baffin Island. When he turned, he saw before him, standing under a skylight so that her face was in a shadow, a woman dressed in crinoline and wearing a large bonnet. When she moved her head, Hall saw that she was an Eskimo. It was Tookoolito. She introduced herself, then her husband, who had followed her into the cabin.

Hall had heard of these two, who were well known throughout Baffin Island. In the early eighteen-fifties a whaling captain had taken them to England, where they had stayed for several years and thrived, arousing enough attention to be invited to meet Queen Victoria and dine with Prince Albert. Showing that some courtly hypocrisy might have rubbed off on him (or that Victoria's plumpness had a particular appeal to an Eskimo), Ebierbing told Hall that the Queen was "pretty." Tookoolito also had been impressed by the Queen, but she had been more impressed by the palace: "Fine place, I assure you, sir," she told Hall. When the two Eskimos had returned to the Arctic, they had brought with them some British habits, as Hall discovered later when he visited them in their camp. When he entered their tupic, he was greeted by the vision of Tookoolito, now dressed in Eskimo fashion rather than in crinoline, knitting socks and preparing tea. He noticed other little signs of their life in England. Tookoolito had a cold, and whenever she coughed, she turned her head aside, putting her hand before her mouth. She kept her hands and face clean and dressed her hair. She told Hall that she was shocked by the language used by American whalemen: "I wish no one would swear," she said. "It is a very bad practice, I believe." (This called for a burst in Hall's journal: "One of the Iron daughters of the eternal snows of the North, standing like an angel, pleading the <u>cause</u> of the TRUE GOD, weeping for the sad havoc made and making among <u>her</u> people by those of <u>my</u> countrymen who <u>should</u> have been, and ever should be, the glorious representatives of Freedom, Civilization, and Christianity!")

Tookoolito and Ebierbing aroused Hall's missionary instincts. He heard that their civilized ways had influenced other Eskimos: cleanliness had become a virtue among some of the women in Cumberland Sound, and a few had begun to knit and to dress after Tookoolito's fashion. Hall believed that she showed the way to "civilize and enlighten" (the phrase often occurs in his journal) all Eskimos. Let working colonies be established as in Greenland, with three or four Tookoolitos and Ebierbings in residence, and civilization would soon spread throughout the Arctic. Educate Eskimos to educate other Eskimos. He immediately began to give Tookoolito reading and writing lessons, and when Christmas came he gave her the Bible that had been presented to him by the Young Men's Christian Union of Cincinnati. He commented, "She feels that she must hasten on in the way to knowledge, that she must 1st learn & comprehend & then teach others, God sparing her life and smiling upon her noble purpose, she will yet be worthy to be remembered as 'MOTHER OF MANY ANGELS.' "

But if Hall desired to teach Tookoolito and Ebierbing, he also knew that they had much to teach him. They owned some European clothes, had some superficial European habits, and spoke English, but they still were Eskimos, tough and skilled in living off the Arctic. He wrote in his journal: "The fact is, to effect the purpose I have at heart—to carry out successfully what I have undertaken to perform—to visit King William Land and lands adjacent—to continue and complete the History of Sir John Franklin and his renowned expedition, I must learn to live as Esquimaux do!" Tookoolito and Ebierbing were to be his tutors.

He learned that the Eskimo's was a world of feast followed by famine. Some Eskimos are notoriously prodigal and seldom prepare for a bad season by saving during a good one, and the Nugumiuts gorged on anything they killed as soon as they killed it; if the spirit was in them, and it usually was, they would make a feast out of a few seals, gathering together for an orgy of eating that seemed to delight their souls as well as their bodies. One day Hall and a sailor from the *George Henry* found the village apparently deserted, but soon heard a joyous ruckus from one of the tents. The sailor lifted the tent flap, put his head inside, then quickly withdrew it, complaining of the terrible stench within. While the disgusted sailor walked away, Hall mustered his strength and went inside. Crowded into the tent were more than a dozen Eskimos, all wielding knives, all smeared with blood and blubber. Some were slashing strips of skin, meat, and blubber with their knives, others were drinking from a bowl of hot seal's blood being passed around among them. Almost eighty years later the French anthropologist Gontran de Poncins witnessed a similar scene in the central Arctic and wrote, "From where I lay their faces appeared to me in profile glistening with fat and running with blood; and with their flattened crania, their hair covering their foreheads, their moustaches hanging low over their mouths, their enormous jaws, they inspired in me so ineradicable a notion of the stone age that I think always of this scene when I read or hear of prehistoric man."[4] Hall, intent on adapting to Eskimo ways, did not think of prehistoric man, and he knew what had to be done. He let it be known that he would like to join in the feast. A woman reached into a pot, brought out four inches of seal vertebrae, and handed it to him. He ate it, found it bearable, and decided to try the blood:

> On first receiving the dish containing this Esquimaux stew, I hesitated. It had gone the round several times, being replenished as occasion required; but its external appearance was not at all inviting. Probably it had never gone through the cleaning process, for it looked as though such were the case. But I screwed up courage to try it, and finally, when the dish again came to those by my side, I asked Koojesse, 'Pe-e-uke?' (Is it good?) 'Armelarng, armelarng' (Yes, yes) was the reply. All eyes were fixed upon me as I prepared to join with them in drinking some of their favorite soup.

Hall found (or at least wrote that he found) the soup excellent, and he passed a crucial test. "Let those who will, think evil of it—one thing is certain, <u>neither my conscience or stomach</u> condemned the deed! . . . <u>I shall 'eat to live,'</u> discarding altogether the common idea—at least for three years— of 'living to eat'!" That he even bothered to mention his conscience is a matter of interest: civilized morality could inhibit in many ways, even in eating habits.

Hall's first seal feast occurred at the end of October. As the season progressed, there were no more seal feasts because there were no more seals, and he began to learn how small the margin for survival could be in a region where slight causes could have large effects. The trouble in the fall and winter of 1860 was caused by temperature—not by cold, as one would expect, but by warmth. The Eskimos depended on consistency of weather, and a sudden thaw in the winter could be as disastrous as a sudden freeze in the summer. In 1860 the bay ice was slow in forming because freezes were followed by thaws or by gales that broke the ice before it thickened. When there was no ice, few seals or walrus could be killed; both were best hunted on the ice. When seals and walrus could not be killed, there was a shortage not only of food but also of fuel, as blubber was virtually the only fuel available to Nugumiuts. Even fresh water was in short supply, owing to the lack of fuel to melt snow and ice. Whenever Hall visited Ebierbing and Tookoolito's igloo that season, he found it cold, dark, and gloomy. The fact that the Eskimos lived in igloos in the winter also caused suffering: the same thaws that prevented thick bay ice from forming also melted igloos. Hall noted in his journal that a thaw in an igloo, eating away the very stuff of the structure, is the equivalent of a conflagration in a house. The village in Cyrus Field Bay was destroyed by a rain on December 22, and many of its inhabitants were forced to live for a time aboard the *George Henry*.

If the Nugumiuts could have moved to another area, their plight would not have been so serious, but the thaws that made life miserable in one area prevented them from moving into another. There was enough ice and snow to make travel afoot difficult, but it was so broken up by the thaws that sledge travel was impossible.

By spending much time in the village, by eating with the Eskimos, and by showing understanding of their difficulties, Hall so ingratiated himself with them that they accepted his presence and let him see things that ordinarily they would have concealed from a white man. Much of what he saw pleased him, but some of it did not. He came to know the shaman, or angeko, who aroused his Christian ire. He disliked the power that the angeko, who was only a youth, had over the whole group: "So complete is this Esquimaux's power over his people that a simple motion of the tip of his finger would be followed by instant action to correspond to the sign." One day the angeko took Hall and Koojesse, whom he had summoned with a gesture, into his tent for a ritual. The angeko invoked the spirit of Kudlago, who, he said, was not resting easily. He said that the spirit could be laid to rest only if the kadloona would offer it one of his double-barreled guns. Hall, who had noticed that the angeko's tent was filled with skins and furs that obviously were tributes from the tribe, was outraged. He suggested sarcastically that he might give the gun if the angeko, who was notoriously lazy, would accompany him on the arduous trip to King William Island during the following summer. The angeko misunderstood and thought that Hall was giving him the gun outright: in his joy, he offered Hall the pick of his three wives, a generosity that did not soften Hall's attitude.

Throughout his journal Hall snorted at the superstitions that he thought debased an otherwise noble people. He understood that such superstitions were part of their way of life and were ancient, but his missionary instinct was never far from the surface: "Possibly it may yet be the honor of our country, through some noble-hearted Christian philanthropist, to bring them to a knowledge of the one true God." He was shocked at their "hilarity" during the Sabbath, and he pitied them for their ignorance of "God—of God's word—of Christ—of Sin— of Repentence—of life Eternal in the Heavens!"

One Eskimo in need of God particularly aroused Hall's pity. Hall had met Blind George when he had first gone ashore at Grinnell Bay, and had seen him often since then. George's life had been an ordeal: his mother had hanged herself; he had lost two children (one mercifully: it had been born covered with black spots and matted with hair); he had gone blind just as he was making a reputation as a guide and hunter; his wife had thereafter left him for Ugarng, taking his one surviving child with her. George spoke some English, and he would often approach Hall with his problems, calling out "Mitter Hall, Mitter Hall!" to attract attention. Once he wanted Hall to ask Ugarng if he could "borrow" his daughter for a while because he was lonely (Ugarng complied), but usually he would simply mutter about his inadequacies. Hall apparently was kind and gentle with George. He took the Eskimo to his cabin and devoted hours to helping him with his English and to encouraging him.

I said to George: "George Pe-e-e-uke (good)!"
He replied in my language, "George no good—poor George
blind—no good!"
I again repeated what I said, petting him on the cheek.
George saw—nay felt—I was in earnest; he grasped my hand
and burst into tears.

To Hall, however, human pity was not enough. He thought
that George needed above all the consolations of Christianity,
and he concluded this entry, "I will do what my poor humble
powers will allow me to open up to him the great Truths of
the Eternal."

But Christian pity was balanced by Christian anger. Hall
often was angry at the Nugumiuts, and, above all, their apparent indifference to death repelled him. On his first trip to
the village he had seen the skeleton of the old woman who
had been left alone to die. Early in January he was forced to
watch helplessly while another old woman endured the same
fate—Nukertou, who had been kind to him whenever he had
visited the village. By chance he heard that she was sick, so
he visited her in her igloo. As soon as Hall saw her on her bed
of snow and skins, he knew that she was mortally ill. For
several weeks, while her relatives ignored her, he and
Tookoolito attended the old woman: they took light into her
dark igloo, remade her bed of snow, fed her, massaged her—
but she grew weaker. On day Hall arrived at the village to
find that a new igloo had been built for Nukertou, but he was
horrified to hear that she was to be put in it only to die; it was
to be her living tomb. For a moment he considered taking the
old woman to the ship, but he knew that he would jeopardize
his relations with the Eskimos if he did. A few days later, he
arrived at the igloo to find its entrance had been sealed shut
with snow blocks. He was told that Nukertou was dead, but,
skeptical, he broke in and found her still alive, though dying.
When Tookoolito joined him, he was forced to recognize how
deeply ingrained was the Eskimos' attitude toward death:
Tookoolito, his civilized, unsuperstitious Tookoolito, shocked

him by saying that because Nukertou was dying, they must leave her alone, "that if we delayed till Nukertou's death, the skin dresses we had on would never do to be put on again." Hall remonstrated with her: "On Christmas Day," he told her, "I gave you a Good Book—the Bible. That book is the Word of God. It tells you and me—every body—to visit the sick, the afflicted, the widow, the helpless, the poor." Tookoolito left him, however, and later he heard her telling Ebierbing about the incident. She was puzzled by Mr. Hall's attitude.

Through the bitter cold night Hall kept vigil over the dying woman, a vigil interrupted only when he heard scraping noises outside and discovered that some Eskimos were trying to shut the entrance again, with him inside. He stopped them and managed to persuade them to join him within for a while:

> Here they remained half an hour with me, then departed. I was again alone with the dying Esquimaux. Nearer and nearer drew her end. Coldness was creeping over her. Indeed, I found the cold taking hold of me. The native lamp, which serves for light and fire, had ceased for want of blubber or oil. There was only my lantern-lamp to give light, and the oil of this kept fluid by the caloric of my encircling hands. During the day my fur stockings had become damp from perspiration, therefore my feet were nearly frozen. Every few minutes I was necessitated to jump and thrash myself—to do anything I could to keep my limbs from frostbites. [Finally, after twelve hours of vigil, Nukertou died.] I placed the lamp before her face. She breathed not. And there I sat on the platform of snow by her side, her disheveled locks matted and tangled with reindeer hair, falling in wild disorder over her tattooed brow. I called to her, 'Nukertou! Nukertou!' but no response came back, the silence of the dead alone remained.

While Nukertou lay sick and dying, the bay ice formed, and by the second week in January the *George Henry* at last was iced in. With improved ice conditions, the Eskimos began to move. Ugarng and several of his friends migrated north to Grinnell Bay, where they hoped to find better hunting, and Ebierbing and Tookoolito planned to join them there. Hall decided to go with them: "Having a great desire to try to do something in the way of exploring, and particularly to accustom myself to actual life among the Innuits ["The People," the Eskimos' name for themselves, which Hall adopted], I at length determined to venture on an excursion by sledge and dogs." On January 10, with the temperature thirty degrees Fahrenheit below zero, he set out for Cornelius Grinnell Bay with a dog team and three Eskimos, Ebierbing, Tookoolito, and Koodloo, cousin of the dead Nukertou. The trip to the bay, Hall was assured, would take only a day and a half.

The first day Ebierbing handled the dogs masterfully and they made fast time as they tracked northward, first across land, then across bay ice. In the late afternoon, when they stopped to set up camp, Hall watched fascinated while Ebierbing and Koodloo cut snow blocks and built an igloo in an hour. Tookoolito made its interior livable. First she put the soapstone blubber lamp into position, lit it, and placed a kettle of snow over it; then she placed boards, canvas, and shrubs, all of which had been brought along for the purpose, on the snow platform that was to be their bed, and on top of them spread tuktoo skins. After she had made the bed, she began preparations for dinner; while dinner (Cincinnati crackling soup, raw salt pork, biscuits, and coffee) was cooking, she did the crucial job of drying and mending clothes— a little dampness or a small tear could bring death at a windy thirty degrees below zero. Hall soon learned why Eskimos never travel without their women if they can help it: "Everything where care is required, even to pipes and tobacco, is placed in the igloo wife's hands." After supper the men smoked for a while, then went to bed, Hall sleeping between Ebierbing and Koodloo. Above his entry for the first day he wrote in large letters, "1st NIGHT IN AN IGLOO!" Thereafter on this trip he kept track of the number of nights he had spent in an igloo: "2nd NIGHT IN AN IGLOO!" "3rd NIGHT IN AN IGLOO!" all the way up to "42nd NIGHT IN AN IGLOO!"

The next day, because their course north was blocked by pressure ridges and massive ice hummocks, they made little distance and were forced to spend another night out on the bay ice. That night the wind blew into a gale, driving in heavy snow from Davis Strait. The storm lasted through the next day, so they remained confined to the igloo for more than twenty hours. In the late afternoon Ebierbing ventured outside.

> Ebierbing has just been out (IV O'clock PM). He reports the astounding news that water appears South of our Igloo only 10 rods, the ice having opened and moved a short distance. This crack or opening runs E. & W., extending Westerly to the land, distant three miles. This shows that the gale of today and last night from the E. has set the sea a-heaving, thus breaking the ice all around us! & if it should shift N. or NW., away seaward we must go.

Although the mainland was only three miles across the ice, the dangers of trying to get there in the storm were even greater than the dangers of staying on the floe, so they tensely waited out the storm in their igloo, feeling the floe shifting under them and hearing the terrible noises of ice masses cracking and groaning. Even after the winds died down early in the night, the floe persisted in its uneasy movements until dawn. In the morning the movements ceased, and Ebierbing cut a hole through the roof of the igloo to peer out at the weather. All was clear.

That day they made their slow way across the storm-wracked, treacherous ice to the mainland, and there, on the southern coast of Grinnell Bay, they fell in with Ugarng, who had preceded them north by several days. They built their igloo beside his and established a comfortable camp. It seemed the ordeal was over. It had been a close call; the next morning, when they looked out at the bay, they saw that the floe on which they had camped had broken up and drifted out to sea.

For several days there was plenty of food. Hall still had some of his rations, and Ugarng had killed a seal the day of their arrival. On the third day in the camp, however, food began to run short, so Ebierbing and Koodloo set out hunting, leaving Hall with the women. That night Hall slept beside Tookoolito and Punnie, one of Ugarng's wives. During the night, according to Hall's journal, the following scene occurred:

> My feet were almost frozen, although well in tuktoo furs and blankets. My cold and aching feet of last night! What could I do! I used every method I could devise to get them warm. At last a smooth, low voice reached my ear: "Are you cold, Mr. Hall?"
>
> I answered, "My feet are almost frozen. I can not get them comfortable."
>
> Quick as thought, Tookoolito, who was distant from me just the space occupied by little Punnie (that is, Punnie slept in the middle), made her way down to the foot of her bed; thence she made passage for her hands directly across to my feet, seizing them and drawing them aslant to her side. My modesty, however, was quieted when she exclaimed, "Your feet are like ice, and must be warmed Innuit fashion!"
>
> Tookoolito then resumed her place beneath her tuktoo furs, intermingling her hot feet with the ice-cold ones of mine. Soon the same musical voice said, "Do your feet feel better?"
> I responded, "They do, and many thanks to you."
> Said this kind & noble hearted Innuit woman: "Well, keep them where they are. Good night again, sir."
>
> My feet were not only glowing warm, but hot through the remainder of the night. When I awoke in the morning, as near as I could guess, there were no less than three pairs

of warm feet all woven and interwoven, so that some difficulty was experienced to tell wh. were my own!

The situation was not an invitation to dalliance. If Ebierbing had offered Tookoolito to Hall, as the angeko had offered one of his wives, intercourse would have been acceptable to the Eskimos, if not to the pious Hall. But Ebierbing had not offered Tookoolito to Hall, and it was usual for men and women to sleep chastely beside one another in the snugness of an igloo; if Hall, by some wild stretch of the imagination, had tried to take advantage of the situation, he might well have been killed in reprisal.

This anecdote brings up the question of Hall's relations with Eskimo women: did he, in his almost ten years of Arctic travel, play the Peter Freuchen or the Stefansson and take an Eskimo bedwife? In his writings he mentions no occasion in which he did but, of course, that could simply be Victorian reticence. (Such reticence is not the monopoly of the Victorians: in the twentieth century Stefansson is mute about his Eskimo wife in his autobiographical writings.) Being somewhat skeptical today about the power of moral inhibition over natural desire, we might want to believe that Hall, who was no eunuch, would have allowed his desires to override his piety, and that his silence about it is hypocrisy or verbal prudery. In spite of our skepticism, however, it is possible that Hall lived out his years in the Arctic without ever involving himself sexually with an Eskimo woman. His piety, although not clearheaded or profound, was genuine and strong, and there is something incorrigibly asexual in his personality and mind as they are revealed in his writing: the mere fact of his telling about the night his feet were cold is an example of his innocence; it would not have occurred to him that the story could be misconstrued.

One other check was racial inhibition. Close as Hall came to the Eskimos, there always was something in him that kept him separate from them, and sexual intercourse with an

Eskimo woman would have struck him as somehow demean-
ing. Hall ultimately was too much a creature of his times,
too filled with a nineteenth-century sense of the superiority
of the white man. He undoubtedly had his secret moments
of lust and frustration, but it is improbable that he ever had
intercourse with any Eskimo woman, and throughout his
writing he expressed open anger and disgust whenever he
heard of white men who had.

Ebierbing and Koodloo returned the next evening from
their hunt, but all that they brought with them was some
black skin and krang (raw whale skin and meat), which they
had cached the preceding fall. The next day bad weather set
in again; Hall and the Eskimos were confined to the igloo
for the three days that followed, living entirely on some
remnants of seal and on black skin and krang. When, after
four days, the weather moderated slightly, Hall decided that
he and Koodloo would make a fast journey to the ship for
supplies, although it meant breaking the Sabbath. Hall had
not reckoned on the debilitation of hunger. Weakened by
the lack of food, he was forced to give up and return to the
camp after only a few hours of struggling in the deep snow
and ice hummocks. It was decided that Ebierbing would
accompany Koodloo on the journey. Hall again was left behind with the women. "Punnie & Tookoolito are now my
company evenings—& nights they are my sleeping partners."
He hastened to add, even in his journal, "That is, so far as
sleeping on the same bed platform is concerned. But under
distinct Tuktoo furs."

When they had been stormed in on the ice floe, Hall had
been appalled by the hunger of the dogs. During that storm,
Tookoolito had cut off Hall's beard (although useful during
the mosquito season, it became a mass of ice crystals during
the winter); when they had broken camp, the famished dogs
had rushed into the igloo and devoured everything remaining within, including the hair of Hall's shorn beard. Now
Hall began to know severe hunger himself. Ugarng returned

from a seal hunt: he had spent two days and a night over a single seal hole in the ice and had not killed a seal. When he and his Eskimo companion Jack killed no seal in the two days that followed, and when Ebierbing and Koodloo failed to return with supplies from the ship, the situation became dangerous. There was very little food, very little fuel.

Tookoolito, Hall noticed, had some scraps of rotten whale meat hung in the igloo:

> One night I asked Tookoolito if I might try the taste of some of the black scraps that hung up. I knew that she had reserved these for the dogs, but nevertheless I had an uncontrollable longing for them. I was very hungry. Tookoolito replied that she could not think of my eating them—the idea made her almost sick.

On January 24 the only food that they had left was a piece of black skin "1¼ inch wide, 2 inches long, and ¾ of an inch thick" (even in dire straits, Hall would be exact in his measurements). Because there was no fuel, the blubber lamp remained unlit: it was dark in the igloo, and the temperature within hovered near zero. Except for a few brief excursions to look for Ebierbing, Hall spent the day huddled in his tuktoo robes, trying to write in his journal. That night at midnight, Jack arrived from Ugarng's igloo bearing the meat and blubber of a freshly killed seal skewered on his harpoon. As Hall moved outside to help him, the dogs attacked, and for a few moments in the darkness at the entrance of the igloo, the famished men and dogs fought for the food. The dogs won: they stripped the harpoon of all of the meat and blubber before the men could drive them off.

Only a few hours after Hall was reduced to fighting with dogs for his food, relief arrived. Ebierbing, exhausted to the point of collapse, appeared with a sledge-load of supplies from the ship and a seal he had killed just that morning. On his way to the ship one of his dogs had sniffed a seal hole, and Ebierbing had marked it with a mound of snow and a squirt of tobacco juice. On his return trip, he had spent an entire night standing with Eskimo patience beside the hole; when at dawn he had heard the seal blowing, he had plunged his harpoon through the tiny opening into the animal.

This time Hall did not have to force himself to join in the seal feast. He watched the Eskimos dismember the animal, and with them drank its blood and ate raw its meat, liver, and intestines. After the feast was over he sat beside the now glowing blubber lamp and read a letter from Captain Budington. Budington wrote that everyone aboard the *George Henry* had assumed that Hall had perished in the gale that had struck two days after his departure from the ship. The village in Cyrus Field Bay, Budington reported, was suffering from famine: not a single seal had been killed since Hall and his party had left. Budington ended by writing that he looked forward to Hall's return to the ship. Hall, however, decided to remain where he was rather than return to the *George Henry*. In spite of the suffering he had endured, he found igloo life "charming" (the curious word is his own) him.

Hall remained in Grinnell Bay with Ebierbing and Tookoolito for another month. The seal hunting improved, and in spite of outside temperatures as low as fifty degrees below zero, life was far more comfortable than it had been during his first twenty days of igloo living. Only one thing disturbed his contentment during this month: the angeko and his wives appeared from nowhere and, much to Hall's annoyance, lived off Ebierbing's and Ugarng's hard labor. "To feed a hungry man was well enough, and a ready act on the part of all of us," Hall wrote, "but then for him to have a stomach as huge and voracious as any polar bear, and try to fill that stomach from our limited supply of food, was more than we could reasonably stand." Hall had no right to use "we," because Ebierbing and Ugarng fed the angeko without complaint. Eskimo charity, it seemed, could be less restricted than Christian charity.

On February 21 Hall finally returned to the *George Henry,* forty-three days after he had left it, guided back by Ebierbing. Although they stopped to kill one seal (the first that Hall had actually seen killed: "the beautiful, eloquent eyes of the victim" affected him, but Ebierbing seemed not at all affected as he dispatched the creature with his knife), they reached the ship in less than a day. After accepting the congratulations of the crew on his survival and eating a warm supper, Hall retired to his cabin. "Once more, then did I enter my own little domicile, where I did not forget to return thanks to Him who had so preserved me in health and safety during that, my first experience of personal life among the native Innuit tribes of the icy North."

Hall, of course, had also been preserved by the "native Innuit tribes of the icy North" themselves; without Ebierbing and Tookoolito, he inevitably would have died. He knew that he had been dependent on the Eskimos for his survival and that they had taught him much about how to survive, but something in him kept him from fully admitting that dependence. When he wrote of his parting with Tookoolito in Grinnell Bay, he seemed almost to imply a dependence of the Eskimos on him: "The parting from Tookoolito was affecting. She evidently felt it; but the hope of herself and husband soon being with me again on my future excursions removed much of the disappointment she then felt at my going away. In fact, both she and Ebierbing were as children to me, and I felt toward them like a parent would."

On the ice floes of Grinnell Bay and in the inhospitable winter mountains of the mainland, however, it actually was the Eskimos who were the parents and Hall who was the child. Not long after his return to the *George Henry,* a terrible incident occurred that showed what could happen to a white man alone in the Arctic. On Hall's return, he was told that several of the crew were suffering from scurvy. In all of his forty-three days away from the ship, Hall himself had never shown a trace of scurvy, not even during the week of near starvation, so he was now convinced that a rigorous regimen and a diet of fresh meat were not only a preventive but also might be a cure for the disease. He and Budington agreed that two of the scurvy-ridden seamen, James Bruce and John Brown, should go across Blunt Peninsula to Frobisher Bay, there to live and work for a while with Eskimos. A week after Brown and Bruce had left for Frobisher Bay they were followed by Koojesse and another Eskimo, who sledged there to trade for fresh meat and walrus tusks. As Bruce later told it, he and Brown felt that they had been cured of scurvy and decided to return to the ship with Koojesse. At the last moment, however, Bruce changed his mind; the cold was bitter, and he preferred to delay the journey. Brown, however, only eighteen years old, was impetuous; impatient to return, he swore, "I'm going on, for by God I'm determined to have my duff and applesauce at tomorrow's dinner." Bruce saw that there was no use in arguing with the boy.

Brown left with the Eskimos, but travel with the loaded sledge was too slow to suit him. Against the advice of Koojesse, he struck out on his own, leaving the Eskimos behind. Late that night Koojesse and his Eskimo companion arrived at the ship and immediately went to bed. It was not until the next morning that they discovered that Brown was not aboard.

The search that followed was a physical and mental ordeal. The temperature remained below zero and the wind was cutting throughout the day; the search parties suffered from cold, exhaustion, and thirst. They soon found Brown's tracks. In his wandering path they could perceive his agony as he realized that he was lost and felt the cold of night piercing him. His tracks meandered from the shore to the bay, back to the shore again, in and out of ice hummocks, around bergs. At one point he apparently had fallen through the broken ice near a berg, and from there on, soaked in bay water, he must have known that he was going to die. Toward morning, his steps had begun to falter, and he made twelve interlocking circles in the course of two miles. After ten hours of search, they found his body. He lay face up on the ice, his hands at his side, the snow around him showing signs of his struggle to get up before he had finally surrendered to sleep and death. Burial in the winter posed a problem, and they left him where he died, covering him with ice and snow. With the coming of June thaws, Brown's body would sink into the bay.

The death of John Brown was a shock to Hall. "O, My God," he wrote that night in his journal, "Thy ways are not our ways! In Thy own inscrutable way, Thou didst see fit to bring us face to face with fact, ultimate fact however horrible it was, & then had us confess to ourselves, shuddering, what things are possible upon God's earth!" The discovery of the frozen body, "cold and rigid as the monuments of ice around us," did not shake Hall's faith in God, but no longer would his faith be so simple and unthinking as it had been. The man who had written less than a year before, "I believe it sacrilege to say that the Elements war . . . The Elements are always at Peace," had then not yet been in the Arctic, had not yet seen its glaciers and sea ice or felt its gale winds and killing cold. That his experiences during those first eight months in the North had somehow reached a climax with Brown's death is clearly shown in the exclamation in his journal: "O, My God, Thy ways are not our ways!"

chapter three

Frobisher Bay— Exploration

J ohn Brown died in the middle of March, and soon afterward Hall settled his plans for the coming year. He knew that it would be at least four months before the sea and bay ice broke up enough for him to start on his voyage to King William Island, but he had evolved another project to keep himself busy in the meantime. "I MUST EXPLORE FROBISHER BAY THIS SPRING," he wrote on March 29, "determining beyond all question the fact of Frobisher Strait being a myth." His interest was partly geographical, partly historical. Koojesse had told him that there was a story passed down by generations of Nugumiuts about kadloonas who had come to their land many years before. Koojesse admitted that he did not know the story in any detail, but he told Hall that he knew a place where there were relics of the kadloonas. Hall wondered if the story might be about Martin Frobisher, although it seemed improbable that the Eskimos would be telling stories about events that occurred almost three centuries before. Some of the books that he had aboard the *George Henry* told the story of Frobisher's three voyages, and in early April he reread them.

Martin Frobisher was a gentleman born, a mariner by profession, a pirate by inclination. During the reign of Queen Elizabeth there was much government-sanctioned privateering, but Frobisher sometimes lapsed from privateering into out-and-out piracy and was several times in London jails for seizing ships that he was not supposed to seize. There was no doubt about his skill as a navigator and commander, however, and in 1575 a group of merchant adventurers, headed by one Michael Lok, put him in command of an expedition that was to search for a northwest passage. The group built one ship, the *Gabriel*, and purchased another, the *Michael*; in June 1576 the two ships, together with a pinnace, sailed from England, heading northwest.

Frobisher's first Arctic voyage began badly. Off Greenland the *Gabriel* and the *Michael* were separated in a storm, and the *Michael* returned to England to report that the *Gabriel*, with Frobisher aboard, was lost. But Frobisher and his crew of eighteen actually were persisting northwestward, in spite of storms that almost tore the tiny barque to pieces. Frobisher was proving his mettle; in the words of his most complete chronicler, George Beste:

> The worthie Captayne, notwithstanding these discomfortes, although hys Mast was sprong, and hys toppe Mast blowen overboorde wyth extreame foule weather, continued hys course towardes the Northwest, knowing that the Sea at length must needes have an endying, and that some lande shoulde have a beginning that way: and determined therefore at the least, to bryng true proofe what lande and Sea the same myghte bee, so farre to the Northwestwardes, beyonde anye man that hathe heeretofore discovered.[1]

On July 20, Frobisher sighted a mountainous land that he named Queen Elizabeth's Foreland (probably Resolution Island), but he was prevented from landing by "exceeding great yce." The *Gabriel* cruised up and down the coast until the ice broke, and then some of the men, under the command of the master of the *Gabriel*, Christopher Hall, went ashore to examine a small island, which they named Hall Island after the master. When the shore party was back aboard the *Gabriel*, Frobisher headed his ship for an opening in the land which he took to be a strait leading to Cathay: "This

place he named after his name Frobishers Streytes, like as
Magellanus at the Southwest ende of the worlde, havyng
discovered the passage to the South Sea . . . called the same
straites Magellanes streightes."[2]

As the *Gabriel* made her way up the "straits," Frobisher
assumed that the land on his left was America, that on his
right Asia. After sailing a hundred miles up the waterway and
passing several islands, he put ashore. There he saw signs
of human habitation, including the remains of a fire. Climb-
ing to the top of a hill, "he perceived a number of small
things fleeting in the Sea a farre off, whyche hee supposed to
be Porposes, or Ceales, or some kinde of strange fishe: but
coming nearer, he discovered them to be men, in small boates
made of leather."[3] It was one of the earliest encounters between civilized man and the Eskimos, and, sad to say, there
was distrust on both sides; sadder to say, the distrust was
justified. Frobisher, assuming that the natives were trying
to cut him off from his ship, sped to it; the Eskimos, in their
turn, hung back when the sailors tried to entice some of them
aboard. After a time there was a cautious interchange of gifts,
and a few Eskimos came aboard. Frobisher was shocked by
their eating habits: "they came aborde his ship, and brought
him Salmon and raw fleshe and fishe, and greedily devoured
the same before our mens faces."[4] He gave orders that such
savages should be treated with suspicion, but five of the sailors
soon went ashore with them and disappeared. Frobisher sailed
as close to the shore as he dared and had trumpets blown
and ordnance fired, but the Eskimos seemed undisturbed.
There was no sign of the men. Frobisher could ill afford to
lose five men out of a crew of eighteen, so he decided to take
a hostage. Ringing a gong and using trinkets as bait, he lured
an Eskimo in a kayak close to the ship; himself a powerful
man, he leaned down and, seizing the Eskimo's wrists, hauled
man and kayak both up onto the deck of the *Gabriel*. The
fact of the hostage had no apparent effect on the Eskimos;
Frobisher decided to sail for England with his reduced crew,

the hostage, and the kayak, leaving the five missing men to their fate.

Aboard the *Gabriel* on its return to England was an inconspicuous object, a piece of stone, that was to change the course of many lives. Frobisher had agreed to hand over to Michael Lok "the fyrst thinge that he founde in the new land," and the first thing was this stone, which had been picked up on the shores of Hall Island. Lok took it to various assayers, who found no valuable minerals in it, but Lok seemed to will his own destruction and persisted until he found an Italian assayer who said that the stone was rich in gold.*

In their excitement over the stone, Lok and others almost forgot that the original purpose of the expedition had been to find a northwest passage and that Frobisher had apparently found one. Lok persuaded others to share his delusion about gold, and on March 17, 1577, the Cathay Company was chartered, with Lok as Governor and Frobisher as "High Admyrall of all seas and waters, countryes, landes, and iles, as well of Kathai as of all other countryes and places of new dyscovery"[6] (the words are from the Queen's grant to the Cathay Company). The Queen herself subscribed £1000 and lent the company a ship. The next expedition was to be a more ambitious and fully equipped endeavor than the first: Frobisher had one hundred and twenty men at his command, three ships, and all the authority of a "High Admyrall." The expedition was instructed to set up a mine on Hall Island, to search for other possible sources of "ore," and to find the five men who had disappeared on the first voyage. Only secondarily was Frobisher to probe farther up the strait to see if it led to Cathay.

Frobisher's three ships arrived at the strait one year after the first expedition had sighted it. When they dropped anchor

---

* When Lok asked the Italian how he had found gold where others had failed, he received the answer *"Bisogna sapere adulare la natura."* ("It is necessary to know how to flatter nature.")[5]

off Hall Island, the crews immediately went ashore to search
for ore. There was none.* Frobisher did not despair, however,
and soon afterward his men found plenty on nearby islands.
It was not long before they saw Eskimos. Frobisher took
no chances: "being in his firste voyage well acquainted with
their subtile and cruell disposition, he provided well for his
better safetie."[8] At first he approached the savages cautiously
and in the company of many other men. After some initial
contacts, they got close enough to observe something of the
Eskimos' way of life. They noted the various utensils, made
ingeniously from bone, teeth, skin, and stone; they saw that
smaller dogs were eaten, larger dogs used to tow sledges: "they
use dogges for that purpose, as we doe our horses." Some of
the men managed to get into a house made of whalebone and
skin; they were horrified at what Beste called the Eskimos'
"sluttishnesse"; "They defile these dennes most filthylie with
their beastly feeding, & dwell so long in a place (as we thinke)
untill their own sluttishnesse lethyng them, they are forced
to seeke a sweeter ayre."[9]

But Frobisher's men, hardly anthropologists, were not content simply to observe. They wanted hostages, both for their
own protection and to use as a bribe to discover the fate of
the five men who had disappeared on the first voyage. Frobisher himself and one other man attempted to abduct two
Eskimos by force. The Eskimos fought back, chased the
Englishmen to their boats, and "hurte the Generall [Fro-
bisher] in the Buttocke with an arrow." Shortly afterwards,
a sailor, "a Cornishman and a good wrastler," succeeded in
capturing an Eskimo youth, who was questioned about the

* George Beste had a curious and rather cloudy interpretation of this:
"it may seeme a great miracle of God, that being only one rich stone
in all that Iland, the same should be found by one of our Countreymen,
whereby it shoulde appeare, Gods divine will and pleasure is to have
oure common wealth encreased with no lesse abundance of his hydden
treasures and golde mynes than any other nation, and would that the
fayth of his Gospell and holy name should be published and enlarged
throughe all those corners of the earth, amongst those Idolatrous
Infidels."[7]

five missing men.[10] He admitted that he knew of the men, but denied the charge that they had been slain and eaten. When a doublet and some shoes were found, hope was renewed that the men were alive, but these were the last signs of them ever uncovered.

Relations with the Eskimos became increasingly strained and finally exploded in violence. On a bluff subsequently called "Bloudie Point" Frobisher's men and a group of about sixteen Eskimos clashed. The Eskimos fought desperately; when their arrows gave out, they used the arrows that the Englishmen had shot at them, even pulling them from their own bodies, but finally realizing that defeat was inevitable and "being ignorant of what mercy meaneth,"[11] many of them hurled themselves from a cliff. After the battle Frobisher's men found and captured an Eskimo woman and her child, who, together with the earlier captive, were later taken to England. All three died within a month of reaching Britain's shores.

The main purpose of the expedition was fulfilled: the three ships were finally filled with stone. At first there was some difficulty in finding deposits, and the expedition was misled by one cliff that glittered so much that "it seemed all to be golde," but it was made up mainly of black lead.* After further exploration, a mine was set up on one of the small islands in a small bay called Countess of Warwick Sound. There, while the larger part of the expedition was out looking for the five missing men and fighting Eskimos, the miners dug almost two hundred tons of stone, which the expedition's assayer swore was precious. Snow fell early in that year 1577; by mid-August the expedition was harassed by severe storms. Frobisher had the stone loaded aboard his three ships, and on August 23 the expedition set sail for England; no attempt

---

* George Beste, the chronicler, remarked that it verified the proverb, "All is not golde that shineth"[12]; his remark should have been directed earlier to Michael Lok and all of the members of the Cathay Company.

had been made to sail to Cathay through the strait, but Frobisher felt that he had done enough.

In England, samples of the stone were tested by various specialists with various results: some believed it valuable, others worthless. The Queen indicated her reserved attitude by calling the new land "Meta Incognita" ("Value Unknown"). A third expedition was mounted. The year following Frobisher's second expedition, fifteen ships sailed with the purposes of bringing back two thousand tons of ore and of planting a colony of one hundred men in Meta Incognita. The enterprises of the Cathay Company were becoming more complicated—and more expensive. Indeed, Frobisher's fleet on the third expedition was the largest to enter the Arctic until the Second World War.

Bad weather plagued Frobisher's last Arctic expedition. As soon as the fleet entered the strait, a storm whipped its ice-clogged waters, and "the yce comming on us so fast, we were in great danger, looking everie houre for death." Not long afterward came "a hidious fogge and mist" that lasted for a week. On July 26 there fell "such an horrible snowe that it laye a foote thicke upon the hatches, which froze as fast as it fell," and early in August there was "an outragious tempest"[13] that almost destroyed the fleet. One storm sank the ship carrying lumber, and the idea of establishing a colony had to be given up. All attention was given to loading the ships with ore as quickly as possible.

There was little contact with the Eskimos. By now the natives of the area, leery of white men, were elusive. Frobisher attempted to approach one group near Bear Sound, "who perceiving his arrivall, fled away with all speede." The next day, with his pinnace at full sail in a fresh wind, he chased a boatload of Eskimos, but they evaded him. Before departing for England, Frobisher had his men construct a house and fill it with trinkets, "thereby to allure & entice the people to some familiaritie against other yeares."[14] There were to be no other years, however, and as soon as his ships were loaded with ore, Frobisher sailed from his strait for the last time.

In England, the value of the stone was at last determined: after long and expensive testing, it was proved worthless. The Cathay Company was forced to assess shareholders 115 per cent of their original investment and to sell all assets, including ships. Michael Lok was virtually bankrupted, and Frobisher himself lost a great sum. Whereas Lok was entirely a business-man and was ruined for life, Frobisher was a skilled sailor and a famous adventurer, and his courage was a salable com-modity. Joining Francis Drake and John Hawkins, he became a scourge to the Spaniards, participating in every major naval action against them, including the defeat of the Armada. The voyages to Baffin Island were only one short phase in his career.

Much of the stone that had been brought from Frobisher Strait at such expense and danger was used to repair roads. The rest apparently was thrown into Bristol Harbor; tons of it were found there when the harbor was dredged only a few decades ago. Frobisher Strait disappeared from civilized man's ken for several centuries. Even while Frobisher was still alive, cartographers mislocated Meta Incognita in southern Greenland, and when John Davis sailed past the Strait in 1585, he renamed it Lord Lumley's Inlet, not realizing what it was. Geographers and explorers of the eighteenth and early nineteenth centuries had more knowledge of the Arctic, and some of them deduced the correct location of the so-called strait and of Meta Incognita, but they had no proof that they were right; on nineteenth-century charts the "Strait" appears in a variety of vague shapes, all of them inaccurate.

Hall had been studying Frobisher's history, and so was prepared when Ebierbing's aged grandmother, Ookijoxy Ninoo, arrived at Field Bay. Hall had heard that she knew all the traditional stories of her people, and, eager to talk with her about the kadloonas who had come long ago, he went to her tupic, taking Tookoolito along as an interpreter. The scene of his talk with Ookijoxy Ninoo remained vivid to him afterwards:

> Her tupic was very small—only large enough to hold herself comfortably in a sitting or reclining posture—but I managed to squeeze in beside her, seating myself on her right side. Tookoolito was outside by the entrance, facing the old lady and myself. The position of Ookijoxy Ninoo was usually a reclining one, she resting her elbows on the pillow place of her bed, and her chin upon her hands. By her side was her little kood-lin [lamp], and in front of that was a small board, on which was a handful of baked beans given to her by some one from the ship, and also a few broken pieces of sea-bread which Tookoolito had saved for her. There was, besides, abundance of walrus blubber and skin for her to eat when hungry. During the time I was in her tupic and listening to her words, a favorite grandchild of hers, Eterloong, was just outside, frequently crying for food. The old lady gave the child a part of the beans and biscuit; but his noise was a great interruption. The weather was very cold—bitterly so; and I often requested Tookoolito to take my place inside, but she preferred my retaining the seat of honor.

The old woman told Hall that she knew well the story about the kadloonas. Hall asked her how many ships had come: "Her reply was, they came every year; first two, then three, then <u>amasuadlo comooarchchua</u> (many—a great many ships)." Hall checked John Barrow's *Chronological History of Voyages into the Arctic Regions,* which he had brought with him: on Frobisher's first voyage he had arrived with only two ships, on his second with three, and on his third with a fleet of fifteen. Oral tradition appeared to agree with recorded history. Excited, Hall pressed Ookijoxy Ninoo for more details.

She remembered that as a little girl she had been told that the kadloonas had killed many Eskimos, and that they had taken others away with them, but that the Eskimos themselves had captured five kadloonas. Hall, remembering the mystery of the five missing men on Frobisher's first voyage, asked her what had happened to them. She said that these men had lived with the Eskimos for at least one winter, and that when spring came they had built an oomien (a large boat), put a mast in her, and sailed away forever. If Ookijoxy Ninoo's tale was true, the mystery of Frobisher's five men was solved: they had drowned, frozen, or starved trying to return to England in their crude boat.

Hall asked the old woman where most of these events had taken place. Some, she said, had occurred at Kingaite (known to white men as Meta Incognita), the highlands on the other side of the bay, but most had occurred on and near the island of Niountelik. On Niountelik, she remembered, she herself had seen timbers, coal, "oug" (something red; Hall later realized that she had seen pieces of brick), and large chunks of a very heavy stone—so heavy that even the strongest Innuit had trouble lifting it. When Hall puzzled about this stone, Tookoolito suggested that it might have been iron.

Only a few weeks before, Hall had made a week's excursion to the region of the island of Niountelik, which was located at the mouth of a small sound in Frobisher Bay. At that time he had not been looking for Frobisher relics, and the area had been snow-covered. Now it began to dawn on him that this sound might very well have been Countess of Warwick Sound, the place where Frobisher had done most of his feverish, ill-fated mining. Hall had two reasons for being excited by what Ookijoxy Ninoo told him. First, it apparently gave him the chance to prove what had always been mere speculation: that the body of water named after Frobisher was indeed the site of Frobisher's Arctic explorations. Second, it was evidence of the extraordinary accuracy and tenacity of Eskimo memory. "I thought to myself, if such facts concerning an expedition which had been made nearly three hundred years ago can be preserved by the natives, and evidence of those facts obtained, what may not be gleaned of Sir John Franklin's Expedition of only sixteen years ago? I was now convinced, more than I had ever been, that the whole mystery of their fate could have been, and may yet be easily determined with even the smallest well-directed aid."

Ever since Hall had arrived at Field Bay, he had been curious about the islands and mountains that he could see southeast of the *George Henry's* mooring. They lay at the very mouth of Frobisher Bay, and they would have been the site of Frobisher's first landing in the new world. Somewhere in the cluster of bluffs, bays, and channels would be Loks Land, named after Michael Lok, and Hall's Island, where Christopher Hall had picked up the piece of "ore" that started Canada's first gold rush. Hall asked Ookijoxy Ninoo about the area. She had no story connecting it with Frobisher, but she told Hall that the Eskimos called it the "Dreaded Land": years before, many Eskimos had disappeared on the ice off its coasts, and it had been avoided ever since. When Hall asked her if she had been there, she recoiled: "Never! NEVER!"

Early in June, Hall traveled by sledge to the Dreaded Land. He had with him Ebierbing and Koodloo, neither particularly eager to make the trip. As they approached the forbidding north coast of Loks Land, Hall himself began to have doubts. A cold fog drifted in and shrouded the entire area, making travel over the treacherous ice impossible. They had to encamp on a tiny island just off the coast to wait out the fog and the gale-driven snow that followed it. It was not a promising beginning. The weather cleared, however, and as they made their way along the shoreline of Loks Land, they saw so many seals that their progress was slow. Nothing, Hall was discovering, could stop an Eskimo from hunting a seal, even when there was no need for its meat and blubber. Ebierbing and Koodloo were, Hall wrote, "almost crazy with joy" as they slaughtered the seals that were all around them on the ice. The very paper on which Hall kept his journal

of this trip was splattered with blood. Ebierbing and Koodloo's joy was complete when they came on a polar bear,
pursued it with the dogs, and killed it with one shot. Ebierbing thanked Hall for bringing them to this land of plenty
that they had always dreaded: there was, he said, "plenty
land, plenty water, plenty seal."*

In spite of their successful hunting, the Eskimos were
nervous about being where no Eskimo had been for many
generations. When Hall insisted that they go through a narrow, deep channel between the sheer cliffs of eastern Loks
Land and Hudson's Island (Hall named it Kane Channel,
after Elisha Kent Kane), Koodloo wanted to turn back: they
were approaching the "big waters" that had carried some
of his people out to the open sea. But Hall persuaded him to
go on with them, and as they emerged at the other end of the
channel, they saw to the east an island, which Hall realized
must have been Frobisher's Hall Island. There was a fine
natural harbor on its south coast, where probably Frobisher
had moored his two small vessels on his first voyage, and
shelving down to the harbor was a beach, where probably
Christopher Hall had picked up the innocuous piece of stone.
Above loomed Frobisher's Mount Warwick.

While the Eskimos hunted seals, Hall climbed the flanks
of Mount Warwick. "On the top of this mountain I found
an Innuit monument which evidently had been erected centuries before, for it was black with the moss of ages." Hall
did not realize it, but he possibly had found a Frobisher relic.
On the second voyage, according to George Beste, Frobisher

* In the summer of 1967 I retraced Hall's route in Frobisher Bay
(dignifying a fine camping trip with the name "field research"). My
experiences in Loks Land were remarkably similar to Hall's. The
Eskimos with whom I traveled, like Hall's, were wary of the region
and did not want to go into it, although they had no specific tales
about it. The reason for its grim reputation was made evident when
we struck thick fogs, as Hall did. Because Eskimos still avoid the
region, it is alive with bear and walrus. The Eskimos with me, like
Hall's, were surprised and delighted—and shot everything that moved,
including a polar bear and several walrus, although they did not need
the meat.

left his boats in the harbor and "passed up into the countrey about two Englishe miles, and recovered the toppe of a high hill, on the top whereof our men made a Columne or Cresse of stones heaped uppe of a good heigth togither in good sorte, and solempnely sounded a Trumpet, and said certaine prayers, kneeling aboute the Ancient [the ensign], and honoured the place by the name of Mount Warwicke."[15] Hall, however, was not given the opportunity to examine the monument carefully. As he stood admiring the view from the mountain, he saw what appeared to be a steamer moving along a lead through the ice close to the north shore of the island. He rushed down the mountain to tell the Eskimos. Now, after a whole year, he would hear news of the outside world, and he laughed to think of how surprised the crew of the steamer would be to see a white man suddenly appear on the shores of the Dreaded Land. But when he and the Eskimos reached the north shore, there was no steamer. Hall was puzzled until he saw, jutting out from the mountain side, a rock formation shaped like a steamer. His disappointment was revealing: in spite of his growing delight in the Eskimo way of life, he still missed the civilized world.

The trip to the Dreaded Land was only of ten days' duration. On his return to the George Henry, Hall did some calculations. When he and the Eskimos had left on the trip, they had taken with them eleven pounds of foodstuffs, but during the ten days out they had obtained over four thousand pounds of fresh meat, skins, and blubber oil. At times the Arctic could indeed be a land of plenty.

While Hall had been in the Dreaded Land, Captain Budington and most of his crew had gone to Frobisher Bay to scout for whales. Hall spent only a few days aboard the ship, then followed them, wanting to see the whaling depot, but also wanting to remind Captain Budington of the boat that he had promised for the King William Island expedition. As soon as Hall arrived at the depot, Budington anticipated him by broaching the subject: "He thought it his duty to open the matter to me at once, announcing what conclusion he had come to, though painful. The Boat which I had made in the States, specially designed & made for my Expedition to King Williams Land, was a suitable one for me—but a whaleboat was unfit." Budington told Hall that the whaleboat was too small and could not carry enough provisions for a journey such as Hall planned. Determined as Hall was, he respected the Captain's judgment.

> This is a serious matter with me—one pregnant with such thoughts I cannot put on paper. I cannot, I will not sell my life foolishly. If the loss of my expedition Boat, which was well planned and strongly made, has taken from me the proper, the only judicious means of carrying out my purpose of going to King William's Land, then I must delay—I must lose one year in returning to the States & preparing again for that voyage.

It was mid-June, forerunning the brief Arctic summer of July and August. Except where the snow had drifted deep in the lee of cliffs, it had thawed, and tiny Arctic flowers were blooming. Mosquitos bred in pools left by the spring run-off, and they harassed Eskimo and white man alike. The bay ice was breaking up. One day early in June, Hall passed by the place where they had left John Brown. The body was still there, but the ice and snow that they had piled on it had thawed; foxes had nibbled on Brown's clothing but for some reason had not mutilated the corpse. A few days later when Hall passed the place again Brown's body was gone, sunk through the thinning ice into the water of the bay. One day in the middle of June, Hall recorded a temperature of ninety-five degrees in the sun; the next day there was a rainstorm. As the ice broke, the eider ducks arrived, and the open waters of the bays were black with them; Hall joined the crew of the *George Henry* in gorging on their eggs, stolen from the nests along the coast. Ugarng and a party of Eskimos shot several caribou late in the month. Finally, in the second week of July, the *George Henry* was released by the ice that had held her since January.

During July, Budington prepared to take his ship on a whaling cruise, while Hall worked on his exploration of Frobisher Bay. For a time it appeared that Ugarng might subvert Hall's plans. Hall had never quite trusted Ugarng since the Eskimo had left him behind after promising to take him on the autumn caribou hunt, and now Ugarng outraged him by trying to persuade Ebierbing, Tookoolito, and other Eskimos to go on a hunting expedition rather than accompany Hall up Frobisher Bay. "Ugarng is ungrateful," Hall wrote.

> Even more—a viper! From the exhibition of U's acts while here this time, Capt. B has great & good reasons for exclaiming:
> "How sharper than a Serpent's tooth
> Is a thankless Child!"

When Ebierbing and Tookoolito resisted Ugarng's cajolery, Hall was flattered because their loyalty to him was so strong. Loyalty was not enough, however: a few days before Hall was due to leave, Ebierbing became seriously ill, and it was obvious that he and Tookoolito would have to remain behind. Perhaps Ebierbing's sickness was put on: although Hall apparently was not aware of it, Tookoolito was due to give birth within weeks.

Hall's little expedition left the *George Henry* on August 9. Crowded into the whaleboat were Hall, Koojesse and his wife, Tunukderlien ("Belle"), Kooperneung ("Charlie") and his wife Akchukerzhun ("Susy"), Koodloo (who had been on the trip to Grinnell Bay with Hall), and a fat Eskimo widow, aunt to Ebierbing, named Kooulearng and known as "Suzhi." Hall had another emotional parting from Ebierbing and Tookoolito.

I told Ebierbing I prayed that when I returned I should find him well again, but that it was possible we might never meet again—that I might die—that he might die—but I hoped if it was to be so, we should meet again—in HEAVEN. Tears were streaming down the faces of all three of us.

They navigated by dead reckoning through dense fog to the narrow waterway that Hall had named Lupton Channel after James Lupton, a Cincinnati businessman, who had given him great encouragement and a pocketknife during the planning stage of the expedition. At the mouth of the channel they were met by a boiling tide running from Frobisher Bay; for hours they had to work against it up the channel, but finally beat through and set up camp on the shores of the Bay.

If tide and weather worked against Hall, so did the Eskimos, who, over Hall's protests, wasted hours during the next day "drowning" ducks—pursuing them in the boat until the birds exhausted themselves from continuous diving and could be picked from the water like so much limp seaweed. As a result, the distance they covered in two days was little more than what Hall had hoped to cover in one. Travel with Eskimos, Hall was discovering, could be irritating to a white man with a sense of scheduled time, but even Hall could not complain about the hunting the next day. The boat was approaching the islands of what Hall hoped would prove to be Countess of Warwick Sound when Koojesse saw a polar bear.

While pulling direct for Oopungnewing—or rather with the intention of rounding it to make for Niountelik where I desired to stop & search for relics of Frobisher's expedition of 1587, Koojesse took up the spy glass, directing it to various Islets lying off S.E. & S. of Oopungnewing 1 & 2 miles distant from Oopungnewing. At last he cried out <u>Ninoo</u>! <u>Ninoo</u>! This was enough to make every Innuit happy, for of all game they delight in <u>Ninoo is the Chief</u>. I took the

glass & saw this "Lion of the North" lying down and apparently asleep. At once I took Koojesse's place at the steer-
ing oar while he, Koodloo & Kooperneung proceeded to load
with Ball their double barrel guns.

The technique they used to hunt the bear was cruel but
efficient. The bear took to the water, swimming toward
another of the islands. When the Eskimos fired, they only
wounded it:

> Polar bear shook his head, turned his course from down the
> Bay to the opposite direction. The effective shot not only
> wounded but enraged the animal. Every now and then he
> would take a momentary look at us, shaking his head. The
> Innuits were now very cautious about making the distance
> between Ninoo & us any less. The white coat of Ninoo about
> the head was now crimsoning with its life blood. The policy
> now became to make Ninoo tow his own carcass.

They forced the bleeding animal toward the island of Oopungnewing, and when it was close to shore they administered
the *coup de grâce* with one shot. On the shore, the Eskimos
immediately butchered it and feasted on its meat, "really
beef-like, bright red & juicy." They saved the bladder and,
according to their custom, inflated it, attached charms to it,
and kept it exposed on a staff for three days and three nights.
    They set up camp on Oopungnewing, and although it was
by then late in the afternoon, Hall hastened to the neighboring island of Niountelik, where he hoped to find Frobisher
relics. The gross Suzhi (she was an extraordinarily large
Eskimo), who knew the area well, went with him as a guide.
As they slowly paced the wind-blown island, eyes cast to the
ground for relics, he asked her about the brick that Ookijoxy
Ninoo had reported:

> I said to her "Noutima brick?" (Where is the brick?) To
> make her understand 'brick' I took up a small stone spotted

over with a peculiar red moss, calling her attention to the red, & then taking off her head ornament, "<u>karoong</u>" (a rounded, polished piece of brass in the form of a semi-circle, fitted to and worn on the head by the Innuit ladies as an adornment), I made motions as if polishing it, for I knew from information I had gained from time to time that Innuits had procured pieces of brick somewhere on or in the neighborhood of the Island on which we were, & used them specially for brightening their ornaments.

They found no brick, and Hall began to be discouraged. There were many relics of old Eskimo settlement, tent rings (rings of stones used to hold down the walls of Eskimo tents), charred wood from fires, shreds of tuktoo skins, and bones of animals and fish, but no evidence of early white settlement. They had searched almost the entire island before they found what Hall was looking for. What they found was not brick but coal:

> I was several fathoms in advance of Kooulearng [Suzhi], hastening on being desirous to make as extended a search as the short time of day-light remaining would allow, when, lifting my eyes from the ground near me I discovered a con-siderable distance ahead what <u>seemed</u> to me an unusual ap-pearance. But a second look satisfied me that what I saw were simply stones scattered about covered with black moss. I continued my course keeping as near the coast as possible, my eyes constantly searching to the right, then to the left, then a little in advance, & so on as I trudged. I was now nearing the spot where I had 1st described the black. It again met my view. I hastened to the spot—"Great God, Thou hast rewarded me in my search!" On casting my eyes all around me, seeing & feeling the character of the RELICS before and under me, I felt as—<u>I cannot tell what my feel-ings were</u>. Anyhow, <u>I was all—all heart</u>. SEA COAL of Fro-bisher's expedition of 1578! NEAR THREE CENTURIES AGO!!

It occurred to Hall that the coal might have been brought

by whalers at a later date, but when he looked more closely
he saw that it was very old indeed: some of it was buried
deep in the ground and was wrapped around with the
roots of Arctic willow. Suzhi had stood by in amazement at
Hall's excitement:

> I held out my hand to her, wh. was full of coal, asking:
> "Kisu?" (What is it?)
> She answered: "Innuit kook'um."
> By this I took it that the Innuits sometimes have used it
> in cooking. Said I, "Innuit ikkumer e-a-u?" (Did the Innuits
> ever use this for a fire to cook with?")
> "Armelarng" (Yes) was the instant response.
> I then asked: "Noutima?" meaning where did these coals
> come from?
> Her response was, "Kodlunarn, oomiarkchua kiete amasu-
> adlo echar" (A great many years ago, white men with big
> ship came here).

Hall wanted to stay in the Sound, to look for more relics
and to establish for certain that it was Frobisher's Countess
of Warwick Sound, but, knowing that the summer weather
would last only another month at the most, he decided to
continue his expedition up the bay and to examine the
islands of the sound more thoroughly on his return voyage.
With Ninoo's inflated bladder aloft on a stake, the small
boat set out again, and for the next several weeks made her
way slowly up the north coast of the bay. They traveled
slowly partly because of conditions: they had to fight tides
as high as thirty feet and frequently were forced to row
into northwest winds that blew the bay into a vicious chop.
But their slow pace was also a matter of choice; Hall wanted
to map the coastline, the islands, and the waters of this unexplored region. Koojesse was helpful in the project, having the Eskimo ability to visualize terrain as a map, to
see it as if from high above, an uncanny ability shared by
many primitive peoples. Koojesse would draw sketch maps
of the coastline as they rowed or sailed past it, basing the

maps on his long acquaintance with the area. Hall checked Koojesse's rough maps and added to them by his own observations with compass and sextant: his lessons in navigation were at last paying dividends, and the maps that were finally produced are extraordinarily accurate.

The winds sometimes would calm, and then the men and women in the boat could hear occasional strange sounds reverberate over the bay, sharp cracks like rifle fire or deep roars like the echo of thunder. At first Hall thought that they were the sounds of distant storms, but the Eskimos told him that they were made by glaciers calving icebergs across the bay in Kingaite, known to whites as Meta Incognita. The calms, Hall discovered, were a mixed blessing. When the winds and waves settled, navigation was easier, but conditions for hunting duck and seal improved—the Eskimos could see their prey easily on the surface of water that was glassy or ruffled only by gentle breezes. Seal hunting in particular delayed their progress. When the Eskimos spotted the head of a seal bobbing on the water, they would quickly fire, not necessarily to kill but to panic the animal into a dive. Then they would stop the boat and all hands would stand up to spy the seal's next appearance. After three or four minutes the seal's head would again break the surface and they would all fire, then row the boat to wherever they thought the seal would next surface. This they continued to do until the seal was forced to make shorter dives and they could come close enough to fire a fatal shot. Such hunting was time-consuming and often involved turning the boat back, losing distance as well as time, but Hall could seldom persuade the Eskimos not to hunt when the opportunity arose. After one hunt he wrote: "I have today thought that for exploring purposes Innuits are not the serviceable auxilliaries I took them to be. When any kind of game is about, they are in for that & nothing else!"

Shortly before he had left on the voyage, he had commented on Eskimo independence in his journal:

They are a people knowing no restraint. <u>They will be</u>
<u>INDEPENDENT in the fullest signification of the word!</u> We
Americans talk about Freedom & Independence. We are far
behind these Northerners. While we are pleased with shad-
ows, these dusky fellows enjoy the substance! <u>DO AS THEY</u>
<u>PLEASE</u>, without anyone having the acknowledged right or
power to say, Why do you do so?

Hall, obsessively independent himself (a few days before this
entry he had written: "I am not bound to swear or speak
according to the dictates of any master"), usually admired the
Eskimos' independence, but when it interfered with what
he wanted to do, he was angered; independence then seemed
irresponsibility. Sometimes, when he was ready to set out in
the boat, he would discover that Koojesse had gone into the
mountains to hunt or had borrowed a kayak to shoot seals
in the bay. Often, when he wanted to move on, the Eskimos
would insist on staying put because of good hunting or
fishing, and occasionally they would take him miles out of
his way because they wanted to go to a place where they had
killed many tuktoo in past years. "Thus was I perpetually
annoyed by the freaks and vagaries of this free and independent people,"[16] Hall was to write in his book.

His annoyance was not really perpetual, however, and
frequently he was delighted to watch the Eskimos exercise
their many skills. Excellent anatomists through experience
in butchering, they could identify any bone that they found
on a beach, naming not only the animal from which it came
but also the exact place where it had fitted into the skeleton.
The men well knew the behavior of animals and fish; they
seemed to intuit where a seal would surface next after diving,
or how a caribou herd would move, or where char would
lie in a stream. The women continually amazed Hall by the
variety of work that they did. One night he went to Koojesse's
tupic to get some blubber oil for his lamp:

Koodloo and Charley made search, found seal-blubber,

brought it in, and passed it to Suzhi, who was in tuktoo—
that is, abed. Of course, like all Innuits when in bed, she
was entirely nude; but she immediately rose on her elbows,
and proceeded to bite off pieces of blubber, chewing them,
sucking the oil out, then spitting it into a little cone-like
dish, made by inverting the bottom of my broken tin lamp.
In this way she obtained with her dental mill in less than
three minutes oil enough to fill two large-sized lamps. It
was a novel scene, that of Kooulearng's [Suzhi's] operations
in grinding blubber for oil; in particular, the incidental
exhibition of what Burns describes as

"Twa drifted heaps, sae fair to see," exaggerated in size,
as in the case with most Innuit women, struck me forcibly.

On their way up the bay they occasionally encountered
Eskimo hunting parties. Only a few miles north of Countess
of Warwick Sound they met a party of Field Bay Eskimos,
most of them former acquaintances, and on the next day they
found an encampment in which lived Koojesse's father, the
venerable Artarkparu. Hall wanted to talk with old Eskimos
in particular, because they knew and told traditional stories.
Artarkparu often had been in Niountelik and had seen the
coal and brick there. He also had seen pieces of iron, "heavy
stones" he called them; he told Hall that when he was young
he and his friends had contests of strength with the heavy
stones, lifting them as high as they could. When Hall asked
how many years the coal, brick, and heavy stone had been on
the island, the old man answered, "Amasuadlo," a great many,
and added that they had been brought by kadloonas. He said
that kadloonas were also supposed to have built a ship on an
island nearby many years before. Several days later, the same
story was told by an old Eskimo woman who was in another
hunting party that they encountered: she too said that the
brick and coal had been on Niountelik for many years and that
kadloonas had built a ship on a nearby island.

Hall was worried about the condition of the whaleboat, and
he persuaded this last party of Eskimos, who had a large oo-

miak (an open sealskin boat), to join with his group temporarily. If the whaleboat began to leak badly, they would at least
have another boat available. The party was led by "Miner,"
one of the Field Bay Eskimos whom Hall had met during the
winter.

The shoreline became less precipitous and barren as they
worked their way up the bay in warm, clear weather. Among
the hills were plains of green, and the Eskimos enthusiastically
told Hall that this was fine tuktoo country. Occasionally they
would go ashore, and Hall would hear the reports of their
guns in the hills. They would come back with great quantities of caribou meat, fat and tender. Hall called it a land of
plenty in his journal, and for once he gave a name that was
suitable, Greenwood's Land. (At least the name sounded suitable, although it came from a Cincinnati industrialist and
iron founder.) On August 23 they found themselves in the
midst of a herd of seals, which ripped the placid surface of the
bay in pursuit of a huge school of Arctic char. Suzhi dipped a
tin cup full of bay water, drank some of it, and handed the
rest to Hall. He sipped it tentatively: it was fresh. Then he
heard the roar of a large river. They had reached the head of
Frobisher Bay.

Hall at first called the river the Cynthia Grinnell River.
"Its waters are an emblem of purity," he wrote. "I know of no
fitter name to bestow upon it than that of the daughter of my
generous, esteemed friend, Henry Grinnell." Unfortunately,
Henry Grinnell's daughter's name was Sylvia, not Cynthia,
but Hall corrected his mistake when he discovered it on returning to the United States, even taking the trouble to cross
out the name Cynthia and to substitute the name Sylvia in his
manuscript journal.

They remained camped in Greenwood's Land at the mouth
of the Sylvia Grinnell River for six days. While the Eskimos
hunted and fished, Hall roamed the nearby hills. The good
weather held, and under the sunlight of Arctic summer the
land looked more and more beautiful to Hall. "Is this not a

land or region Self Supporting?" he asked in his journal. "A colony here planting the seeds of Civilization & Christianity would not only be able to support themselves but add wealth to the people establishing it." Those Canadians who now live in the government colony of Frobisher Bay, which sprawls near Hall's old encampment, could well scoff at his enthusiasm over this piece of Arctic real estate, but he had come from the grim lower reaches of the bay, and his enthusiasm on seeing the green hues of the plains after the snow and ice of a long winter is understandable. Eliminate the ugly barracks, radio antennae, and dumps that now clutter the landscape, and Greenwood's Land would still look beautiful to someone coming from the rock desert of Loks Land or Hall Island.

On August 29 Hall's expedition, together with Miner's party, now consisting of twenty Eskimos and two boats, broke camp and rowed west across the head of the bay to Kingaite or Meta Incognita. This short trip provided the final proof that Frobisher Bay was not a strait; in celebration, Hall went to the top of a hill behind their next camp, and there sank a pole, from which an American flag flew.

> And how glad was my heart as I planted the flag of America upon that mountain-top, and beheld it fluttering in the breezes of heaven in the sun's light. The red, white, and blue—the argent stars—seemed gifted with a speaking spirit that said, "God hath ever blessed and ever will bless this emblem of freedom and power!" Yes, said I, mentally, that banner now floats where white man never stood before. The American flag precedes all others in proclaiming that this is the inceptive moment when civilization, with all its attending virtues, makes hither its advance.

They remained only a few more days at the head of the bay. Although he was suddenly plagued with boils and sores, Hall explored afoot the land near the mouth of another river—Jordan River as he called it (not after the scriptural river, but after Daniel B. Jordan, a paper-box manufacturer of Cincinnati). Across its large tidal mud flats he found a limestone mound of considerable size; at its base and along its flanks were thousands of fossils (Lower Silurian, as he discovered when he had some examined at Yale on his return to the United States). This mound he later named Silliman's Fossil Mount, after Benjamin Silliman Jr. of Yale.

The time had come to head back down the bay to the *George Henry*. It was September; ice was forming on still waters, and already there had been several snow squalls. When they set out the tide was ebbing rapidly, and Suzhi, who was experienced in boating (she was so strong a rower that Hall had to adjust for her power with his tiller or she would swing the boat around), joyously pointed out their speed as they rode the outgoing waters. Hall too was pleased, until he looked down under the surface; as the boat gathered velocity, the rocks that jutted up from the bottom of the shallows rushed by with terrifying rapidity. A few minutes later, the tide had fallen enough for their jagged tips to be exposed; the boat might just as well have been riding rock-strewn, dangerous rapids, and indeed the sounds were those of a monstrous river. By what seemed to Hall a miracle, they missed all the rocks and found themselves at last safe ashore on an island that Hall immediately named "Preservation."

The male Eskimos had all preceded them down the bay in the oomiak to hunt tuktoo. For several days Hall waited for them impatiently at the place where they had arranged rendezvous. His boils had become worse, and he was suffering from a painful abscess in his shoulder. A return journey from the unknown is often a greater psychological strain than the outward journey, which, however hard, has always the mitigating pleasure of anticipation. Hall had been living with Koojesse and the others for more than a month now, and his nerves were frayed. He vented his anger in his journal:

> Another morning has come & the hunters are still out! They deserve a severe thrashing wh. is the only remedy I can think

of for their "Selfish Independence." I know not when I have
felt so much & so often like administering physical chastise-
ment. Moral suasion with these creatures is entirely out of
the question. Force & severity on the very first infraction of
a reasonable rule or law, would soon bring them within the
rule of Civilization! As it is, I must submit to anything and
everything in the way of gratification to these unruly people.
I am surprised that Koojesse should treat me so. I indulged
in the hope that he was tinctured with enough of Civilization that he would act the manly part with me, but I find
it otherwise! He, like the other 2, acts the SAVAGE!

He scrawled pages of enraged commentary on Eskimo irresponsibility, vowing that never again would he make a voyage
with only Eskimos to keep him company.

Koojesse and the other men arrived after three days, bur-
dened with tuktoo skins. Miner's party decided to separate
from Hall's in order to stay up the bay for hunting, so Hall
again had only one boat and six Eskimos. For all his anger at
Koojesse, Hall had to admit that he showed skill as he guided
them safely through tidal shoals even more dangerous than
those they had already navigated, but the two men were now
at loggerheads. Hall would ask Koojesse to put in at an island
that interested him, or to go closer to the mainland, or to
change direction for some reason, and the Eskimo would sullenly refuse. Hall had hoped to return down the coast of Kingaite almost to the mouth of the bay, then cut across to
Countess of Warwick Sound, thereby completing his exploration of the bay. One day, noticing that Koojesse had suddenly
changed the direction of the boat, he asked him where they
were going.

He points across the bay—I suspected this in the way he was
directing the boat—He acts the devil with me. I must say
that I believe my life is in danger—but God is with me here
& everywhere—if I die at the hands of this treacherous
people I die in faith that I am in performance of my duty.

God deliver me from such scenes as I have witnessed among
the men Innuits I have with me. Consultations—savage looks
—are now and then to be seen.

Koojesse, knowing the waters of the bay, probably had
good reason for refusing to hug the Kingaite coast with its
dangerous tidal rips, and Hall was undoubtedly in a state
of nervous irritability, but his fears for his life were not
altogether unfounded: he had seen the Eskimo capacity
for violence break through their usual placid surface several
times. In the spring, one of his dogs had been mutilated
by this very Koojesse: in a fury, Koojesse had taken out
his knife and slashed off one of its ears. Only a few days before, Hall had seen Charlie hurl a lethal seal hook at his
wife for no apparent reason. He knew that small things
could trigger a black and dangerous rage in them.

Once Koojesse had brought the boat safely across the
bay to its north coast, however, tempers seemed to improve,
and he began again to do what Hall wanted. They touched
on the north coast somewhat northwest of the Countess of
Warwick Sound, and spent the next several days retracing
their outward route. Finally, on September 21, Hall found
himself back at the Sound that had so much aroused his
curiosity. They landed at Niountelik and set up camp there,
but Koojesse soon took Hall across to another island in the
Sound, a small island that the Eskimos called Kodlunarn
because white men (kadloonas) had been there many years
before. According to Koojesse, this was the place where the
five white men about whom Hall had heard from Ookijoxy
Ninoo had built their boat. As soon as Hall landed, he
began to find evidence of human habitation that could
not have been Eskimo:

> Coal; flintstone; fragments of tile, glass, and pottery; an
> excavation which I have called an abandoned mine; a trench
> by the shore on an inclined plane, such as is used in building
> a ship on the stocks; the ruins of three stone houses, one of

which was twelve feet in diameter, with palpable evidence of its having been erected on a foundation of stone cemented together with lime and sand; and some chips of wood I found on digging at the base of the ship's trench.

The "ship's trench," which was on the north coast, was the product of considerable labor, for it was cut partly out of solid rock. According to the Eskimos, the trench had been used by the five white men to build their boat, and Hall accepted this explanation.* The other trench, about one hundred yards inland, was probably what Hall thought it was, a mining excavation. It was six feet deep, eighty-eight feet long, and lined with debris thrown up by Frobisher's diggers. Having stripped the surface of the island of its "ore," Frobisher had probably dug an exploratory trench to see what lay underneath.

On Frobisher's third expedition he had built a house: "This daye the Masons finished a house whiche Captaine Fenton caused to be made of lyme and stone upon the Countesse of Warwickes Ilande, to the ende we mighte prove againste the nexte yere, whether the snowe coulde overwhelme it, the frosts breake uppe, or the people dismember the same."[17] Not far from the mining trench Hall found a large quantity of lichen-covered stone laid out in a rectangle, undoubtedly the foundations of a house. He also found two smaller piles, which might or might not have been the ruins of houses. On some of the stone he found the remains of mortar, and nearby were quantities of flint. (The large amount of flint found by Hall and by later visitors to the island might be explained by the fact that in the sixteenth and early seventeenth centuries flint was often used as ballast.)

* Duncan Strong, archeologist on the Rawson-MacMillan Expedition, which visited the island briefly in 1927, believed that it was a dry dock used to repair Frobisher's smaller vessels, but possibly it had been used as a ramp from which Frobisher's stone was loaded into boats to be taken out to the ships.

On the next day Hall went to the mainland, only a few
hundred yards from Kodlunarn Island. He was wandering
there when he heard one of the Eskimos shouting from the
shore:

> The Innuits started on the run, and so did I, for I was sure
> that something of interest had been found. Arriving at the
> spot, what was before me? A relic of three centuries! Iron—
> time-eaten, with ragged teeth! This iron, weighing from
> fifteen to twenty pounds, was on the top of a granite rock,
> just within reach of high tide at full and change of moon.
> The iron stain from this specimen was in the rock; other-
> wise its top was cleanly washed. This was just what I wanted
> to find—some of the heavy stone which the venerable
> Innuit woman, Ookijoxy Ninoo, had told me about the
> previous winter.

Snow squalls and high winds kept them in the sound for
several more days, which Hall used to explore the other
island and portions of the mainland. He found more coal
and flint and, just before they departed for Field Bay, another chunk of iron, imbedded in the "ship's trench." Hall
decided, probably correctly, that these chunks of iron were
"blooms" smelted by Frobisher's miners to test the ore on
the island. Any iron brought over from England for the use
of blacksmiths would have been "pig" cast in ingots, whereas
these "blooms" were crude half-spheres weighing about
twenty pounds, the sort of iron smelted in primitive furnaces
dug in the ground. Frobisher's men had lime available for
lining such furnaces and hard coal or possibly charcoal for
fuel, and the ore that they mistook for gold was actually
magnetite (containing some pyrite), which would have
smelted into iron.

When the weather cleared, Hall packed his relics in any
containers available, including his socks and mittens, loaded
their little boat, and then set off for Field Bay and, he hoped,
the *George Henry*. Hall was anxious on the short voyage

because Budington, not wanting to risk spending another winter in the North, especially as the autumn freeze was already beginning, might well have left for the United States. They reached Field Bay in the dark of night, and Hall thought that his fears had been confirmed as they slowly made their way toward the whaler's old anchorage in Rescue Bay. But suddenly the dark shape of the *George Henry* loomed up before them. Hall's Eskimos shouted and fired off their rifles in celebration of their arrival.

The good news that Hall received on his return was that Tookoolito had safely been delivered of a male child, her first baby, not long after he had left for Frobisher Bay. The bad news was that the *George Henry* had secured no whales since he had been gone. Budington, discouraged with the voyage, had decided to sail for home in the middle of October, which gave Hall another month for his explorations. He was glad to have the month; further conversation with the Eskimos convinced him that he should return once again to Countess of Warwick Sound to search for more relics. Even Blind George confirmed the traditional stories that Hall had been hearing. Standing before a table, the blind Eskimo, drawing on memories from the time when he could see, used the table as an imaginary map and pointed out the location of the different islands in the sound in relation to one another, telling the story of the kadloonas who had lived on them. Hall handed George one of the blooms and, touching it with his lips, George said it was like others he had seen and felt. When Hall asked Ebierbing how such stories remained current for so long, the new father replied, "When our baby boy gets old enough, we tell him all about you, and about all those kadloonas who brought brick, iron, and coal to where you have been. When the boy gets to be an old Innuit, he tell it to other Innuits, and so all Innuits will know what we now know."*

* Unfortunately, Ebierbing's explanation no longer holds true. Since the great influx of outsiders during World War II and after, the

Hall was particularly excited by news of another relic, said to be on the island of Oopungnewing. According to several Eskimos, it was heavy like the blooms, but was smooth and red. For a time Hall thought that it might be copper, but after talking to Ugarng he decided that it was probably a rusted iron anvil. Ugarng had been to the United States, and in describing the object, he formed his fist to represent a hammer, struck downward, and said, "All the same as blacksmith." If for no other purpose, Hall decided that it would be worthwhile returning to the sound to find this obviously important object. The Eskimos who had accompanied him up Frobisher Bay all balked at returning, except for the hardy Suzhi, who was happy to go anywhere. With Budington's help, however, Hall recruited a crew, and the Captain also donated some supplies. "Shall such a friend ever be forgotten?" Hall wrote. "Will this humble, poor heart of mine ever cease to thank <u>God</u> that <u>He</u> hath blessed my pathway through life with such a friend as Captain B.?" In future years, Hall regretted writing so effusively about Captain B.

Hall's plans to return to the Countess of Warwick Sound were defeated by weather. He and his little party set out in a boat on October 7, but after only a few hours high winds forced them ashore. During the next several days they were able to travel only as far as Lupton Channel because the winds increased to gale force, reminding Hall of the storm that had driven the *Rescue* ashore the previous autumn. Regretfully he returned to the *George Henry*, where he found Captain Budington and the crew in good humor: a few hours after Hall had left, they secured two whales and they had seen many others since. Budington had decided

---

Frobisher Bay Eskimos have lost their oral tradition, and they no longer tell stories about Frobisher—or about Hall. Nowadays there is nothing remarkable or memorable about kadloonas coming to their land.

to risk remaining in the area for another ten days in hopes of making up with one spectacular week for a bad year of whaling.

The gamble was not a good one. The entry in Hall's journal for October 17 began, "Shall I put upon paper my feelings of tonight? Or shall I leave them to be <u>imagined</u> after stating the bare facts from whence they originate? At present it is thought <u>that we are ice-imprisoned in Rescue Bay for the</u> <u>WINTER</u>!" He continued: "A few hours ago, we were all anticipating the short time that remained before the G.H.'s sails were to be given to the wind. But <u>now</u> we are all thinking of <u>preparations</u> for the <u>acquirement</u> of the wherewithall <u>to live</u> in these regions of cold, ice and snow." That morning, Hall had climbed to the top of a mountain overlooking Field Bay. When he had reached the summit, he had surveyed the panorama below him:

> I took the spy glass, and proceeded to make a prolonged observation. I first directed the glass toward the vessel, which was at a distance of seven miles; I then directed it to Davis's Strait. This I saw was filled with a heavy <u>pack</u>. I swept with the instrument down along said strait to the extremity of Hall's Island. No black water—naught but <u>pack</u>, <u>pack</u> met my view! . . . Monumental Island was white, and its sides presented no black rock peering out; and the same was true of Lady Franklin Island. The pack appeared very rough, much pinacled ice was among it, and it was especially to be seen around the first island of the extreme land next to Davis's Strait. As far as the eye could reach by the aid of the most excellent glass, up and down the strait, no open water met my view.

Within three days the waters of the bay itself froze, and the *George Henry* was trapped in ice for another winter.

Food and fuel would be a serious problem. Budington sent the men to gather driftwood from the beaches, and the jawbones of the recently secured whales were sawed, chopped, and split like so much birchwood. Immediate food rationing was imposed: for the remainder of the autumn and winter, unless large quantities of seals were killed, the men would have two rather than three meals a day. Budington decreed that they would use the Eskimos for hunting; they would buy or barter for whatever the natives killed. Hall contributed what was left of his expedition's supply of biscuits and pemmican to the ship.

By early November, the ship and the men were prepared for the cold, dark months that lay ahead. The men had at least enough food to survive, and were kept warm enough to maintain bodily health, but the problem of mental health was another matter. Budington, an experienced Arctic sailor, condoned and even encouraged many distractions that offended the pious Hall. Occasionally parties were held aboard the whaler, with singing, dancing, and some drinking. There also were "theatricals," and the men whiled away many hours playing games. Hall's popularity aboard the ship was considerably diminished when he complained to Budington about their gaming on the Sabbath:

> I told Capt. B. in expressing the pleasure it would afford me by his having the men discontinue playing games on Sunday, that it was not that I considered myself better than anybody else—that I too was a great sinner—but because I felt that it would be for his own good—that certainly when he (Capt. B) was upon his Death bed he would never regret the act.

Budington ordered that there would be no more gaming on Sunday, but Hall could hardly have ingratiated himself with captain or crew by his stiff-necked piety.

What is sometimes called "cabin fever" is an elusive and insidious sickness of the mind, whether it takes its course in a trapper's shack or aboard an iced-in whaling vessel. At first some men turn inward in ominous silence, whereas others become loud and self-assertive, but all look out at the others with irrational distrust. A single word or gesture can hatch a grievance that will be nursed with bile during weeks of self-destructive introspection. A tiny mannerism, a tendency to eat with the mouth open, to snore, or to laugh too loudly, can become the focus of an intense communal hatred. Envy, fear, spite, and guilt stalk the ship. In the fever's later stages, there is an apathy that is spiritual death.

In Hall's journal for the month of December 1861, we can see incursions of cabin fever eroding the minds of the men aboard the *George Henry*. Hall himself became hypersensitive. One evening while eating with the second mess, he either realized or imagined (one indication of the fever is the blending of real and imagined offenses) that the crew believed that he was eating *their* food—that he was a parasite aboard the ship. He retreated to his cabin, where he brooded and went on a hunger strike. If that was the way they felt, he thought, then he would show them: he would not eat a morsel of their food. He would starve to death, and that would show them. Budington came to see him, and he explained to the captain what had happened. With patience, Budington soothed his hurt feelings.

Tensions mounted among the crew. One man stole bread. Another stole gunpowder, which he used as barter for his own private dealings with the Eskimos. The youngest sailor aboard broke out with syphilis. There were fights, and soon many of the men sank into apathy. Budington, who had been a whaling captain for a long time, knew that something had to be done. In January he sent most of the crew out to live with the Eskimos for a while, hoping that the harsh, active regimen would jolt them back to life. The experiment was a failure: most of the men returned to the ship after only a few days, complaining that they could not endure the Eskimo way of life. Ebierbing laughed to Hall about them: "They all be same as small boys." But those who did remain out for a week or more suffered. One returned with frostbitten toes, which Budington had to amputate. (As one of his toes was being cut off, the sailor shouted, "Damn that toe to hell," shocking Hall, who wrote in his journal: "Under the circumstances it was enough to make one's blood run cold so extraordinarily wicked was the speech.") An officer wrote to his captain from an Eskimo camp:

> CAPTAIN—SIR: Ooksin got one small deer today, and I send this to you for yourself, and hope that soon we may have the luck to send you more. They see quite a number of deer every day, but half the time their guns will not go. I hope that you are well, for I know that your mind is troubled, as I heard that all of the men have come back to the ship. We are quite hard up here now, for all the 'black skin' is gone, and I have only about ten pounds of whale meat left; but I shall not come to the ship, for I might as well die here as there, for all I know.

The writer of the letter, Third Mate Reuban Lamb, did return, however, as did all the others, straggling back like beaten dogs. One group of men brought news that snapped Hall out of his lethargy: they said that the Eskimos who had been with them had left a sick woman behind to die by herself. By now Hall had encountered this custom several times, but he still would not accept it; the fact that some Eskimos had visited the remains of old Nukertou a few weeks before to leave offerings of food near her corpse and to talk with her spirit did not mitigate what he considered to be outrageous brutality. Hall, Ebierbing, and Reuban Lamb set out by sledge to try to reach the woman before she died. In spite of biting cold and high winds, they made good time to the place where the woman was supposed to be, on the mainland near Countess of Warwick Sound. Drifted snow had entirely covered the igloo village. To Hall's eyes there was nothing but a flat plain of white, but Ebierbing found places where he thought there would be igloos under the snow. Hall poked down through the surface with a seal spear and located three igloos. Ebierbing helped Hall to lower himself into the third, and there he found the woman, dead and frozen. He prayed for her soul, then climbed out of the igloo and sealed it shut again with blocks of snow. Six of the Nugumiuts had died since Hall had arrived at Baffin Island. "How my heart weeps to behold this people dying off without an equivalent compensation in births," he wrote in his journal. "A few years & there will be no race."

The winter was cold and depressing, and Hall, unusually inactive, accomplished little. He joined Eskimos on occasional hunting trips. He spent hours listening to their tales about the kadloonas who had come to Countess of Warwick Sound. In his tiny cabin, he brooded about his failure to reach King William Island, where he was certain he would have heard other tales about Franklin's expedition, and he laid plans for his next expedition. Part of his plan was to take Ebierbing and Tookoolito back with him to the United States. On January 8 he wrote:

> This P.M. I have called on my Innuit friends Ebierbing and Tookoolito. They are going to accompany me to the United States. I take them with the object of having them as interpreters on my still proposed voyage to King William's Land and Boothia Felix. Among the Innuits who spend their lives in the vicinity of the places named, there exists the history of Sir John Franklin's expedition from about the time the Erebus and Terror became beset in the ice, near King William's Land, to its final dispersion; and of all events connected therewith. I repeat: the history of Sir John Franklin's expedition exists among the Innuits now living on and in the vicinity of King William's Land, Montreal Island, and Boothia Felix Peninsula.

In the meantime, he decided that he would re-explore Frobisher Bay before the ice broke in the spring, this time using dogs and sledge. Tookoolito was still weakened by the birth of her child (childbirth for Tookoolito was an ordeal; three times she nearly died of it), and she and Ebierbing remained behind, so Hall again traveled with Koojesse and several other Eskimos whom he did not entirely trust. They set out early in the morning of April 1. Hall left without saying good-bye to Tookoolito, who had overslept, but after almost an hour on the trail he saw a small figure striving after them. Tookoolito, baby nestled Eskimo-fashion on her back, had struggled over the hummocky ice merely to say farewell.

His second trip up Frobisher Bay lasted six weeks, but his journal for those weeks is lost, and he gave only a hasty account of the trip in his book, *Arctic Researches and Life Among the Esquimaux.** Although he probed up some inlets that he had passed by in the previous summer and saw new parts of the Kingaite coast, he accomplished little in the way of exploration, mainly retracing the route that he had taken on his boat voyage.

If he made no geographical discoveries, however, he did learn much about the techniques, hardships, and dangers of sledge travel. He was fortunate in having clear weather most of the time, but inevitably there were some storms. Blinded by dense, wind-driven snow, he several times was forced to rely entirely on his compass for direction, a dangerous pro-cedure not merely because they could become lost, but be-cause they might wander out onto the bay ice, which in the high winds could break up around them and trap them on drifting floe, where they would be at the mercy of wind, cur-rent, and tide. That the ice was dangerous in the spring, Hall learned one clear day when he was out on the bay surveying some islands. A high wind came up. To the south was open water, and Hall suddenly heard the noises of shifting, cracking ice. He and the Eskimos rushed to the shore across the uneasy floe, and reached safety just as it began to drift. The spring

* The account is hasty probably because it was written in the spring of 1864, when Hall was rushing to complete the book before he left on his second expedition.

winds and thaws also made living in an igloo disagreeable: no sooner was an igloo completed than it began to thaw. The Eskimos therefore began to make half-igloo, half-tupic dwellings, with snow walls but skins instead of a snow dome.

Except for a few brief periods, they had good hunting. They secured some walrus, harpooning them on the edge of the bay ice, and most of the time seals were plentiful. Seals had pups in April and May, and Hall delighted not only in the tender meat of the young seals, but also, like an Eskimo epicure, in the mother's milk that was sometimes found in their stomachs. He witnessed a cruel technique often used to hunt seals in the spring. A mother seal nurses her young in a "seal igloo," a little cave burrowed in the snow directly over an access and escape hole in the ice. One day one of the Eskimos found a seal pup outside of its igloo. Koojesse tied a line around the pup's flippers (Hall might have been softening the truth here: according to Franz Boas, who was with the Nugumiuts twenty years later, the Eskimos using this technique skewered the pup on a hook), and put it back inside the igloo. The pup immediately dove through the hole in the ice into the water, where, presumably, it cried for its mother. Koojesse waited patiently for the mother to be lured within range of his seal hook, but on this occasion she did not appear; he had to be content with only the pup, which he strangled, thus preserving its valuable blood.

On this trip, Hall also twice experienced the sensations of the hunted rather than the hunter. One day when he was using his sextant on the top of a hill above their camp, he heard a growl. He looked around him and saw nothing, but when he heard another growl he headed for the camp so hastily that he tripped and rolled most of the way down the hill. When he told the Eskimos about the incident, they assured him that he had probably escaped from either a polar bear or wolves. Several hours later, as they were making their way across some bay ice, they saw four wolves following them at a hot pace, "snapping their teeth, and smacking their

chops, as if already feasting on human steaks and blood."
Hall and the Eskimos hid behind ice hummocks and fired at
the wolves with rifles, driving them off only when one of the
animals was wounded.*

Two days after this encounter with wolves, Hall and his
party came on a polar bear and her half-grown cub near the
base of one of Kingaite's bold mountains. Koojesse cut the
draught lines, releasing the dogs, and the cub, pursued by the
pack, became separated from its mother. While the Eskimos
went to the slopes of the mountain after the old bear, Hall
cautiously approached the cub, which was being attacked
by eleven dogs. Suddenly the young bear broke away from
the pack and, "jaws widely distended," went for Hall. Hall
had a seal spear in hand; he set himself for the shock and
received the bear's charge on the spear point. He expected
praise from the Eskimos when they returned to find him
standing in triumph over the body, but, much to his disappointment, they seemed indifferent. Soon he discovered
that they were not merely indifferent—they were displeased.
They had failed to kill the old bear but had wounded her.
They were frightened that she would return to search for her
cub. Already enraged by her wounds, she would be very
dangerous when she found that the cub was missing. Hall
wished to stay in the area to explore it more thoroughly, but
the Eskimos insisted that they move on, and they even took
evasive actions as they sledged away from the coast, hoping to
confuse the bear if she followed their trail. Much to Hall's
relief, they never saw her again.

Hall arrived back at the *George Henry* on May 21. More
than two months passed before the ship was released from the

---

* Four years later, on his second expedition, Hall was to see another
method of discouraging wolves: the Eskimos of Foxe Channel soaked
knife blades with blood and imbedded them, blade out, in the ground.
Wolves would lick the blades, not feeling their cuts because of the
numbing cold. The more they licked, the more blood there was on the
blades. They licked until, tongues lacerated, they collapsed from loss
of blood.

ice, and for several tense weeks late in July Hall and Budington feared that they faced yet another winter in the Arctic.
During the months of waiting, Hall made several short trips.
He and Ebierbing sledged to Grinnell Bay, where Hall explored and mapped some inlets and islands. When small leads
began to appear in the ice, Hall took his boat back to Loks
Land to examine more thoroughly its complex of islands and
channels. He returned twice more to Countess of Warwick
Sound, once with a company of eleven Eskimos to help him
search for relics. (He found many, but not the "anvil," which
had disappeared.) During the second trip to the sound Captain Budington arrived in a ship's boat to announce that the
George Henry was at last freed from the ice.

She sailed for home on August 9, only twenty-four hours
after Hall learned that she was free. The ice might have closed
in again at any moment, and no time could be wasted. While
the crew prepared the ship, Hall helped Ebierbing and Tookoolito to move aboard with their baby and their gear.
Knowing that he might use the Eskimos for lectures and
exhibits, he had asked them to take along some fishing and
hunting equipment and complete winter and summer outfits.
He also had decided to take two dogs for the same reason,
Ebierbing's "Ratty" and his own favorite Greenland dog,
"Barbekark." No sooner were all aboard than Budington had
the boats manned to tow the ship out of the becalmed bay
into Davis Strait. Most of the way down the bay, the *George
Henry* was accompanied by Eskimos in their kayaks and
oomiaks, all waving and shouting "Terbouetie!" ("Farewell").

Hall spent the days of the cruise to Newfoundland thinking
about what he had accomplished and what he would accomplish on his next expedition. He had completely failed in the
stated purpose of his first expedition, not having come even
close to his intended destination, King William Island. But he
had proved that the so-called Frobisher Strait was a bay, and
packed in boxes in his cabin were relics indicating that it was
indeed the place of Frobisher's explorations almost three

hundred years before. He had learned much about Eskimos and their way of life, and he had proved to his own satisfaction that he could live as they lived. And if he could learn to survive in the Arctic, why could not Franklin's men? If there were survivors from the *Erebus* and *Terror,* he would find them on his next expedition. If there were not, then he would at least solve the mystery of their fate: the stories told by the Nugumiuts about Frobisher had convinced him that he could find out in detail what happened to the Franklin expedition if he could talk to the Eskimos in the area of King William Island.

Hall's reliance on Eskimo stories about kadloonas was to cause him trouble. He never entirely learned that such stories had to be assessed carefully. The problem was not that the Eskimos lied (although they were capable of improvising to please their auditor; they considered it good manners to tell him what he wanted to hear); rather, the problem was that the stories might mix incidents together or might be about something or someone other than what he thought them to be about. During the spring of 1861 Hall was told a story by some Eskimos from Baffin Island's south coast who briefly visited Field Bay. They said that several years before, some kadloonas had arrived in their land in two open boats. The men in the boats were healthy and had plentiful supplies; after staying only a few days, they rowed away toward the open sea. Hall had thought about this story and, perhaps clutching at straws, had decided that the men were survivors of the Franklin expedition. When the *George Henry* put into St. John's, Newfoundland, he made the mistake of telling the story and his interpretation of it to a newspaper reporter who interviewed him. Several days later the reporter's story appeared in the St. John's newspaper, featuring the headline "TWO BOAT'S CREWS OF FRANKLIN." When Hall arrived in New York, he discovered that in 1859 a British whaling vessel, the *Kitty,* had been crushed by ice in Hudson's Strait, and its crew had escaped in two ship's boats: undoubtedly these were the men whom the Eskimos had seen. It was embarrassing. The St. John's story had been picked up by the British press and Hall was afraid that, appearing a fool or a fraud, he would be doubted in his other discoveries. That was only the first time that he was to be misled by Eskimo stories about kadloonas.

The *George Henry* arrived at St. John's on August 23. The pilot who came aboard outside of the harbor brought news: the United States was no longer united—the Civil War had begun four months before. Three days later, the *George Henry* set sail again, heading toward a war-torn country.

chapter four

Interim

On September 7 the *George Henry* was met by a pilot boat just off Montauk Point. Aboard was a *New York Herald* reporter, who interviewed Hall and the crew as the *George Henry* was piloted into New London harbor. Even in time of war, Hall's return merited one of those interminable nineteenth-century headlines in the *Herald* a few days later:

THE NEW ARCTIC DISCOVERIES

* * * * *

ARRIVAL OF THE GEORGE HENRY
AT NEW LONDON

* * * * *

Return of Mr. C. F. Hall, the
American Explorer

* * * * *

Highly Interesting Discoveries—
Mountains of Fossils

* * * * *

BRITISH EXPLORERS CORRECTED

* * * * *

The Fate of Frobisher's Expedition
of 1576

* * * * *

RELICS THREE HUNDRED YEARS OLD

* * * * *

ARCTIC LIFE AND PRIVATIONS

*****

The Voyage of the George Henry

*****

Statements of Her Second Mate,
Mr. Gardiner, and Mr. Hudson,
the Steward

*****

THE INNUIT FAMILY,
&c., &c., &c.

At New London Hall found a letter from Henry Grinnell,
saying that he was unable to meet the ship because of sickness
in his family. "You probably may be in the want of a little
change on your arrival to defray your personal expenses at
New London," the letter concluded. "I therefore give you
liberty to draw on me for $100." Hall settled Ebierbing, Too-
koolito, their child, and the two dogs with the Budingtons in
Groton, drawing on Grinnell's money to pay expenses in advance, then hastened to New York to see his patron. He stayed
in New York for only a few days, telling Grinnell about his
experiences and discussing his plans for another expedition.
Then he left for Cincinnati to see his wife and children. He
was obsessed with returning north, and on his way to Cincinnati he wrote Grinnell a hasty letter repeating what he had
told him in New York: "Instead of reading, thinking, or talking 'WAR' on my way, I kept revolving in my mind expedien-
cies relating to carrying out my purpose of renewing a Voyage
to the Arctic Regions next Spring." Even as Hall penned this
letter on September 16, Jackson, who had captured Harper's
Ferry the day before, was marching to join Lee at Sharpsburg,
while McClellan was delaying attack on the Confederate
forces. The day that Grinnell received the letter was the blood-
iest day of the entire war; when the battle was done, more
than twenty thousand Federal and Confederate casualties lay
bleeding on the fields near Antietam Creek. Not long after, in

spite of Hall's stated determination not to concern himself
with the war, he made his one and only gesture in its direction: he wrote a long letter to Salmon P. Chase volunteering
his services. He told Chase that he had heard about the depredations of the Confederate steamer *Alabama*. "I could not—
I cannot keep down my soul longer. I offer my heart's blood
with a cheerful devotion to my country." He wrote that he
would organize some of the whaling men of New London and
obtain a whaling vessel. Would Chase arrange to commission
him, his crew, his vessel to go out after the *Alabama*? Chase
apparently ignored this rather flamboyant offer, and Hall, perhaps miffed at being ignored, returned to his proper business.
In the two years that followed, he ignored the national struggle as if it did not exist, mentioning it only twice in all his
letters and journals of the period. While the eyes of the nation
were turned south, Hall's remained fixed on the north.

During his stay in Cincinnati Hall brooded about what had
to be done to fulfill his dream of another expedition. He
knew that again his main problem would be raising money,
and that to raise money he would have to publicize his ex-
ploits, giving lectures and possibly writing a book. While in
Cincinnati, however, he refused several invitations to lecture
because he thought that lecturing would distract him from
another scheme that he had in mind: he planned to donate
some of the Frobisher relics to the English people, delivering
them to England himself. England, after all, was at peace and
might be more sympathetic to Arctic exploration than the
embattled United States. Hall also knew that Lady Franklin
was still agitating for further investigation of the Franklin
disaster, and he hoped that he could persuade her to give
generously to his next expedition.

Allowing only two weeks to wife and children, he returned
east in the middle of October, eager to leave for England
immediately. In spite of his enthusiasm, however, Henry
Grinnell dissuaded him from making the journey. He assured
Hall that the money could be raised in the United States and

that therefore there was no reason to encumber himself with the expense of going abroad. Possibly Grinnell also secretly believed that the overenthusiastic Hall would only be humiliated in London, and lose more than he might gain by making a personal appearance there. Grinnell took some of the edge off Hall's disappointment by arranging for him to give a lecture at the American Geographical and Statistical Society early in November, and for the next several weeks Hall was kept busy preparing for his appearance there. He had decided that in lectures, and in the book that he knew he must write, he would emphasize the discovery of the Frobisher relics; he spent long hours in rooms at the Geographical and Statistical Society and the Astor Library reading all that he could find about the Frobisher voyages, and he wrote to Clements Markham, Secretary of both the Royal Geographical Society and the Hakluyt Society, asking about the availability of the Hakluyt Society reprints.* In his researches on Frobisher, Hall wanted both to provide himself with material for his lectures and to prepare himself for possible English skepticism about his discoveries; he feared that the St. John's newspaper's reports about the "two boat's crews of Franklin" would sour the English and cause them to discount all that he had done.

The meeting of the American Geographical and Statistical Society was held on November 6. After an introduction by Henry Grinnell, Hall made some preliminary remarks about his gratitude to those who had supported the expedition, then went on to tell his story. At the outset he admitted failure in the stated purpose of the expedition, the search for Franklin; then he talked mainly about Eskimos, praising their honesty, generosity, and independence. Soon, by referring to their traditional tales, he made the transition to his main subject,

---

* The Hakluyt Society at that time had no reprints of the Frobisher chronicles, but Hall's discoveries and queries helped to stimulate the Society into printing its 1867 edition of Frobisher materials, which was dedicated to Henry Grinnell.

the voyages of Martin Frobisher and the question of the location of Frobisher Bay. Reading passages from a rare copy of Hakluyt that he had borrowed from the historian George Bancroft, he related the geography inferred from the chronicles to the large maps of Baffin Island and Frobisher Bay that were displayed behind him. He concluded by discussing the relics, which were spread out on a table before him. His lecture was greeted with enthusiastic applause.

Present at the meeting was forty-five-year-old William Parker Snow, an English explorer and writer who had an adventuresome and wildly erratic career behind him. Snow had gone to sea at an early age, sailed to Australia on a merchantman, and for a time engaged in mysterious and probably illegal trade in the East Indies. He had returned to England to join the Navy, from which, finding it too restrictive for his tastes, he deserted; he had been caught, arrested, and punished, and served out the remainder of his enlistment on the coast of West Africa. After his discharge, he had gone to England to try his hand at newspaper writing, but soon had given that up and migrated to Australia, where he and his newly-wed wife managed a hotel. After the hotel and his health both failed, he had returned again to England and become a secretary, working for Macaulay among others (Snow transcribed the first two volumes of the *History of England*). In 1850, when the excitement over Franklin's disappearance was at its peak, he had volunteered to serve as purser, surgeon, and first mate aboard the *Prince Albert,* the ship sent out by Lady Franklin in that year. It was Snow who, during this cruise, first heard the Eskimo Adam Beck tell his terrible story about Eskimos slaughtering white men. After the *Prince Albert* returned, Snow wrote a book about his experiences, *The Voyage of the Prince Albert in Search of Sir John Franklin.* Then, still restless, he had taken command of a vessel owned by the South American Missionary Society. For several years he had sailed the dangerous waters around Tierra del Fuego,

Patagonia, and the Falkland Islands, but this job ended suddenly when the Missionary Society fired him from his command for disobeying orders, leaving him and his wife to find their own way from Tierra del Fuego to England. When they finally arrived in civilization again, Snow wrote another book —*A Two Year Cruise off Tierra del Fuego, the Falkland Islands, Patagonia, and the River Plate*—an angry book full of accusations against all those who had harassed him. The book sold well, but Snow used up the profits in a suit against the Missionary Society, and found himself destitute when the court decided against him. Penniless, he and his wife went to New York. He had been in New York not quite a year, living by occasional hackwork for publishing firms, when he attended the meeting of the American Geographical and Statistical Society at which Hall spoke.

As Hall was soon to discover, Snow was undependable, disputatious, litigious, and possibly paranoid, but their relationship began in a most friendly fashion. Snow asked probing questions after Hall's lecture, then stood up to state that he believed Hall had made some major discoveries. Hall was relieved: there before him was one Englishman who apparently believed in what he had done. Not long after, in a letter to the English geographer John Barrow (son of the late Secretary of the Admiralty), Hall mentioned his meeting with Snow. "It has given me great pleasure to meet Capt. W. Parker Snow of your country," Hall wrote. "He needs no commendation at my hands—suffice it to be said, when I learned his devotion to the Cause he so long ago espoused [like Hall, Snow firmly believed there were Franklin survivors], I took his hand, & my heart spoke, 'THOU ART MY BROTHER.' "

The hit of the evening was the sudden appearance after the lecture of Ebierbing, Tookoolito, and their son, Tukerliktu, the little "Butterfly," as Hall now called him (Tookoolito called him "Johny"). In the weeks before the lecture,

Hall had instructed Budington to have Tookoolito prepare full summer costumes of sealskin and to gather together bows and arrows, fish spears, dog harnesses, and other Eskimo paraphernalia. Several days before the lecture, Budington had escorted the three Eskimos and the two dogs, Ratty and Barbekark, from Groton to New York. Although the dogs apparently did not make their appearance at the American Geographical and Statistical Society, the Eskimos did, and as the *Herald* reported, "Their presence created quite a sensation."[1] The crowd that milled around them was particularly impressed by Tookoolito, who graciously answered questions in her soft-spoken English.

Hall now considered himself primarily an explorer, but his talents as an entrepreneur and publicist were still on tap, and his decision to bring the Eskimos from Baffin Island had undoubtedly been affected by his awareness that they could provide him with the publicity he needed to raise money; indeed, they could raise money themselves. The day after the lecture, the Eskimo family and the dogs began a week's engagement at Barnum's Museum, where they were so popular that the engagement was extended to two weeks. While they were appearing at Barnum's, Hall also was approached by J. A. Cotting, who wanted to arrange an exhibition at Cotting and Guay's Aquarial Gardens in Boston.

Hall's arrangements with Cotting and Guay brought him into strange contact with one of the most famous scientists of the century, Louis Agassiz. When Cotting called on Hall in New York, he brought with him a letter from Agassiz addressed to Henry Grinnell, praising Cotting as "a most enterprising gentleman" and stating that at the Aquarial Gardens "exhibition has been conducted with the desire of making it useful & instructive rather than to minister to the propensity for fanciful & marvelous curiosities." In short, Agassiz wrote, Cotting and Guay would exhibit Ebierbing and Tookoolito with dignity. Hall immediately signed on the dotted line, but he soon regretted having done so. A few days before the Eskimos were to travel to Boston, he requested an advance of one hundred dollars, but received only fifty, enclosed in a letter so cool as to be insulting. When the two-week engagement in Boston ended, Hall tried unsuccessfully to collect one hundred and forty-five dollars plus forty-five for expenses still owed to him. By this time he had hired Charles Daboll, a friend and neighbor of the Budingtons in Groton, as an agent to assist him in his various projects. He dispatched Daboll to Boston to investigate Cotting and Guay, and the agent soon wrote that the firm was so nearly bankrupt that there was little hope of collecting from it. Hall then had the effrontery to write to the formidable Louis Agassiz, stating that it was because of Agassiz's letter that he trusted Cotting and Guay, and hinting clearly that Agassiz should therefore pay the one hundred and ninety dollars still owing. Agassiz naturally ignored Hall's impertinence, and so the Boston venture was a total loss. Hall wrote Budington, "This is indeed bad business having dealings with 'show' people, whose sole business is to grasp & hold the Almighty Dollar."

Although Hall apparently had no qualms about exhibiting the Eskimos to make money for himself, he did worry, with good reason, about the effect on their health of being week after week "in hot furs & in hot rooms." Early in December, when the manager of Barnum's Museum asked to have the Eskimos again for four weeks at a high price, Hall refused. He wrote to Mrs. Budington:

> He cannot have them again. I do think it would ruin their healths to go through another siege as when they were there. Money would not induce me to run another such risk of their lives. They must not go into any more Show-Establishments. I was very sorry immediately after I made the arrangements I did with Barnum & that Boston Concern. My only reasons for allowing such agreements to be made were on account of my circumstances.

Although Ebierbing, Tookoolito, and their child were never again made to appear in "Show-Establishments," Hall did use them in his lectures. By December he and Daboll had arranged a series of lectures in Providence, New Haven, Norwich, Hartford, Hudson, and Elmira. Featured very prominently on the posters that Hall had printed was a woodcut of the Eskimos, dressed in tuktoo skins and standing in front of an igloo village. Ebierbing, his wife, and the child would appear part of the way through the lecture, and the dog Barbekark, led on stage in full harness by Ebierbing, also played a part. (Ratty, after tasting the pleasures of civilization by escaping on the streets of New York for several days and by chasing sheep in the fields near the Budingtons', was judged too obstreperous for public display.)

In spite of war, Hall's lectures were a success. At first it seemed that the war might interfere—when arranging for the first of the lectures in Providence, Daboll received a discouraging letter from the president of the club that he had approached to sponsor the event: "In justice to you I must say that I get but little encouragement to go on with the lecture from our members. Those that are not in the army are so discouraged by the condition of our country that they are not willing to do much for this enterprise." Discouragement with the condition of the country in mid-December 1862 was to be expected: on December 13 Burnside, who had replaced McClellan, had failed to dislodge Lee at Fredericksburg, and more than fifteen thousand casualties had been added to the growing toll of the war. But Hall went ahead with the Providence lecture and the lectures that followed it, usually speaking to capacity houses that received him enthusiastically. A lecture about the Arctic probably was a relief to his war-weary audiences. In advance newspaper publicity for the later lectures, he made good use of a testimonial that had been given to him by Professor Benjamin Silliman, Jr., of Yale, who heard him speak in New Haven:

Mr. Hall possesses much knowledge not found in books—
the fruits of his own experience—and the discoveries he
has made in the polar regions are regarded by geographers
as of decided importance.—Indeed he did not himself realize
their importance until since his return, after more than two
years exile there. No civilized man has heretofore been enabled to identify himself so completely with the Esquimaux
as Mr. Hall. Speaking their language and adopting their
modes of life and voyaging, he is enabled to reach with
safety and even comfort, regions hitherto deemed inacces-
sible. Old Martin Frobisher has become *redivivus* under the
very unexpected revelation made by Mr. Hall. The native
family who accompany Mr. Hall are alone worth the notice
of all who feel an interest in the history and varieties of
the human family.

Hall finished his lecture tour on January 20, just as
Ebierbing, Tookoolito, and the baby were becoming sick
after months of public exposure. Hall wrote to the Budingtons, asking them to accept the Eskimos back into their
household again. When Captain Budington came down to
pick them up, "Butterfly" was so ill that Hall and Budington
both thought that he was going to die, but the baby recovered
enough to be moved, and Budington escorted the three
exhausted Eskimos and the still-rambunctious Barbekark to
the peace and quiet of Groton, while Hall settled down to
work on the many pressing matters that he had been forced
to ignore during the lecture tour.

One was his book. In November, not long after his appearance at the American Geographical and Statistical Society, he had given his manuscript journal to Harper
Brothers, and they in turn had handed it over to William
Parker Snow, who had done contract editorial work for
them before. Several weeks later, Hall was delighted to
receive a copy of Snow's eulogistic report on the book:

The writing of the MS. is so fine and close that it takes much
time to go over, but I may venture to say that very few
works if any that I have read on the Arctic Regions (and I
believe I have read nearly all) will surpass this of Mr.
Hall's. . . . In the Journals of Mr. Hall there are passages of
exceeding great beauty. There is incessant variety of incident. The faithfulness with which he narrates the habits and
customs of the singular people with whom he came in contact deserves especial attention. His genuine, unaffected,
manly piety, and the honest love he displays toward those
poor children of the Icy North is strikingly evident.

Snow went on to say that although some editorial work
would have to be done, the book should be made up mainly
of extracts direct from the journal: "his own words and
language will be found best suited and well adapted for the
printed work." He concluded his report: "I hope the Work
will not be lost. It is due to America, and, indeed, to the
whole civilized world that these records of individual labour
in the cause of Science and humanity, especially so faithfully and interestingly narrated, should be preserved." Perhaps Snow was so enthusiastic because he hoped to be hired
to edit the book (as indeed he was), but this unqualified
praise is ironic in view of what he was to say about Hall and
his work at a later date.

On December 4 Hall had signed a contract with Harper
Brothers. The publishers agreed to advance five hundred
dollars, the money to be paid in weekly installments of
twenty dollars to William Parker Snow, whom Hall had
hired to work on the book. In his agreement with Hall,
Snow had vowed that he would "suitably prepare it for
publication to entire satisfaction of said Hall, and to see it
through the Press, devoting at least forty-eight hours each
week to these purposes."[2] For the following month and a
half, Hall concentrated on his lectures, allowing Snow to
go ahead with the preparation of the book, but when Hall
finished lecturing he checked on Snow's progress and dis-

covered that little had been done. For the next several
months he was forced to needle the stubborn Englishman;
in return Snow complained that Hall's needling was distract-
ing him from the work at hand. Relations between the two
men became increasingly strained as the spring went on.

Nevertheless, Hall devoted only occasional moments to
Snow and to the book. After finishing his lecture tour, one
main project dominated his thought: the preparation of his
next expedition. As when he had prepared for the first
expedition, he began with ambitious plans and high hopes.
A meeting with Grinnell in November had set him off with
exultant, almost hysterical, optimism:

> My heart too full to record the happiness of the meeting
> tonight. Jottings will suffice. My usherance into the parlor—
> soon entered my dearest friend Mr. G. the warm grasp—
> his face as if the reflex of Heavenly thoughts—the noble
> expressions of his conclusions—'There must be something
> more done in Search of the Franklin Expedition'—his son
> to be devoted to the Cause—to go with me to King Williams
> Land—& if need be he (H. G.) would contribute $10,000 to
> the Search. This like an electrical heart-shock to me. Even
> as my loved friend ceased utterance to these words, I was
> in his arms—my hands clasping his—my lips to his noble
> brow—& we mingled our tears together. Never—never in my
> life was I happier!

Because Hall did not wish to depend entirely on Grinnell
unless he had to, however, he laid plans to approach the
United States government, although obviously its attentions
were turned elsewhere. He wrote to Captain Budington:

> I intend to enlist Government Powers of Washington in my
> favor with the view of getting aid to the amount of $25,000
> to $30,000. There is ground to hope that I shall succeed.
> There are prominent men in Providence, New Haven,
> Hartford, New York, Washington, Philadelphia, Cincinnati
> &c that will do all they can to help me on.

One of his most promising "prominent men" was Richard
Chapell. Chapell had for many years worked in the whaling
firm of Williams and Haven and still maintained a close
relationship with it, but he had become an important whaling agent in his own right, with seven ships under his name.
He knew men of power in Washington, among them Secretary of the Navy Gideon Welles; he was enthusiastic about
Hall's project and offered as much help as he could, including
a letter of introduction to Welles. Hall himself wrote to his
former Cincinnati backers, including Salmon P. Chase, who
was now Secretary of the Treasury, and to other men of
political stature. In a long letter to Senator Henry Wilson
of Massachusetts, he outlined the results of the first expedition and his plans for the second, then concluded: "Columbus had his advocate at the Court of Ferdinand and Isabella.
I trust my selection of you as mine at a greater Court than
Spain ever knew, will prove before three years have passed
that the World is benefitted by it." To Hall, Columbus
was always the image of the Explorer overcoming all odds,
and he simply assumed that Senator Wilson would be flattered by the analogy that he drew, although the Senator
would function only as an advocate.

Hall planned to go to the capital, taking the Eskimos with
him. He wrote to Budington, warning him that they should
not be photographed until that time; he wanted to wait
until they could appear before "the President & other dignitaries of our Country."

His hopes of government backing died hard, but their
death was inevitable. Slowly Hall realized that Washington
was too interested in the war to pay heed to him or his
project. The armies east and west were preparing for the
late-spring offensives that would explode at Vicksburg and
Chancellorsville, and the nation was tense in anticipation.
In April Hall went to see Horace Greeley, who expressed
himself about the war with characteristic force:

> Called on Horace Greeley, Ed. of Tribune. 1st time I have
> met him since my return. Just before I left in 1860, had
> interview with Greeley in same place—his editorial rooms.
> In this interview today Mr. Greeley expressed that he could
> have no sympathy with my present movement for he be-
> lieved not another idea should be entertained by any man
> who loved his country but crushing the Rebellion. He said
> he wished it was law for every man to stay in his country to
> work with the sole view to put down Rebellion North &
> South. He believed all Expeditions should take their course
> that way (suiting this expression by pointing his finger
> Southerly & Westerly). Much more he said of similar
> character.

Hall was discovering that others, especially in Washington,
shared Greeley's opinions, and he became so discouraged that
he did not even bother to make his trip to the capital. From
a distance, the "treacherous savages" of his Frobisher Bay
boat voyage were looking better and better to him. "Away
with politics," he exclaimed in a letter to Budington. "I am
bound for the North—the far North where Peace reigns and
noble people live." If the government would not cooperate,
he would again have to collect from private sources.

It was a bad spring for Hall. Early in March Tookoolito
and little Tukerliktu, still weak from their appearances at
lectures and "Show-Establishments," grew dangerously ill.
They were with Hall in New York at the time, and he decided that they should immediately be removed to Groton,
but the baby died before he could take them there. The
next afternoon Hall took the shattered parents and the body
of the child on a boat to New London. Arriving at midnight,
they were met by Captain Budington, who took them to his
home and to the warm sympathies of Mrs. Budington. Two
days later they buried little "Butterfly" in a plot near the
Budington's house. Hall wrote to Grinnell from Groton:

> I deeply regret to inform you that the mother is in a very

precarious state of health. On Monday we all thought her
dying, but she finally revived. One of the best physicians of
New London attended her & the succeeding day she seemed
better. In the P.M. she again became worse. The loss of her
idol child is overwhelming her—she often calls: "Where's
my 'Johny'?—Where's my 'Johny'?" On one occasion I answered her that little Johny was in Kudleparmeun (which
means Heaven) & with God (of Whom I had often told
her). She answered: "I want to go too—I want to be with
my little Johny and God."

Hall stayed in Groton until Tookoolito showed signs of
recovering, then returned to New York. His troubles were
just beginning.

He continued to hope that he could get off in the late
spring or summer, and he was willing to sacrifice his plans
for a large expedition and a ship of his own in order to do
so. Even as he worked on other schemes during the spring,
he periodically inquired about the possibility of immediate
transportation on a whaler to Baffin Island or Hudson's Bay,
but he was always rebuffed: the ship was already full, it
was going to the wrong place, or it was leaving too soon
for him to make it.

In the meantime, he formulated another plan and met
with Grinnell and Richard Chapell to present them with a
detailed proposal:

PROPOSED EXPEDITION TO
BOOTHIA AND KING WILLIAM'S LAND
for the final determination of
all the mysterious matters relative to
SIR JOHN FRANKLIN'S EXPEDITION

I — A vessel of about 200 tons to be furnished & pro-
visioned for two years & six months, the same to be
under my command.

II — This vessel to be fitted for whaling, the object being
to have the whole expenses of the expedition paid by
the proceeds of whale-bone and oil.

III — The vessel to sail on or before the first of June of the present year—to make direct for the North side of Frobisher Bay, there to take aboard three or four men Esquimaux with their wives—also dogs and sledges—then to make for Hudson's Strait—thence to Hudson's Bay, West side south of Southhampton Island, thence up the channel of Sir Thomas Rowe's Welcome to Repulse Bay.

The proposal went on to detail Hall's plan to work his way in a boat through Fury and Hecla Strait to Boothia and King William Island while the whaler went whaling. He listed as members of his party Walter Grinnell, Frank Rogers (First Officer on the *George Henry*), and William Sterry (the *George Henry's* jack-of-all-trades), all of whom had volunteered to go with him. Grinnell and Chapell were both enthusiastic about the proposal, and Grinnell repeated his offer of ten thousand dollars, suggesting that Williams and Haven might invest another ten thousand. A few days later Hall went to New London to consult with Williams and Haven, who balked at the proposal, probably because they wanted the stated primary purpose of any of their vessels to be whaling, whereas Hall's proposal, although it allowed for whaling, made his expedition primary.

Hall perforce began to look for a ship to buy. One day he called on "the brothers Fox" of New York, who owned a schooner in which he was interested. He told them that Henry Grinnell would purchase the ship, and the elder Fox inquired how much Grinnell would be willing to spend. For a time the two men jousted, Hall asking how much the schooner would cost, Fox repeatedly asking how much Grinnell would spend.

Following this, Mr. Fox proceeded to impress on me how very high the prices of vessels are now. He recapitulated some of his transactions in the purchase of several small vessels. The figure varies from $6,000 to $12,000 or so. About this time there entered a gentleman in the office who was, as I soon learned, a ship-broker. Without letting this gentle-

man (who, of course, was a stranger to me but an old
acquaintance to the Messrs. Fox) know anything of the
conversation, the elder Mr. Fox turned to him and asked:
"What's the price of a 1st class schooner, say of about 150
tons, well found & ready for sea?"

The gentleman thought a moment & then asked, "Copper
fastened?"

Mr. Fox added, quite loudly for the man was quite deaf:
"Yes—yes. Copper fastened all beneath the water-line."

"Well," answered the gentleman, "About twelve hundred
to fifteen hundred dollars!"

Both the Foxes & myself were silent for a moment, then
followed hearty laughs from Foxes and the writer of this.

The ship broker had misunderstood the situation, assuming
that Hall was selling and the Foxes buying, and so had suggested a low price to help his friends. After they all enjoyed
their laugh, the older Fox told Hall seriously that he would
not sell the ship for less than ten thousand dollars, too high
a price for Hall's budget.

His lectures had netted him barely enough to support
himself and the Eskimos for a few months, and either Henry
Grinnell had withdrawn his offer of ten thousand dollars or
Hall had chosen not to take advantage of it. As his hopes
for a "self-paying" or a government-backed expedition faded,
he set about raising money by private subscription. He wrote
to Budington early in April: "It gives me great pleasure to
communicate how kindly I have been received by prominent
men of this city since I have begun calling on them to invite
their presence to a contemplated meeting next week. The
sky is brightening." The "prominent men," whom he had
met largely through Henry Grinnell, included Augustus
Ward, James C. Brevoort, James Beekman, and Judge Charles
Daly, all men of wealth and influence. The meeting was a
special gathering of the American Geographical and Statistical Society, convened to consider Hall's problem. The attendance was small, but Hall was encouraged by the results:

after debate about whether it would be easier to collect a thousand dollars apiece from fifteen men or one hundred dollars apiece from one hundred and fifty men, it was decided that the American Geographical and Statistical Society and the New York Chamber of Commerce should form a joint committee. Hall wrote to Budington that the two societies would "join hands & put through all matters pertaining to the raising means for my proposed Expedition—if this be carried out, there can be no doubt but the Expedition will be a settled fact."

So encouraged was he about his prospects of going north by early summer that he wrote to Harper Brothers asking to be released from his contract; he argued that since he would soon be leaving for the Arctic, he would not be able to see his book through its preparations. He said that he would return their advance payment and that on completion of the next expedition he would immediately go back to work on the book. To Hall's great relief, Fletcher Harper agreed to extend the contract, setting a much later date for the publication of the book, and refused the return of the advanced payment, saying that he knew Hall was in bad financial circumstances. "What more noble from a member of a House that but a short time ago was a perfect stranger to me," Hall wrote in his journal that night. "LONG LIVE HARPER BROTHERS."

His bright skies were soon darkened, although at first with only small clouds. He received a gentle but irritating rebuff from one of his prospective donors, Edward Everett, whom he had invited to a special meeting of the Chamber of Commerce to be held in his honor:

Altho' it has never been in my power to make a special study of Arctic Adventures, I have never failed to bestow the humble tribute of my admiration on the perseverance and enterprize of the gallant Adventurers in that field, especially on our countrymen. Your own researches have seemed to

164

me to be of a most interesting and meritorious character, and you will carry with you my warmest wishes for your success. I fear, however, I must excuse myself from attending and taking part in the proposed meeting. The application to me to attend and address public meetings of various kinds are to numerous (more than one a day, upon an average), the difficulty of making discriminations to great, and my health to much impaired, that I am obliged to decline all applications but those of an obviously exceptional character.

Two days later Hall learned that both dogs had died; then Reuban Lamb, Third Mate on the *George Henry*, and one of the men whom he had hoped to have as an expedition assistant, could not go north. The day after that, he called on one A. A. Low, who condescended to him, arousing his old sense of social inferiority:

The impression was left on my mind that Mr. L. was cold and indifferent to me. I confess I am in want of what makes a man worthy of respect and consideration in the eyes & mind of the wealthy class of my countrymen—to wit, fine clothes, gold watches & the like! Not so, however, my noble-minded friend, Mr. Grinnell. He knows I am poor & yet he always treats me as though I were rich.

Hall was able to absorb these minor setbacks and disappointments only because he anticipated action by the American Geographical and Statistical Society and the Chamber of Commerce. The Chamber of Commerce was to meet April 22 to consider the proposition that it form a joint committee with the American Geographical and Statistical Society. Hall spent long hours preparing a speech for the occasion; he planned to emphasize the potential commercial value of Arctic exploration, especially to the whale fisheries, and he was confident that he would be able to persuade the organization to help. He was disappointed when at the last minute the meeting was postponed for a week because notices had not been sent to the membership, but he remained confident: six hundred notices were sent out on the following day. A week later, he arrived at the Chamber of Commerce, speech in hand, only to discover that so few persons had appeared that the meeting could not be convened. This was a terrible blow to his pride and his hopes.

His pride was somewhat assuaged on the following day when the *Herald*, always sympathetic to his endeavors, attacked the Chamber of Commerce, calling it "a set of old women"[3] for not taking an interest in his project. The *Herald* announced that the Royal Geographical Society had met in London several weeks before and had praised Hall for his accomplishments on Baffin Island. At that meeting were some of the greatest men in the field of Arctic exploration and geography, including George Back, John Rae, Sherard Osborn, John Barrow, Jr., and Clements Markham. The occasion was the arrival of Hall's Frobisher relics, which were laid out on display. Those present apparently were unanimous in declaring that the relics were probably Frobisher's, and also praised Hall for his exploration of the bay and for establishing close relations with the Eskimos. A week after the *Herald* reported the meeting, Henry Grinnell received a letter from his son Cornelius, who had attended it. Cornelius corroborated the *Herald*'s story and added, "It was delightful to witness the respect and kind feeling exhibited by the eminent discoverers present for the labors of a brother explorer. If Hall could only reach King William Land & find the records of Franklin, what a name he would make for himself!" Hall, naturally, was flattered by this sudden and somewhat unexpected recognition of his accomplishments by the English.

But he was in the United States, and his prospects were grim. So bad were his personal circumstances, in spite of Grinnell's occasional donations, that he was forced to borrow sums as small as seventy-five cents, and under the date of May 2 there is the following entry in his journal: "Started down the Bowery, sold damaged old hat to make a raise of 37 cts!"

He had reached a new low. "I may here record my opinion—
I cannot succeed in getting the necessary co-operation of my
countrymen to carry out my proposed Expedition. God only
knows my struggles. But single handed & alone, I will yet accomplish my purpose."

Even as he set himself to carry on alone, there was an up-
swing in his fortunes. At another of those meetings that were
so crucial to his career, the American Geographical and Statistical Society on May 7 again brought up the subject of his
proposed expedition. Among other things, the members discussed the meeting of the Royal Geographical Society and the
apparent English interest in Hall's work. Judge Charles Daly,
according to the *Herald*, "bore strongly upon the mortifica-
tion that would be felt by the American public should Captain Hall not be sustained in a matter of so much public
interest by our own institutions, instead of throwing him
upon the patronage and support of foreign governments."[4]
Daly concluded by resolving that a committee be formed to
assist Hall in collecting money. By this time Hall had reason
to be skeptical about the effectiveness of such a resolution,
but in the weeks that followed he began to receive contributions. J. C. Brevoort, a wealthy retired diplomat and amateur
scholar who was rapidly taking a place beside Henry Grinnell
in Hall's estimation, gave him one hundred dollars for his
personal expenses. Augustus Ward, who, Hall confided to
Budington, "is worth over 3 Million Dollars," contributed
another hundred dollars and told Hall to order the finest
pocket chronometer that he could find at Tiffany's; Hall purchased a five-hundred-dollar timepiece, which he thereafter
always referred to as "my Ward Chronometer." A subscription list was made out, and soon other men were subscribing
sums ranging from twenty-five to one hundred dollars.

Hall began to negotiate for a ship. He asked Budington to
search for a 50- to 75-ton vessel, but Budington advised him
to purchase a larger ship that was for sale in New London at
the price of $3400. Hall agreed, and in early June he found

himself in possession of a 95-ton schooner, the *Active*, paid
for with money collected either through the American Geographical and Statistical Society or by Henry Grinnell. At
the same time, Captain Henry Robinson of Newburgh, New
York, donated a small yacht, which Hall immediately sold,
hoping to use the proceeds from the sale for necessary im-
provements on the *Active*. Because Budington had committed
himself to Williams and Haven for a whaling cruise, Hall
hired another sailing master, Henry Dodge, who had been on
the Hayes Expedition in 1860. William Parker Snow volunteered to be First Officer under Dodge, and Hall tentatively
accepted the offer, although he distrusted Snow more every
day. He even signed on a naturalist-photographer, Washington Peale, whom Hall in a letter described vaguely as being
"of the well known family of Peales of our Country" (he was
the grandson of James Peale and grandnephew of Charles
Wilson Peale). Hall also had a long list of other volunteers
to choose from.* All went smoothly, so smoothly that Hall
wrote to A. D. Bache of the United States Coast Survey requesting rush delivery of certain instruments: "It is now
arranged that I leave the port of New York on about the 1st
of July in a vessel of 100 tons, the vessel specially selected &
Strengthened for Ice Navigation." He told Bache that he
planned to sail to Frobisher Bay, where he would take aboard
some Eskimos, then to Hudson's Strait, Foxe Channel, and
through Fury and Hecla Strait. He would examine Boothia
Peninsula and King William Island for signs of the Franklin
Expedition and then, if possible, make his way west to the
Bering Sea. He was becoming very ambitious, and hoped to
sail the northwest passage.

Exactly what happened to destroy these fine plans is un-

---

* During the spring he had received many letters from young strangers
offering their services. The sudden desire to go north on the part of
these youths might be explained by the progress of the war—early in
March, Congress had passed the Enrollment Act, our first national
draft law, and in May and June the death toll mounted sharply at
Vicksburg and Chancellorsville.

clear. Hall's journal is mutilated at the crucial point, and the pages covering the remainder of the summer have been slashed from the book, probably by Hall himself. Apparently he had not been able to gather enough money to support the expedition, and was forced to sell the *Active* to support himself. That he had trouble getting money at this time is not surprising: during June, Lee's Army of Northern Virginia moved northward and, in the first days of July, encountered the Army of the Potomac at Gettysburg. In the East, these were the most harrowing weeks of the war, hardly the time to finance and organize an Arctic expedition.

Hall had a problem other than financial. In the middle of June, he quarreled with Captain Sidney Budington. The two men had become close friends. Budington had earned Hall's respect during their two years in the Arctic, his affection in the ten months since their return to civilization. In Hall's letters and journals he repeatedly praised Budington for his strength, loyalty, and kindness. Together the two men had nursed the dying Eskimo baby and the sick mother; together they had worked on Hall's various plans for his next expedition. Hall called the Budingtons' house in Groton "home," and he often left New York to stay there for a while with Sarah and Sidney, their two daughters, and Ebierbing and Tookoolito, who now lived with the Budingtons most of the time. "You and your noble wife are ready to do everything to assist me," he once wrote to Budington. "I can ask for no better friends." In another letter he wrote, "Your letter of yesterday tells me in unmistakable language your deep and abiding feeling for me. I wish I were worthy of such kindly favors as you & yours ever have proffered to me. How gloriously looms up your devotedness to me! What were friendship if it did not shine in these hours of my troubled life? Believe me, I long to see you & your noble wife." Hall was closer to Budington than to anyone he had ever known— or ever would know—yet suddenly he quarreled bitterly with him.

Budington was partly responsible. Without consulting Hall, he went to see Henry Grinnell about Ebierbing and Tookoolito. It was mid-June, and Budington told Grinnell that he did not believe Hall would be able to go north until the next year. Budington himself was scheduled to go on a whaling cruise to Baffin Island in July, and he suggested to Grinnell that he should take the Eskimos with him because they were yearning for their homeland. Grinnell told Hall about the conversation, and Hall flew into an unreasoning rage. "Captain S. O. Budington," he addressed his friend: "Confident am I that the time will come when you will deeply regret the strange & unaccountable treatment you exercised toward the writer of this & the Esquimaux during the last week. We are not aware that we ever have done you a wrong. I trust neither I nor the Esquimaux will ever trouble your house again." He also wrote a statement for Grinnell to sign; it purported to be a letter from Grinnell to Budington, but the writing and the sentiments were Hall's own: "From the short interview I had with you the other day relative to the Esquimaux, I do not wish it understood that I would throw the first obstacle in my friend Hall's way. If he thinks that he will still persevere in his Arctic enterprise & that it will be best for him & the cause he has espoused to retain the Esquimaux, we certainly will not throw the least obstacle in his way—rather will we help him on all we can." Grinnell, caught in the middle of a squabble that was not of his making, probably did not agree to sign it.

Ebierbing and Tookoolito moved from Groton to Hall's furnished rooms in New York. When Budington left for the Arctic in July, neither he nor Hall had made any effort toward reconciliation, but in the autumn Hall received a gentle letter from Sarah Budington, and he replied in kind, asking her for news of her husband: "Write all the news you have of him. How I wish I could see him. Earthly troubles must be forgotten & forgiven. Capt. B & I have been friends. We must be still. I shall ever remember him as a friend &

brother." Mrs. Budington had touched Hall by telling him that in July the *George Henry* had been driven aground and sunk in Hudson's Bay; the loss of the old vessel flooded Hall with memories of his long months in the Arctic with Budington. Six years later, when Hall returned from his second expedition, he apparently reestablished his friendship with the whaling captain. But Hall was an unforgiving man; real or imaginary offenses gnawed at him, and he could nurse hatreds for many years. The scars of his quarrel with Budington were never entirely healed, and in the last months of his life they were to be torn open again.

For Hall, the six months that followed his quarrel with Budington were months of despondency and relative inactivity. He and the Eskimos lived together in New York while he concentrated mainly on his book. He knew that he could not sail until the following summer, and he was resigned to taking passage on a whaler rather than commanding a vessel of his own. In September he made a halfhearted attempt to solicit an appropriation of thirty thousand dollars from the State of New York, but otherwise he was unusually passive. By now he must have accepted the fact that a nation at war could not concern itself seriously with the private endeavors of an Arctic explorer. With Lee's retreat from Gettysburg, some pressure was taken off the northeast, but Lee's army was still intact, and a Union attempt to take Charleston in September failed. Through the autumn months Grant and Bragg fought bloody battles in Tennessee, at Chickamauga, Lookout Mountain, and Missionary Ridge. As the war dragged on, Hall was less and less likely to find any large-scale backing.

In a room provided by Harper Brothers, Hall worked on his book. "I had rather made a dozen voyages to the regions of ice and snow than prepare one book for publication," he wrote that autumn. William Parker Snow was officially still on salary, but Hall was increasingly dissatisfied with his work. The Englishman was so harassed by real or imaginary personal troubles ("My troubles are fearful," he once wrote Hall, who noted on the letter, "What this <u>fearful trouble</u> be I cannot imagine") that he was unable to concentrate on anything else, leaving Hall to do much of the work. Nevertheless, Hall renewed their agreement in September, with some changes: because Snow had been dilatory, Hall insisted on specifying that he work "at least five days a week and six days when he can," going on to define "day": "Eight and a half hours faithful work make a day." In November, Snow complained that this arrangement was difficult for him. "I will give you forty-eight hours honest labour upon your work per week at the sum you name, viz. fourteen dollars per week, bestowing upon it all the faculties of my mind and body. But I profess that those forty-eight hours be not fixed by the day. I may need some time occasionally to attend to my own future affairs." Hall not only acquiesced to this request, but also made another agreement in December, raising Snow's salary to twenty dollars a week and giving him an advance bonus of sixty dollars; to do this, Hall himself had to request an additional sum from Harper's, raising to one thousand dollars the total amount that he had drawn from the firm against his future royalties. During the winter and early spring of 1864 Snow continued to work only haphazardly, and he and Hall had several strained meetings. After one of these meetings, during which they had quarreled, Hall uncharacteristically wrote to Snow, asking that he come to Harper's, where they could "swear upon the altar of brotherly friendship that we will be friends—that no act & no word, no thought shall ever be between us that would serve to mar or sever the bright links binding true, <u>tried & noble friends together.</u>" Not long after, however, the altar crumbled. Apparently Hall lost his temper and, according to Snow in an angry letter of recrimination, he used "harsh words—unjust and opprobrious terms." Snow went on in this letter: "I deny the whole of your untrue allegations. There need be no more words between us. I told you, in a friendly way, why I could not be the mere servant you wanted to make me." He concluded by making a veiled threat of legal action: "If you will persist in your unjust and insulting conduct to me, I can only say let impartial persons judge between us." For the time being, Snow did not bring the matter to court, but he was only biding his time.

The quarrel, one of many in both men's lives, reflects badly on both. There is no doubt that Snow did not work well for Hall; he harassed his employer with his personal difficulties; he frequently broke appointments; he seldom did what he said he would do. His letters and books show him to have been difficult—undependable, irascible, full of self-pity —and his later actions show that he could blind himself to truth and act with an intemperance that verged on paranoia. But if Snow was a bad employee, Hall was a bad employer— driving, intolerant, and tactless. Both men were touchy egotists and quick to take offense, but Hall had the advantage over Snow in their relationship and should have bent to his assistant. Unfortunately, he was not a bending man.

Snow later was to claim that he wrote Hall's book, but examination of Hall's journals shows that this claim is unjustified: the book was simply an edited and cut version of the journals, and Hall himself did much of the editing and cutting during dreary months in late 1863 and early 1864 while he waited until he could again begin to organize his expedition.*

In May, having finished the book, Hall began again to work on his expedition. First he arranged free passage to northern Hudson's Bay on a whaler, the *Monticello,* one of Richard Chapell's vessels. She was due to sail in mid-June. Early in May, he spoke before the Long Island Historical Society, in a lecture reminiscent of those given two years earlier. Ebierbing and Tookoolito, dressed in their summer sealskins, sat

* Although he completed the book in late April, it did not appear until he was on his way north. It was first published in an English edition entitled *Life with the Esquimaux,* then in an American edition entitled *Arctic Researches and Life Among the Esquimaux.*

on stage behind Hall, with their hunting and fishing im-
plements beside them. After the lecture, some of Hall's
wealthy patrons published an announcement in New York
newspapers:

TO THE PUBLIC

Capt. C. F. Hall, who twenty months ago returned from a
two years and four months' exploration of the Arctic Region,
intends to set sail on the 15th of June for another and more
thorough voyage of discovery. During his former voyage he
lived among the Eskimos, acquired their language, and
satisfied himself that he can live with these people in safety
and health. He is prepared as no other explorer has been
before him for making a thorough investigation of the important portion of Arctic land and water to which he pro-
poses to devote himself.

   This region still holds an important portion of the secret
of the ill-fated Franklin Expedition, which our countryman
confidently expects to lay bare. It is, moreover, of value to
our whaling and sealing interests, and the reports on its
natural history will possess scientific value. These considera-
tions which have led him to devote the best years of his life
to Arctic research, induce also those whose names are appended to this notice to ask their fellow-citizens to join
them in procuring for the brave explorer such an outfit as
shall set him fairly on his way, and enable him to perform
thoroughly the task which he has set for himself. Our
countrymen have won an honorable fame by their courage
and endurance in Arctic research. It is, therefore, not fit
that one who has already shown such perseverance, fortitude,
and ingenuity in his previous voyage as Captain Hall has
done, shall be permitted to leave our shores lacking anything which can further his laudable object. . . . In order to
complete the outfit, a sum of about $3,000 is yet required,
and while it is Captain Hall's intention to sail at any rate,
whether thoroughly fitted or not, it is hoped that our public-
spirited citizens will not permit this intrepid explorer to
depart from our city lacking anything which can help to

preserve his life or enable him to perfect his explorations in the inhospitable regions to which he is bound.

Subscriptions in money, or donations in kind of supplies, or goods for the expedition, may be handed to any of the undersigned, who will see that they are properly applied in aid of this praise-worthy enterprise.

J. CARSON BREVOORT.

JAMES W. BEEKMAN.

A. W. BURR.

HENRY GRINNELL.

E. & G. W. BLUNT.

JOHN AUSTIN STEVENS.[5]

Enough was collected by donation and subscription to supply Hall with at least the necessities. He ordered an expedition boat to be built in New London; pemmican was prepared by a New York merchant; instruments were purchased and borrowed, the Coast Survey donating a sextant and a dip circle. Everything was going well enough for him to plan a quick visit to Cincinnati to see his wife and children —for the first time in almost two years—before he left.

He had not reckoned on William Parker Snow. In May, Snow had written an adulatory advance review of Hall's book for *Harper's New Monthly Magazine* (that the self-proclaimed ghost writer of a book should review the book for a magazine published by the book's publisher should surprise no one familiar with the ethics of the nineteenth-century book trade). Obviously Snow had written this review for pay, not out of conviction, and once it was done he declared independence from Harper's. Just before Hall left for Cincinnati, Snow wrote a scathing letter to the New York *World*:

HALL'S 'ARCTIC' EXPLORATIONS

To the Editor of The World:

Sir: With every desire to see Arctic explorations carried on, especially by individual enterprise—which is generally the most successful—I have no actual feeling of opposition to Mr. Hall's undertaking. But I cannot (either in common justice to myself, nor from respect and esteem for the many brave men of America and England who really have explored the Arctic regions) allow the arrogant pretensions, false assumptions, and the misstatements of Mr. Hall to go forth without strongly denouncing them.

Snow went on to deny the originality of Hall's plans for his new expedition, claiming that he, Snow, had thought of them first, and he snidely cast doubt on Hall's discoveries on his first expedition: "What Mr. Hall has done is yet to be shown and proved: for it is singular that he brings forward no white man's evidence to sustain him, nor does he meet any Arctic men of experience and scientific knowledge on the subject." (Both statements are false.) Snow hammered away at Hall's most vulnerable spot, his lack of professional training in the sciences, and he contrasted Hall's limited knowledge of the Arctic with his own: "What I have done in exploring the Arctic and Antarctic seas, and my general services, are patent to the whole world through the testimony of hundreds of letters from eminent men and the encomiums of the press and learned societies here as well as in England." Snow went on to exaggerate his own Arctic experience and to underestimate Hall's, stressing maritime at the expense of overland travel.[6]

Snow was not content merely to write a letter. In the second week in June, just as Hall was about to leave for Cincinnati, Snow brought suit, claiming that money was still owed him for his work on the book. The time that Hall would have spent with his wife and children was spent instead in New York's Marine Court. Henry Grinnell and Fletcher Harper accompanied Hall as defense witnesses, and Dudley Field was his lawyer. Snow did not have a chance of winning the suit. Hall had kept receipts carefully and was able to prove that, far from owing Snow money, he himself was owed $78.85 for advances. The suit was thrown out of court.

Snow was to remain bitter about the incident for the rest of his long life (he lived to be eighty), and for several years, while Hall was north on the second expedition, he fired off fre-

quent angry letters to American newspapers. In a typical
rambling letter to the *Morning Post,* filled with wild accusations and self-pity, he told the story as he saw it. He wrote
that, "cunningly compelled by my engagements," he had
been forced to be silent, but that now he could tell the truth:
Hall had lied about his previous discoveries, Hall had cheated
Snow, Hall's second expedition was a fraud. He complained
that he had not even been given a copy of Hall's book, which
he said he virtually had written. He said that in the United
States "it is only the rich who may say aught against others,
not the poor, no matter how truthful it be." He said that Hall
was deliberately trying to discredit the accomplishments of
English explorers, and that he, Snow, was mistreated in the
United States because he was an Englishman. Snow had become venomously anti-American, and he concluded this letter
with a strident, incoherent war cry to the English. The Americans, he wrote, had been planting their flag in the Arctic, and
the British should renew their Arctic endeavors in competi-
tion with "that pushing and enterprising flag" by sending out
another expedition to search for Franklin relics:

> Let me then once more, as of old, venture to raise my voice.
> Do with me what you will; say of me what you please;
> beggar me still more by unfair opposition, party men; but
> oh! mighty press of England and you wealthy and powerful
> ones in and out of official life, heed me. Off with another
> expedition at once, by Bering Straits and from the East, if
> you care for the honour of our dear old flag. What boots the
> cost in gold? What is it compared to the lustre of our too
> much battered name? It [American exploration] serves the
> more to cry aloud in thunder tones, for the children of
> old Baffin's and Frobisher's land, and of old Elizabeth's once
> proud and haughty domain, to again arouse themselves
> under another beloved and Queenly Sovereign. Away then,
> just once more, hardy, bold, and fearless voyagers![7]

During the next three years, whenever one of Hall's dispatches from the Canadian barrens was published in a news-

paper, Snow would immediately write a letter to the paper questioning whatever Hall had written. When in 1866 there was a long silence from Hall, Snow loudly announced to the press that Hall obviously was lost and that a rescue expedition should be dispatched immediately. He allowed a note of triumph to creep into the announcement, and evidently he had a vision of humiliating Hall by leading the rescue ex-pedition himself. But no expedition was sent. Few persons listened to Snow any longer, and in 1867 he returned to a bitter and cantankerous semiretirement in England. Many years later, Snow found a copy of the English edition of Hall's book in a bookstore, purchased it, and vented his spleen on its margins with angry comments: "What a lie!" "I wrote this!" "Liar!" "The whole by W.P.S."

Hall did not have to endure Snow's insults. By the time that the Englishman began his letter-writing campaign, Hall was already far to the north, out of range of such harassments. On June 30, accompanied by Ebierbing and Tookoolito, he traveled to New London. On the following day he embarked on the *Monticello*, Captain Edward A. Chapel commanding. Their destination was northern Hudson's Bay. From St. John's, Newfoundland, where the ship put in for a short time, Hall wrote to Grinnell and Brevoort:

> I have now a work before me that might make some shudder to undertake. It is a great undertaking for one man, I will confess; but, having once put myself in the course, I must and will persevere. I hope by the aid of Heaven to succeed, and at the end of three years I shall return to my friends, who may rejoice that they withheld not in the time of my great need.

Hall was underestimating the difficulties that he was to face and the time that he was to spend on his second expedition. He was destined to be in the Arctic not for three, but for five arduous years.

chapter five

Roe's Welcome, Repulse Bay, Igloolik, King William Island

As the *Monticello* picked its way through the floe ice of Hudson's Strait after an uneventful cruise, Hall could see to starboard the jagged peaks of Meta Incognita and the distant glow of Grinnell Glacier. He thrilled to think of what lay on the other side of them, only fifty miles away: Frobisher Bay, *his* bay. He was not returning there, but the knowledge that it was so close warmed him. On August 20, ten days after he saw the glow of the glacier, the *Monticello* anchored off Depot Island, a mosquito-infested speck of rock and lichen in northern Hudson's Bay, at the mouth of Roe's Welcome Sound. Miserable as it was, Depot Island was a well-known whaler's rendezvous, and within a week the *Monticello* was joined by seven other vessels.

Hall soon decided to hire an assistant from one of the whalers, a young German seaman named Charles Rudolph. Rudolph told Hall that he had spent a winter with Eskimos a few years before and looked forward to spending more such winters. He appeared strong-minded and strong-bodied. In the presence of the mate of Rudolph's ship, Hall warned the sailor that the expedition would be an ordeal, but Rudolph, swearing he would be able to endure any hardship, signed a three-year contract to work under Hall for twenty-five dollars a month.

A few days later, the tender of the *Monticello* carried Hall, Ebierbing, Tookoolito, Rudolph, and their equipment north from Depot Island. The captain of the tender had agreed to take them to Wager Bay, a hundred miles up the west coast of Roe's Welcome, but by serious error he dropped them off forty miles to the south of the agreed-on point. Hall and Hubbard Chester, the mate of the *Monticello*, argued with the captain, but he insisted that he was right. The error perhaps cost Hall an entire year; because of it, he was not able to winter at Repulse Bay as he had planned.

After they had cached some of their supplies ashore, Hall's little party coasted northward in the *Sylvia*, his expedition boat, looking for signs of Eskimos. Only a few hours after they set out, Ebierbing spotted an Eskimo standing beside a beached boat, and Hall immediately headed the *Sylvia* in toward shore. Ebierbing was jittery; as they came closer, it seemed to him that the strange Eskimo was loading his rifle and acting hostile. Over Ebierbing's protests, Hall insisted that they continue to head inshore; when the boat went aground, he leaped into the muddy shallows and waded toward the Eskimo, who had not moved. "The next moment my hand was in that of noble <u>Ouela's</u>, as fine a specimen of an Eskimo as ever I met," he wrote to Captain Chapel of the *Monticello* some months later.

Ouela and his people, who came from Repulse Bay, used the region south of it as their hunting grounds. Far from hostile, he greeted Hall as a friend; having often received gifts from whalers, he looked on any white man as a potential benefactor. At once he led Hall and his party to a small cluster of tupics at a nearby place called Noowook. There Hall met some of the men and women who were to delight, frustrate, and anger him in the coming years—a wilder-looking, handsomer people, he thought, than the Frobisher Eskimos. He was relieved to discover that Ebierbing, Tookoolito, and even he had little trouble talking with them, in spite of some differences in dialect. He was flattered by the warmth of their welcome: no sooner had he set up camp than Artooa, one of Ouela's brothers, presented him with six caribou tongues and some salmon, and that night Armou, a cousin, did him the honor of sleeping in his tupic. The next day, Artooa and Nukerzhoo, a half-brother, took Hall, Ebierbing and Rudolph on a caribou hunt. In the evening Hall, determined to win their cooperation, even participated in an ankooting ceremony presided over by Artooa, the chief angeko of the group. Hall soon referred to the Eskimos at Noowook as "these kind-hearted children of the North," asking himself rhetorically: "Where else in the world could a more free-hearted, generous people be found?" In his optimism he forgot some of his uglier experiences at Frobisher Bay.

   Their friendliness and cooperation were necessary to the success of his expedition. Not only would he have to depend on them as guides and assistants; he also hoped that, like the Frobisher Bay Eskimos, they would have stories about "koblunas" who had come into their lands. (The shift from the Frobisher Bay "kadloonas" typified the dialect differences between the areas.) Hall wasted little time before asking them about white men whom they or their forbears had seen or heard about, especially to the north and northwest of Repulse Bay. Having studied the histories of all the expeditions that had been in northern Hudson's Bay, Roe's Welcome Sound, Repulse Bay, Fury and Hecla Strait, and the peninsulas of Melville and Boothia, he believed that he would be able to distinguish among the various expeditions and identify stories that had to do with the Franklin Expedition.

   He knew that the Eskimos of Repulse Bay and Igloolik had seen at least two expeditions in the preceding half century. In 1821–3 Commander William Edward Parry of the British Navy, searching for a northwest passage, had sailed the *Fury* and the *Hecla* east of Southampton Island to Repulse Bay, wintered off the south coast of Melville Peninsula,

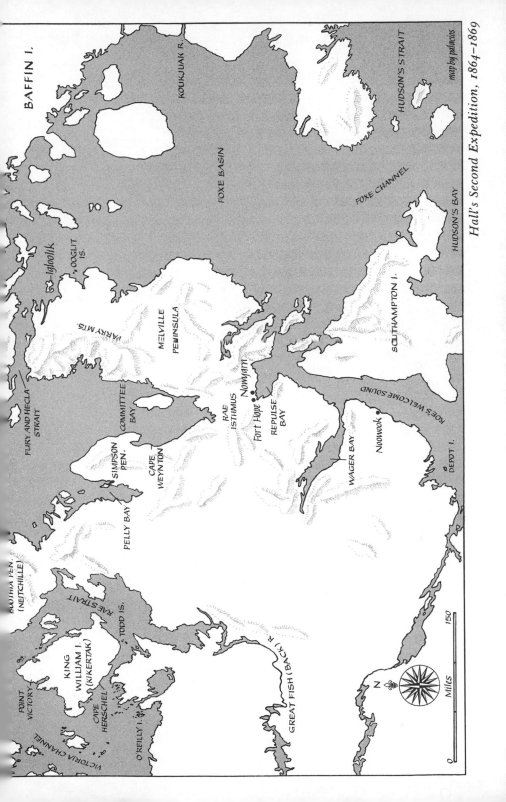

BAFFIN I.

KOUKJUAK R.

HUDSON'S STRAIT

map by palacios

FOXE BASIN

FOXE CHANNEL

HUDSON'S BAY

Igloolik

OOGLIT IS.

BARRY MTS.

MELVILLE PENINSULA

SOUTHAMPTON I.

FURY AND HECLA STRAIT

COMMITTEE BAY

Nowyarn

RAE ISTHMUS

Fort Hope

REPULSE BAY

ROES WELCOME SOUND

SIMPSON PEN.

CAPE WEYNTON

PELLY BAY

WAGER BAY

Noowook

DEPOT I.

BOOTHIA PEN. (NEITCHILLE)

RAE STRAIT

TODD IS.

KING WILLIAM I. (KIKERTAK)

CAPE HERSCHEL

O'REILLY I.

POINT VICTORY

VICTORIA CHANNEL

GREAT FISH (BACK) R.

N

Miles

0   150

Hall's Second Expedition, 1864–1869

and then sailed up the east coast of the peninsula to Igloolik. Parry had hiked from there to a promontory overlooking a narrow strait that headed west, which he named Fury and Hecla Strait. It was so jammed with ice that it could not be navigated, so he had spent his second winter at Igloolik, seeing much of the local Eskimos.

Parry had been in the area forty-three years before Hall. Doctor John Rae had explored it twice for the Hudson's Bay Company, eighteen years and also ten years before Hall. On both journeys Rae had traveled light, with small boats, few men, and a minimum of supplies; the most adaptable of British Arctic explorers in the nineteenth century, like Hall he learned to live off the land. Rae had wintered at Repulse Bay on both of his expeditions, and had explored the land and water to the west and northwest, proving, among other things, that Boothia was a peninsula and that a northwest passage did not cut through it. It was on his second expedition that Rae heard from Eskimos that many koblunas had died to the northwest; when he returned to London, he brought with him Franklin relics and the terrible story of cannibalism which so shocked the British nation.

Hall explained to Ouela, Armou, Artooa, and the others where he wanted to go, pointing out on an Admiralty chart Repulse Bay, Boothia Peninsula, and King William Island. He discovered that they called Repulse Bay "Iwillik," Boothia "Neitchille," and King William Island "Kikertak." He made the mistake of saying that he was searching for koblunas who had disappeared years before near Kikertak—a mistake because Eskimos often tried to please explorers by telling them what they wanted to hear. They would not usually lie, but they were capable of mixing various stories to create an ideal story—that is, the story that their auditor was hoping for. Sometimes the materials were actually confused in their minds, but occasionally, taking an artistic delight in the process, they seemed to make a deliberate construct.

Hall's first talk with them about the purpose of his voyage

delighted him: "They at once told me that there were two ships lost near Neitchille many years ago, and that a great many koblunas, whites, died—some starved and some were froze to death—but that there were four that did not die." He had not specified that the koblunas he was searching for had lost two ships; the Eskimos themselves had volunteered this information, and it seemed to confirm that they were talking about Franklin's men when they mentioned the four survivors. Hall felt that he was already on the track of a major discovery, but when he told them that he wished to move on immediately to Repulse Bay, they discouraged him. It was too late to kill tuktoo there, they said, and the seal hunting would be bad there in the winter. Besides, crossing the mouth of Wager Bay in the overladen. Sylvia would be dangerous during windy September. But if he stayed with them at Noowook through the winter, they promised, they would supply him with food and furs and would go with him to Repulse Bay in the spring.

Hall decided to winter at Noowook. Artooa and Shoo-shearknook, another of Ouela's brothers, helped him find a sheltered place for his tupic, out of the cold northwest winds that blew during the fall. In October the Eskimos built igloos, Ebierbing supervising the construction of the one that Hall would share with him and Tookoolito. It was a complex structure, a cluster of linked igloos, with an entrance tunnel, two storerooms, a vestibule, a cook room, and a central sleeping and living room. Hall soon settled in for the winter, which he thought would be an easy and comfortable one.

> I never before knew any Eskimos so provident as this tribe or clan I am with. I doubt not they have four hundred or more reindeer, killed last summer, on deposit within the distance of a circle of 20 miles in diameter. We are now living on polar-bear and walrus meat. Five polar bears, some musk-oxen, a great many partridges, and four walruses have been killed since arriving among the natives, besides a large number of reindeer.

For a while at least, relations between him and the Eskimos were excellent. He supplied them with medicine, tobacco, and ammunition; they drew from their caches of meat to feed him and his party. They hunted together and exchanged visits in their igloos. Occasionally they gathered for a festivity, twenty-five of them crowding into a single igloo to play games, dance, and sing. The men would strip to the waist and beat the keylowtik, an instrument like a tambourine, or punch one another in a test of endurance; the women, sitting on the bed-platform with their infants, would clap, sing, and laugh. The noise was Rabelaisian, the stench from bodies and blubber lamps overwhelming. One night the usually abstemious Hall even sat up with Ouela, Armou, and Ebierbing (Tookoolito having been banished to a neighboring igloo) to drink two bottles of Hubbell's Golden Bitters, which advertised itself as "Good for Dyspepsia."

> We were all gloriously drunk. When I awoke, I never had such a sick, terrible feeling head in my life. And yet at the usual hour I was up, but I was glad to get between my tuktoo furs again ½ hour later.

Although for a time his relations with the Eskimos were good, Hall had his troubles. The cold could be dangerous, with its inevitable threat of frostbite, but it also could be simply inconvenient. The caribou meat had to be thawed by rubbing with mittened hands; breathing on it could frostbite lips and tongue. Hall's ink froze solid, and he had to boil it down into a putty, which he mixed with thawed snow as the occasion demanded. His self-registering thermometers did not function properly; the mercury apparently froze in the extreme cold. With the change in regimen, especially in diet, his health broke. He was plagued again with boils, which to his horror spread to his eyelids and for a time almost blinded him. On October 5, when a gale struck Noowook, his brief entry in his journal records the low point of the autumn: "The storm — bad — blind — sick."

As his body adjusted to the way of life, his health improved, but he was harassed by other problems. Charles Rudolph fell far short of his promises and boasts. In his journal Hall called him "the Great Baby" and "the down-hearted, homesick child." Rudolph, refusing to work or hunt, spent most of his time sulking in his igloo. He told Hall that he feared starvation, and when Hall pointed out that the Eskimos had immense caches of caribou meat, he declared that "he did not think he could live without bread and salt meats." So moody did Rudolph become that Hall, always quick to suspect the worst, began to fear for himself. He stayed awake at night worrying about the German: "I believe at times that I am in danger," he noted in his journal. Finally, he and Rudolph terminated their contract and Rudolph, accompanied by some of the Eskimos, returned to the whalers.

As the winter passed, Hall discovered that the angekos of Repulse Bay and Roe's Welcome had even more arbitrary powers than those of Frobisher Bay. On the very day that he arrived, Artooa, in his role as the most potent angeko of the group, had decreed that no iron was to be filed until the ice formed, a minor inconvenience but only one of many that were to strain Hall's patience. He made it policy to follow their customs whenever possible, especially their numerous and complex dietary taboos. When an Eskimo woman presented him with a large part of a frozen caribou carcass, he had to use a hatchet to cut it so that the pieces would fly westward. When he ate the meat, he was told that he could not use walrus oil on it, only seal oil. He hoped to cook the head for soup, but he was firmly informed that this could not be done until after the walrus season was over: cooking the head would hurt the walrus hunting.

He even submitted to ankooting himself, loathsome as the ceremony was to his devout soul. During his plague of boils, Artooa offered to ankoot him, and, rather than offend Artooa, he accepted. One function of the angeko was to account for trouble in terms of past events. Artooa announced to Hall that there were several causes of his illness; for example, during his expedition to Baffin Island he had eaten food that had not been prepared in Innuit fashion. But the main cause, according to Artooa, was an enemy. Hall's ears pricked up at this: "There was one man in America who was a great enemy to me—he sought to do me all the injury he could—would rejoice in my sickness & greatly so at my death—if he had the opportunity, he was such a bitter enemy he would kill me." For once, Hall listened attentively to an angeko; into his mind flashed the choleric visage of William Parker Snow. "I must say," he wrote in his journal that night, "this Angeko makes some very good guesses."

Although he tried hard to accept Eskimo mores, he was angered when they offended his own Christian morality. By this time he knew that he could not allow his anger to show, and that he could not simply forbid the Eskimos to obey an angeko, but he fought back as best he could. One night Artooa, in his role as angeko, declared that he and Ebierbing should exchange wives. Tookoolito, at least partly converted to Christianity, was unwilling, but Ebierbing, who was suffering from rheumatism and was convinced that the angeko could cure him, insisted on her cooperation. On Hall's advice, Tookoolito prepared for her ordeal by clothing herself in layers of skins. "In fact," as Hall wrote, "she was as it were mailed from neck to ankles." When Artooa arrived, he and she lay down "in tuktoo" together.

> After the fellow had got into bed, he awaited his moment until he thought I was asleep & then he proceeded. The lamp sent forth its full blaze all night. My place was within a foot of him. In his pertinacious attempts, how the fellow worked & puffed! What a cloud of vapor at such respiration! From the moment Artooa got into bed beside Tookoolito (11–30 PM) to the moment of my call to T. (1–45 AM)

his course was almost an uninterrupted one to get Tookoolito awake and to get her skin tights open.

At 1:45 Hall called out to Tookoolito to insist that she get
his breakfast. While she moved quietly about the igloo
setting water to boil, Hall lay comfortably and smugly in
bed reading the *Life of Thomas Simpson,* Artooa beside him
tense with anger and frustration. Finally the angeko got up
and stomped out of the igloo. That day there was a frenzy of
ankooting as he cast taboos about him. For once Hall had
triumphed over him, but Artooa was not to forget or forgive
the frustration of what Hall called his "arrogances."

During the winter, Hall gathered much diverse information about koblunas. Most of it had to do with Parry and
Rae, some coming firsthand from Eskimos who had witnessed
the events that they described, the rest coming second- or
thirdhand from their friends and relatives. Some of the information was detailed and factual, some vague and mythic.
Early in December, Erktua, an elderly Eskimo woman, arrived from Repulse Bay. Hall had heard about her and
looked forward to talking with her, for she knew much about
the Parry expedition, having been in Igloolik in 1822–3.
She did not disappoint him with her tales, and among other
things she gave him a fine example of the mythologizing of
fact. During the winter of 1822, Parry flogged an Eskimo
named Ooootook for the theft of a shovel, a shocking application of British naval discipline to a people who could not
possibly understand it. Parry seemed to believe that the
effect was salutary and that the Eskimos learned a lesson from
Ooootook's example. He might indeed have frightened the
people of Igloolik into temporary submission, but, as
Erktua's version of the story showed, the punishment had
different long-term consequences from those he might have
wished: Ooootook became a figure of heroic proportions.
According to Erktua, Ooootook was a mighty angeko. She
said that the British sailors first tried to shoot him, but the

bullets veered off; then they whipped him, but he was unscathed; then they hacked at him with knives, but the knives could not cut into his flesh. When he was locked up below decks, he called on a spirit that shook the ship so violently that the koblunas, fearful that it would split asunder, finally released him.

Erktua had other stories about Parry which appear in no printed records of his expedition. The old woman had had the world in her time, and even in her advanced years her blood ran hot as she recalled for Hall her former amours, among others not only William Edward Parry, that elegant and proper naval officer, but also his second-in-command, George Lyon. Hall recorded Erktua's reminiscences dutifully in his journal, writing along the margin, "ESPECIALLY PRIVATE!" Parry was Erktua's first paramour, Lyon her second: "Erktua furthermore says that when Parry found out she had slept with Lyon, & Lyon learned that she had done the same with Parry, they became jealous; and for this Erktua ever after refused to sleep with either again." When Parry's ships left Igloolik, Lyon, who had found his satisfaction elsewhere after Erktua refused him her favors, left two Eskimo sisters pregnant with his children.

Several months after hearing this shocking (to him) story, Hall paid a visit to the whalers at Depot Island. When he returned, he added a note along the margin on which he had written "ESPECIALLY PRIVATE!": "I have reason now to insert the following opinion: that Erktua is a notorious falsifier—in other words, a liar." The reason: during his absence, Erktua had been spreading rumors about Hall, saying that he had tried to solicit her through the offices of Tookoolito.

In spite of this example of Eskimo fabrication, Hall still tended to believe stories that he wanted to believe. During the winter, he heard a series of tales that excited him because they concerned not Parry, Lyon, or Rae, but F. R. M. Crozier, Franklin's second-in-command. In his journal entry of December 6, in large letters and with a pointing hand in the margin, is this heading:

FOUR SOULS OF SIR JOHN FRANKLIN'S EXPEDITION HEARD
FROM — ONE OF THESE F.R.M. CROZIER! THREE OF THESE
MAY YET BE ALIVE. THE INNUITS THINK THEY ARE.

Crozier had been a midshipman on Parry's expedition; much to Hall's surprise, the Eskimos knew his name. They said that this man Crozier had first come with Parry *not* as an eshmuta, or chief, but that he had returned many years later as an eshmuta, and that he was one of the men who had been with the two ships that had been sunk near Neitchille. Tooshooarthario, one of Ouela's cousins, had come on Crozier and three other men wandering lost and hungry not far from Neitchille. Crozier was weaker than the other men, because, as Hall recorded it, "Crozier was the only man that would not eat any of the meat of the koblunas, as the others all did"; that is, Crozier, unlike the others, would not commit cannibalism. According to Ouela and his brothers, Artooa and their cousin Shooshearknook had fed Crozier and his companions seal meat. In the weeks that followed, one of the four men died of some sickness, but Crozier and the others grew fat and healthy. Finally, they left Tooshooarthario and headed south toward the lands of the koblunas. "The Innuits here think the two men & Crozier are alive yet—think that they may have returned to Neitchille if they found they could not get home to the Kobluna country, & live again with Innuits."

This was the story that the Eskimos told Hall on December 6, which Ouela, Artooa, and Shooshearknook all swore they had heard directly from their cousin Tooshooarthario. In the days and evenings that followed, Hall gathered more details from the three brothers and from other Eskimos at Noowook. What emerged was a fragmentary but at least partly coherent tale.

Mother Ookbarloo, Ouela's mother, told him that the

Eskimos of Neitchille believed that the koblunas who came
on the two ships brought bad luck, so two powerful angekos
ankooted so much that fish and animals stayed away from
the area. "The two angekos of Neitchille were very bad, for
they ankooted on purpose to have the koblunas that were in
the two ships in the ice all starve to death." Some time later,
Mother Ookbarloo said, some Innuits of the Neitchille area
found a big tent ashore "and there saw starved and frozen
Koblunas all dead—many with the flesh all cut off of the
bones."

When Ouela's cousin Tooshooarthario found Crozier and
his three companions, they had guns and plenty of ammunition. After recovering their health, they shot birds. The
Eskimos there, who had never seen or heard a gun, were
terrified; in fact, when Crozier left, he tried to give the
cousin one of the guns, but the cousin would not accept it.
"He was very much afraid of it—afraid that it would kill
him it made so much noise." While Crozier was staying with
Tooshooarthario, he told the Eskimo that before the other
men from the two ships had died, they had battled with
Indians (Etkerlins). One day Crozier had been out hunting: "Suddenly one Indian very near him jumped up from
behind a big stone & threw his lance at him, hitting him
in the forehead. The lance passed right across the forehead
just above the eyebrows & cut a long ugly gash in it."
Crozier shot and killed the Indian. The next day he and
his men were attacked by others but succeeded in driving
them off with their guns. It was after this fight that so many
koblunas froze and starved to death.

Crozier and his two companions left Tooshooarthario in
the late summer or fall, heading southward toward Ootkoo-
seekalik, the estuary of the Great Fish or Back River. They
traveled overland, but they had with them a boat that would
"hold wind." Ebierbing told Hall that the Eskimos probably
meant a rubber boat; the Franklin Expedition had indeed
carried such boats.

This is a bare outline of the story that Hall pieced together at Noowook. Some aspects of it were more complicated than they appear in outline—for example, there was a problem of names. Although the Eskimos knew Crozier's proper name, they also had an Eskimo name for him, Eglooka. At times they called him Crozier, at times Eglooka. The problem lay in the fact that other explorers had been given the same name, or at least names that sound very similar. Parry had been called Aglooka (Parry's transcription) and James Ross was called Argloogah (Ross's transcription). Apparently the name had some unknown generic meaning that could make it apply to koblunas other than Crozier. Eager to confirm preconceived conclusions, Hall made too much of questionable differences in transcription in order to preserve exclusively for Crozier the name that he heard as "Eglooka."

In mid-December Ouela and several other Eskimos traveled to Depot Island to pay a visit to the whalers. Hall sent with them a long letter to Captain Chapel of the *Monticello*, relating his discoveries and saying that he himself would go to Depot Island in the near future. When Ouela returned ten days later, bearing gifts from the whalers, Hall greeted him warmly and asked for news. What he heard turned his good cheer into anger. Chapel had arranged with Ouela that he return to the *Monticello* with his wives and with other Eskimos as soon as possible,˙ to go with the ship to Marble Island. Probably Chapel wanted hunters, but Hall had another interpretation: "A moment's reflection sufficed for me to think that CAPTAIN E. A. CHAPEL of the 'Monticello' had probably concocted this plan for the object of getting Ouela's wives to his ship for his own <u>licentious accomodation</u>." Whatever Chapel's motivation (Hall later retracted his slander), he was undermining Hall's plans by taking the Eskimos away. Hall depended on them for help, and his project would be seriously threatened by their loss. He determined to go to Depot Island himself immediately after

the New Year. In the meantime, he did his best to secure
the services of as many men as he could. On New Year's
Eve he entertained the entire village in his igloo, plying
even the women with brandy punch. (In his journal, he
tried to rationalize away his sense of guilt by arguing that
his great end justified his means.) When everyone was
muddle-headed and euphoric, he delivered a long, long
speech, beginning with a bow and a refrain that he repeated
throughout the address: "Listen, my brother Innuits . . ."
He pointed out that he had been with them many moons
and that they had become as brothers, but some koblunas
had robbed them, taught them profanity, infected them
with disease. He told them his noble purpose, and he promised that he would share his firearms and ammunition with
them in the years to come. "So long as I am in your country,"
he concluded, "let us be as we have been for four moons
past—a band of brothers and sisters. I thank you all very
much. Good-night." His stupefied audience, receiving the
speech enthusiastically, asked him to give another. In their
enthusiasm, Ouela and the others promised that they would
stay with him rather than work for the whalers.

Hall was proud of his oratory, but he knew that its effects
would wear off almost as fast as the brandy punch. When he
left for Depot Island, he tried to persuade the Eskimos to
stay behind, fearing that the whalers would be able to change
their minds, but sixteen of them insisted on going with him.

As they made their way down the ice of Roe's Welcome,
Hall brooded on a new enterprise:

> Give me the means to get to such Northern Lands & Waters
> as are unvisited by civilized man & then I will be in my
> great glory. After visiting King William Land & clearing
> up the mysteries relative to Sir John Franklin's Expedi-
> tion, I hope to be enabled to make a voyage to the North
> Pole. A few thousand dollars with well-directed efforts will
> give the civilized world a knowledge of all that portion of

God's beautiful footstool over which the Lesser Bear makes
his daily circuit.

His second expedition had hardly begun, yet he was already
contemplating his third. During the next several years, he
often reverted to the subject in his journal.

Wintered-in a few miles west of Depot Island were five
whalers, snow banked high against their hulls, their decks
well housed: the *Monticello* and the *George and Mary* of
New London, the *Black Eagle* and the *Antelope* of New Bedford, and the *Concordia* of Fairhaven. "What a change within
a few moments!" Hall wrote not long after boarding the
Monticello. "From the life of the Esquimaux, a minute's
jump brought me into that of civilized men—and civilized
food!" Chapel greeted him on his arrival, immediately order-
ing the steward to bring him pie, cake, and cheese. That
evening they went across to the *Antelope*, where there was a
makeshift theater, to watch a performance of *Damon and
Pythias* put on by the "Hudson's Bay Theater Company."
On his various visits to New London and Groton, Hall had
met most of the captains, including Captain George Tyson
of the *Antelope*. The following night, Tyson invited him to
dine aboard his ship:

> O, what a glorious dinner for me! Baked beans & pork,
> preserved Beef, preserved vegetables of various kinds, in-
> cluding green corn, preserved cherries, mince pie, coffee
> and preserved milk! Where and when did I ever enjoy
> more a dinner? Do not, Messrs G & B [Grinnell and
> Brevoort; Hall often directly addressed them in his jour-
> nal], think me wild when I place such emphatic sentences
> here in relation to the food I am now supplied with. I like
> civilized food as well as any man.

During the next month, Hall tasted the pleasures of a
northern whaler's approximation of civilized living. There

were frequent games, exchange dinners, theatricals, even masked balls. His stay at Depot Island was at least physically a comfortable interlude.

In spite of the whalers' hospitality, Hall had trouble with them in the very way that he had anticipated when he tried to persuade the Eskimos to stay behind at Noowook. The whalers, needing Eskimos to supply them with meat and to transport blubber during the spring floe whaling, cajoled, flattered, and bribed Hall's little group to gain their services for the coming years. Chapel persuaded Ouela to stay on with him, although he assuaged Hall's anger by promising that he would keep Ouela for only a few months and would send a boat to Repulse Bay during the following year to assist Hall by picking him up when he returned from King William Island. All in all, Hall decided, Chapel was a "TRUE FRIEND OF THE CAUSE." Not so were most of the other captains, who simply suborned the Eskimos whom Hall considered to be his and offered nothing in return. When Hall argued with Captain Jeffries of the *George and Mary* that he had made previous arrangements with the natives, "Jeffries at once responded that 'he didn't care a d——n for all my previous arrangements'—he, for one, was going to look out for himself." Hall stormed off the ship after this exchange, to affirm that night in his journal: "Rather than have serious trouble with a man who acts more like a MADMAN than otherwise, I will let matters take a peaceful course. My mission is one for humanity. Let it be fulfilled peacefully if possible."

Hall had come to Depot Island with sixteen Eskimos. When he left, he had only three with him, including Ebierbing. As if this were not bad enough, trouble was beginning to develop between himself and the few Eskimos who stayed with him. During the trip back to Noowook, Ouela's brother Shooshearknook began to "play the devil" (Hall's favorite phrase for all kinds of trouble making). He refused Hall and Ebierbing any share of his walrus meat,

although he stuffed himself and even fed his dogs with it.
He stole some of the precious bread that the whalers had
given Hall. Things did not improve when they arrived at
Noowook. Hunting had been bad there, and Shooshearknook
conspired with his brother Artooa and with the other natives at Noowook to desert Hall. "At the end of a little over
six months' wintering along side of Shooshearknuk, he
shows the cloven foot," wrote Hall. Most of the Eskimos
moved out of Noowook to another camp, some twenty miles
away.

Hall had hoped to set out for Repulse Bay in the late
winter and, after establishing a base there, to make his journey to King William Island in the spring. With the desertion
of the Eskimos, he decided that his plans would have to be
set back a whole year. He probably would not be able to
reach Repulse Bay until the summer; he would have to
winter-over there, then leave for King William Island in
the spring of 1866. "I shall endeavor to be cautious in all my
movements," he wrote to Chapel. "It must be remembered
that I propose to go to that part of the world where some
one hundred and thirty men—choicely picked men—the
very flower of the English Navy—all perished save three."

Before he could set out for Repulse Bay, he had to endure
several more months of frustration and discomfort. The
weather was bitter, and sometimes during storms he thought
with pity of Franklin's men. Meat and blubber were scarce;
much of the time, he had to live on old caribou heads and
haunches, eating the putrid brains, cracking the bones for
their bitter marrow, and even consuming the skin from
around the noses and hoofs. Without blubber, there was
little light or heat:

> How cheerless is our igloo! The widely extended moss-
> wick of our fire-lamp, which usually sends forth a radiant
> heat, is now narrowed down to a simple wick point, and
> makes the gloom more dismal by its glimmering light than

total darkness, for long and cast-down faces are now faintly seen that otherwise would be veiled from each of us.

He suffered pains in his back, chest, and shoulders from the hours that he spent hunched over, covered with tuktoo skins, trying to write in his journal. Even his special "freezeless" ink froze, bursting its bottles, and he stored it outside in icy blocks. Periodically, he would leave the igloo to cut a chunk of ink.

On April 1, with the return of Ouela from Depot Island, the situation improved. Ouela went to the Eskimo camp and persuaded his brothers Artooa and Shooshearknook to rejoin Hall's party. On April 15, when Hall finally set out for Repulse Bay, he was accompanied by thirteen Eskimos. They made a leisurely journey northward, pausing for a month to hunt seals at Wager Bay. (Hall bitterly noted in his journal on the day they arrived there that his original plan had been to land there when he first left the *Monticello*, but it had taken him nine months to make it.) They reached Repulse Bay on June 10.

The remainder of the summer was spent moving from camp to camp in Repulse Bay, hunting first seals and then caribou as the summer blended into autumn. In August a few whaling ships appeared, among the first ever to cruise the area. One brought news that the Civil War had ended and that Lincoln had been assassinated. Not long after the whalers departed, Hall and the Eskimos succeeded in killing a whale, harpooning it from the *Sylvia*. Caching the meat and blubber for their own use, Hall also carefully preserved the fifteen hundred pounds of bone, hoping to sell it to the whalers when they returned the following year.

In September he prepared his winter camp on the North Pole River near Fort Hope, where Rae had wintered in 1847 and 1854. Little remained of Rae's habitation except a stone oven, which Hall used as a cache, but Hall often thought of the English explorer and decided to follow his route from Repulse Bay to Boothia when he made his sledge trip in the spring. In the meantime, however, he had to endure another long Arctic winter of waiting.

Hall thought that he was familiar with the ways of Eskimos, but the fall and winter of 1865–6 strained his patience to the utmost. On September 16 Tookoolito gave birth to a boy, whom Hall immediately named King William. Much to Hall's annoyance, before and after the birth Tookoolito carefully observed the taboos both of her own people of Baffin Island and of the Repulse Bay Eskimos. For a time she lived in seclusion and avoided drinking cold water; she ate only stewed caribou meat, prepared only by herself with her own utensils. As the months passed and she continued to live under what Hall considered to be a superstitious regimen, his annoyance sometimes flared into anger—at her and at her culture. He did not like to be reminded that her Christianity was only a late and superficial modification of her native beliefs.

His relations with the other Eskimos would be warm for weeks on end; then he would do or say something untoward and find himself living with strangers whose masklike mongoloid faces filled him with fear and loathing. During the autumn and early winter, all of the Eskimos except Armou and his family lived separate from Hall, Ebierbing, and Tookoolito; while Hall and his little group settled at Fort Hope, Ouela and his people established a winter camp at Nowyarn, ten miles away. Amicable relations were maintained for some time, goods and supplies were exchanged, and Hall thought that all in all the separation was probably wise. Then Ouela lost two of his brothers: Shooshearknook died suddenly of some disease, and Artooa, hunting alone in his kayak, capsized and drowned. Soon after Artooa's death, Ouela arrived at Fort Hope:

> He said that he would like very much for me to go to Nowyarn & live there the remainder of the winter, for he

felt quite lonesome since his two brothers' deaths—that no
one could seem more like a brother to him than myself.
When Ouela told this to Tookoolito & Ebierbing, as he
did not with a tearless eye, I felt to do almost anything
within my power to show that I deeply appreciated such
fraternal feeling extended to me from so noble a soul as
Ouela's. Ouela is a man that would command respect,
honor & admiration in civilized lands for his truly eminent,
genuine & inherent virtues.

Hall moved to Nowyarn. Within a week of the move, he
made this entry in his journal:

> How terrible is my situation here, the only white man
> among a savage people! As I have said before, never again
> will I put myself in the power of an uncivilized race. The
> life I am living is one worse than his who is being
> 'murdered by inches.' It is true that at times everything
> goes along smoothly; but how unstable is the base! A
> whisper, a tip of the finger is enough to throw all seeming
> order here into an earthly hell.

As for Ouela: "Should I live many, many years & should
this party show me a thousand favors, he could not wipe out
the stain that has been effected by his late wrongful acts."
It seemed to Hall that Ouela was trying to starve him to
death by refusing to give any of his food to the explorer
or his party. The Eskimo behaved so sullenly that Hall was
afraid to stand up to him: "There is a huge block of whale
blubber now before my eyes. My very mouth waters for a
good eat off of it, but I fear to touch it, knowing that it is
Ouela's will that I should not."

By bribery with tobacco, he managed to maintain at least
amicable relations with the other Eskimos for a time, but
after a few weeks he again felt the strain of living with their
superstitions. There was, for example, the affair of "Queen
Emma," one of Ouela's wives, who fell seriously ill during
the autumn and began to waste away. One night late in

December, an old Eskimo woman dreamed that Queen
Emma was sick because she had committed a terrible crime:
in the dream, she had given birth to a tiny dead infant about
the length of a forefinger, and had never told anyone about
it. The crime was not in the supposed birth, but in Queen
Emma's secrecy about it. The old woman spread the news of
her dream to the encampment. Queen Emma, protesting
her innocence but presumed guilty because no one would
doubt the truth of the dream, was sealed up in an igloo with
her enraged husband and several old hags, who dictated
severe restrictions in her diet as a spiritual purgative. Hall
watched helplessly as the poor woman, already seriously ill,
went into a rapid decline. "O, that I were allowed to save
her! But nothing can any person do that would sooner
bring him into disrepute & danger than to meddle with such
superstitious notions as entertained by these people."

Tookoolito, still living under the taboos forced on her
since the birth of King William, witnessed Queen Emma's
ordeal with sympathy. Hall was pleased when she expressed
anger at the treatment of Queen Emma, hoping that she
would declare her own independence from the superstitions.
"I told Tookoolito that I was glad to find that she was beginning to feel how perfectly useless it was for her & Ebierbing to try to live as the Innuits around us do. Said I, you
see that the way Queen Emma and yourself are obliged to
live, you both will soon die. Here T. told me that she would
live as I desired her." The next day, Hall triumphed when
Tookoolito ate bread and drank coffee for the first time since
the birth of her child. His triumph was short-lived. When
he offered her some meat, she refused: "She must not, she
says, eat meat the same day that she eats bread & coffee.
Otherwise her little King William might take sick and die.
How utterly impossible it is to knock or reason these absurd,
superstitious ideas out of an Innuit's head."

Resolute in his determination to leave for King William
Island in the spring in spite of his troubles with the Eskimos,

Hall set about preparing his equipment and provisions in March. Although Ouela and some of the other natives refused to go with him, a few, including Ouela's half-brother, Nukerzhoo, agreed to make the journey. Just before Hall departed, he and Ouela became friendly again, Ouela agreeing to give messages and letters to the whalers who were supposed to arrive at Repulse Bay in the summer.

On March 31 Hall set out with Ebierbing, Tookoolito, little King William, three other Eskimo couples, and five other children—an unwieldly caravan. He had earlier decided to follow John Rae's route, striking north from Fort Hope across Rae Isthmus to the head of Committee Bay as the first leg of the journey. The expedition started badly. A gale struck when they were only a few hours out, and they remained stormbound in hastily built igloos for three days. During the storm, King William showed the first signs of an illness that was to make the journey agony for both his mother and Hall. When the weather cleared, they made a day's trek, then stopped for a week; King William's illness had become so serious that Hall dared not travel with him. During the stop, Hall once again had to endure ankooting, this time in a form that he considered highly dangerous. He attempted to treat King William as best he could with what few medicines he had, but after two days of this, Nukerzhoo decided to become an angeko and cure the baby.

He attached a leather thong to the head of one of the women, made her lie down, and asked questions of a Spirit: when the Spirit answered "yes," he pulled on the thong to raise the woman's head—when it answered "no," he did nothing. Soon his questions became pointed: Should the baby take any more of the kobluna's medicine? (No movement of the woman's head.) Had Tookoolito followed the taboos that she should have? (No movement.) Should Tookoolito give up bread and tea? (Vigorous nodding of the woman's head.) Hall tried to argue with Tookoolito, but she submitted to the will of the new angeko. She said that if she did not obey, the Eskimos would curse her and Ebierbing and probably would desert Hall.

After a week they moved on, but very slowly. The Eskimos clearly had little desire to reach King William Island; they dawdled, they pretended to hunt, they insisted on stopping for ankooting. When Hall talked to them about King William Island, they were filled with dire warnings about starvation and unfriendly Eskimos. Hall confided to his journal that if they deserted him, he would persist in going ahead by himself, but soon after he was given an example of the Eskimo knowledge and courage that made them invaluable. Late in the night of April 14, a pack of about twenty-five wolves attacked their dogs. Nukerzhoo and the other men ran straight from the igloo at the pack, shouting and waving their arms. The wolves retreated, then attacked again, to be driven off once more by the Eskimos.*

In eighteen days Hall's party traveled only thirty-two miles. In the week that followed, their pace quickened; they gained the head of Committee Bay and began to work their way up its west coast. They reached Cape Weynton twenty-eight days from Fort Hope. Hall knew that Rae had made the same trip in five days without dogs; proud of his own ability in Arctic travel, he felt humiliated.

On April 29, just north of Cape Weynton, they came on a group of Eskimos from Pelly Bay. Hall was delighted to learn that one of them was the mother of Tooshooarthario, the man who had found Crozier wandering in the barrens; he was even more delighted when the head man of the group showed him two spoons, one of which was clearly marked with the initials F. R. M. C. (Francis Rawdon Moira Crozier). Soon he was engrossed in a long talk, hearing tales about the two

---

* At about this time, Hall also was given an example of Eskimo resistance to pain: Ebierbing borrowed his forceps and removed one of his molars by himself. "He said my tooth puller instrument slipped off three times, but the 4th time brought it out. He said he could see stars in his eyes. This all done so silently by E. that I knew nothing of it till the 3 pronged ugly fellow was out of his mouth."

ships that had been iced-in near Neitchille many years before. Some of the older members of the group said that they had been aboard the ships and that they remembered the eshmuta, whom they called Toolooark. They said that he was old and gray-headed and wore something over his eyes (Tookoolito told Hall that they probably meant spectacles). He used to shake the Innuits' hands vigorously, gave them food, and was always cheerful. He was sick when they last saw him, they said. Hall had no doubt that he was hearing about Sir John Franklin himself (the description would apply equally well to Sir John Ross, however). The Eskimos had other tales that filled in some details of the Franklin disaster. They told Hall that one of the ships sank very suddenly—so suddenly that the koblunas did not have time to get supplies out of her. They deserted the other, and she drifted southward. Some time later, they said, Eskimos of Ookgoolik (O'Reilly Island, south of King William Island) found two boats on sledges near a beach. In the boats were dead koblunas.

After the talk, Hall was shown other relics of the Franklin Expedition: more spoons, a fork, a pair of scissors, a mahogany barometer case. After some bargaining, the Eskimos handed them over to him.*

The Pelly Bay natives had other stories that frightened Hall's companions and destroyed what hopes he had of reaching King William Island that year. They said that they had left Pelly Bay partly because the Seeneemiutes, a fierce clan of Eskimos who shared the region with them, had become aggressive. There had been depredations of settlements, wife-stealing, even murder. They warned that the Seeneemiutes were prepared to plunder and murder any group that entered the area of Pelly Bay. Hall's Eskimos listened with such apprehension that he knew they would refuse to move any farther in the direction of King William Island. Reluctantly, he decided to turn back. Before he left, however, he cached

---

* Hall carefully preserved these relics. They are at present in the vaults of the Division of Naval History at the Smithsonian Institution.

provisions near Cape Weynton, a practical measure but also a symbol of his determination to return. "Thanks be to God, I have yet the heart to persevere in what I have taken upon myself to do," he wrote on the day he left. "Obstacle after obstacle has yet to be overcome before I shall triumph, but by the aid of High Heaven, I will yet succeed."

The return journey was made a nightmare by King William's worsening illness. The baby had become weak and torpid, and Tookoolito, over Hall's objections, followed Eskimo custom by giving him away to another couple, supposedly a cure for illness in a baby. On May 13 she found him dead. Only a few years before, she had lost little "Butterfly," and now King William was gone. For an hour she carried the dead infant in her arms, giving him up only after long, gentle persuasion. That afternoon, they buried him on a hill near their camp; Hall buried a piece of paper with him, on which he had written:

> These are the mortal remains of Little King William, the only child of Ebierbing and Tookoolito, the interpreters of the last Franklin Research Expedition. Deposited here May 13, 1866, the day of its death. God hath its soul now and will keep it from all harm.

Near the grave he erected a monument. Three stones formed the base, representing faith, hope, and charity; on top of these were piled two others in the form of a cross.

Hall and his group arrived back at Repulse Bay at the end of May. Understandably, he was discouraged at his failure to reach King William Island, but with his characteristic resilience he reasserted his determination to try again:

> Today my King William party was ended, for the present at least. On the return of the successful tooktoo party of this day [the natives had gone caribou hunting as soon as they arrived back], I invited all the men into my kommong, and there I served each with moderate drinks of capital

good Bourbon whisky. We talked, smoked, and drank—
talked smoked and drank till every heart felt that it should
be friendly to everybody. One matter is worthy of record:
all the men of my party are still determined to accompany
me next spring, when I purpose to <u>try again</u>.

Hall settled down to another year of waiting. He knew that
he could not make his next try until the following spring,
when conditions again would be right for extensive sledge
travel; in the meantime, he planned to make only local
explorations in Repulse Bay, examining and mapping it.
This endeavor would be worthwhile, but he also wished to
remain in the area for another reason: whalers were due to
arrive sometime during the summer, and he believed it im-
perative that he see them. The reports of the Pelly Bay Eskimos that the Seeneemiutes were dangerous had forced him to
conclude that he should hire white men to assist him on his
next journey. At Cape Weynton, he had written in his journal, "I find it necessary to organize a company mostly made
up of white men all well drilled in military tactics & completely armed for the protection of lives and property of such
an expedition as mine passing through a country inhabited by
savages who now have become warlike." He hoped that the
whalers would provide him with a miniature army.

Behind this decision also lay his experiences with the Pelly
Bay and Repulse Bay Eskimos. Their superstitions and customs not only offended his own beliefs but also made accomplishment of his goals difficult—they were so inhibited
by taboos that it seemed almost impossible to get them to
travel at a reasonable pace. He had come to the Arctic hoping
to find freedom and independence. For a time in Frobisher
Bay, he thought that he had found them in the natives. "They
are a people knowing no restraint," he had written of the
Frobisher Bay Eskimos. "<u>They will be INDEPENDENT in the
fullest significance of the word</u>: We Americans talk about
Freedom and Independence. We are far behind these

Northerners." Since that time hard experience had changed
his ideas and made him look back at his earlier beliefs with
irony. "I once thought Innuits the only persons in the world
that were perfectly free," he wrote in his journal on the return trip from Cape Weynton, "but I now know how mistaken I was. . . . It is custom—custom of the old dead Innuits
that must be followed or everything will go all wrong with
these people."

His life with the Eskimos while he waited for the whalers'
arrival was made difficult not only by their customs but also
by the fear of violence breaking out among them. The Pelly
Bay Eskimos had followed his party from Cape Weynton,
setting up camp near Nowyarn, and relations between them
and the Repulse Bay Eskimos were at best uneasy. When they
challenged Nukerzhoo and the other Repulse Bay men to such
contests of strength and skill as boxing, wrestling, and knife-
throwing, Tookoolito told Hall that he should not allow it,
warning that the sport could easily turn to murder. She had
heard that the Pelly Bay people sometimes put pointed bones
in their mittens when they boxed; they would aim for the
temple of an opponent, deliberately trying for a killing blow.
Hall managed to stop the "sports," but in July he apparently
was given an appalling example of the Pelly Bay people's
capacity for violence. The references in his journal to the
event are strangely oblique and obscure, but several years
later he wrote a summary of the expedition in which its outline emerges. "Then the terrible times!" he wrote, referring
to mid-summer 1866. "Wife of old Kokleearngnun [elder and
chief of the Pelly Bay group] hung as a Peace offering by her
own son & relatives; & soon after my good old friend Kokleearngnun hung and disemboweled!" In Frobisher Bay, Hall
had seen Eskimo elders allowed to die, but this was his first
encounter with the custom of actually killing them. That
Kokleearngnun had apparently asked to be killed did not
make his death, or that of his wife, any more acceptable to
Hall. Why he is so obscure about the subject in his journal

(only mentioning that Kokleearngnun's son had told him that he had hanged his parents) remains a mystery.

Relations between the Repulse Bay and Pelly Bay Eskimos were not improved when Ouela, who had been away hunting when they arrived back from Cape Weynton, returned to Nowyarn. Hall soon learned that Ouela knew some of the Pelly Bay men and, sometime in the past, had quarreled with one of them. The meeting between the two men was charged with latent violence; both prominently displayed their knives. Although in time they reached a *modus vivendi,* Hall knew that the slightest wrong word or action could cause bloodshed. Late in the summer, when one of Ouela's wives died (Queen Emma, who had never recovered from the persecution that followed the old woman's dream of the stillborn baby), the angeko told Ouela that the presence of the Pelly Bay people was the cause. Hall was expecting a murder, or even tribal warfare, when the whalers at last arrived and distracted the Eskimos from their growing hostilities.

Six whaling vessels came to Repulse Bay early in August. Having lived almost a year alone with Eskimos, Hall found their presence a great comfort, and frequently went aboard the ships for dinners and entertainments (including a candy-making and corn-popping party). Almost immediately, he set about trying to hire some men for his planned spring journey to King William Island. The whalers decided to winter over at Repulse Bay. Hall told the captains that he would assist them during the fall and winter by assigning the Eskimos to hunt for them. In return, he expected the captains to provide him with some men in the spring, with the understanding that he would get them back in time for late summer whaling. At first Hall assumed that the captains were agreeable to the plan, but during the winter it dawned on him that they were simply using the Eskimos (whom Hall considered to be "his") without guaranteeing the services of any white men in return.

In late January he faced still another problem. Dogs were

at a premium. There were about seventy dogs in the area, but the whalers kept them all busy transporting meat and blubber. Foreseeing the possibility that he would be unable to get any dogs for his spring sledge trip, Hall realized that he would have to obtain some of his own. He decided that he would have to make a trip north more than two hundred miles to Igloolik and buy dogs there.

He left Repulse Bay for Igloolik on February 7, with only Ouela, one of Ouela's wives, and his youngest child as company. (He did not take Ebierbing and Tookoolito because Ebierbing was suffering from a severe attack of rheumatism.) It was forty degrees below zero on the day they left; February was the worst possible month to make such a trip, but Hall could not wait if he were to be back in time to start for King William Island in mid-March.

Predictably, sledging to Igloolik with Ouela was, in Hall's words, "hellish." They were frequently stormbound during the twenty-day trip, but the weather was less trouble than was Ouela. Hall surmised after a week that the Eskimo was trying to wreak vengeance on him: "There is evidently some damnable scheme in this man's head to satisfy his long desire to punish me—or in plain words to kill me—for the trouble I once had with his 2 now deceased brothers." He noted that Ouela "eats 5 times more than myself—he is very hoggish." Not only did Ouela gorge himself, he also gorged his wife, their child, and even his dogs, while feeding Hall as little as possible. The mood of the trip was epitomized in a scene that occurred just before they reached Igloolik. They were sitting in an igloo eating their evening meal. Ouela's child, which Hall in his journal sarcastically called "the little Idol," gobbled down his portion; then, seeing Hall still eating, he began to cry and to reach out for Hall's portion. When Hall refused to hand his food over to the child, Ouela stood up and stomped out of the igloo. He did not speak to Hall for more than a day.

Hall spent two weeks in Igloolik. He found the Igloolik

Charles Francis Hall, engraving based on the photograph (Plate 9) taken during the winter of 1870.

Sir John Franklin
(from Nourse's Narrative).

Hall's beloved patron
Henry Grinnell.

Captain Sidney Budington.

Captain George Tyson.

Elisha Kent Kane in winter quarters
aboard the Advance, *1854. From left*
to right, Kane, Isaac Hayes, William Morton.
Kane was one of Hall's idols,
Hayes one of his adversaries, Morton
one of his mates on the Polaris *expedition.*

Tookoolito, date unknown.

[LEFT] *Tookoolito, Hall, and Ebierbing in their Arctic clothing.*

6

*A typical page of Hall's Frobisher Bay journal,
with illustration of an aurora.*

[LEFT]   *Ebierbing, date unknown.*

Poster used to advertise lectures that Hall delivered
during the Civil War after the Frobisher Bay expedition,
showing Ebierbing, Tookoolito, and little "Butterfly."

*Charles Francis Hall, in the only known photograph,
taken in Washington in the winter of 1870 (see p. 250);
from left to right, Colonel James Lupton,
Major T. H. Stanton, Hall, Penn Clarke. The engraving
(Plate 1) that is our best image of Hall was based
upon this photograph.*

The Polaris.

Doctor Emil Bessels, date unknown; photograph in the National Portrait Gallery, Washington.

*Tyson's party photographed at St. John's (see pp. 295-6),
with Frederick Meyer standing at the right,
Tyson at the left. In the middle: Ebierbing and his family;
in the middle right: Hans and his family; the only other man
identified in the photograph is the steward, John Herron,
in the middle of the back row, wearing a hat.*

Emil Bessels's sketch of Hall's funeral;
in the background, Bessels's observatory,
near which three men wait at the
graveside for the funeral party.

TO THE MEMORY
OF

C. F. HALL

LATE COMMANDER

OF THE

NORTH POLAR EXPEDITION

DIED NOV. 8. 1871,

Aged 50 Years.

Tookoolito beside Hall's grave,
sketch by Emil Bessels, now at the Center
for Polar Archives, National Archives.

The ruins of Bessels's observatory; in the background,
"Observatory Bluff," behind it the coast of Ellesmere Island.
Thomas Gignoux is walking past the ruins.

[OVERLEAF] *The Nares Plaque, placed*
at the foot of Hall's grave by the Nares
Expedition in 1876 (see p. 336).

natives the most pleasant, hospitable, and cooperative Eskimos he had met. They willingly showed him around the area, taking him to various places associated with Parry's stay in 1822-3. He was even impressed by their angekos, who struck him as more earnest and honest than those who practiced the art to the south, and he let them ankoot him for frostbite. The people of Igloolik also were willing and eager to do what he had hoped: trade dogs for the goods that he had brought with him. He left with a fine team.

Unknown to him, Ouela also had been doing some trading —not for dogs, but for a new wife. Hall discovered this only on the day that they left on their return trip, when, going out to the sledges, he found a handsome young widow perched expectantly on his sledge with a child and all her gear. He berated Ouela, saying what the Eskimo well knew: that to travel with two women and two children at that time of year was foolhardy. Ouela sullenly refused even to listen, but by some judicious bribery Hall persuaded the widow to desert her new husband. Ouela, frustrated and angry, made the return trip to Repulse Bay even more hellish than the trip to Igloolik. Hall became sick soon after they left, and Ouela, seeing his advantage, tormented him by denying him food and by making him do menial "woman's" labor. After one particularly painful day, Hall wrote in his journal, "I had great reason at times to shoot the savage down on the spot, and know not how long it may be before I shall have to do so terrible an act to save my own dear life." There was ominous foreshadowing in this entry, although Hall did not know it; the time was coming when he would indeed pull a trigger to save his "own dear life."

Hall did not arrive back at Repulse Bay until March 31, fifty-two days after he had left for Igloolik. Even as he first sighted the whaling vessels in the bay, he could see that they were busy preparing for the spring whaling. What he had feared would happen did happen: the whaling captains told him that they could spare no men, so his arduous trip to

Igloolik had been wasted. He had dogs but no men, and he was so weakened by the trip that he could not consider leaving for King William Island even if it were possible. Bitterly, he faced yet another year of waiting.

Some measure of his despondency and defeat during this year is given by the state of his journals, which are incomplete, with long gaps between half-hearted, scrappy entries. He had lost much of his drive and with it his usual enthusiasm for recording his accomplishments and his hopes. He made only one extensive trip, returning to Cape Weynton to check the cache he had left there the previous year. The rest of the time, from March 1868 to March 1869, he remained in the area of Repulse Bay, not altogether inactive but accomplishing little to further what he had so often called his "grand enterprise." He helped the whalers by making detailed surveys of some parts of the bay and by joining the Eskimo hunting parties that the captains sent out after caribou and musk-ox. He also finally persuaded them to lend him some men in the late summer. By fall, he had arranged a year's contract with five: Frank Lailer, Peter Bayne, Patrick Coleman, John Spearman, and a man named Antoine, whose last name is unknown. They were to assist him in any way that he saw fit, and he gave them fair warning of the discomforts and possible dangers that they would have to endure. Like Charles Rudolph before them, they all swore that they would bear up even in the worst conditions.

He also continued to gather stories about Parry, Rae, Franklin, and Crozier, and one that he heard in the late fall of 1868 snapped him out of his lethargy. Some Igloolik Eskimos who had come down to Repulse Bay during the summer told him that they had seen two koblunas near Igloolik only a few years before, "one tall man, the other considerably shorter." Then, in January, some Pelly Bay Eskimos told Hall that they had seen on Simpson Peninsula an inukshuk (a monument of piled large rocks) topped by a thin stone pointed east toward Igloolik, and, on the shore, the broken mast of a ship. If Crozier had gone eastward from King William Island in an attempt to get to Igloolik (where he had been a midshipman with Parry), then he might well have gone over Simpson Peninsula and left a marker for possible rescuers. By late winter Hall was more convinced than ever that at least two survivors of the Franklin Expedition, one of them possibly Crozier, were living somewhere in the north part of Melville Peninsula. He did not seem to be bothered by the fact that these supposed survivors had not immediately gone to the Igloolik Eskimos for help, as Crozier certainly would have.

He had a decision to make: Should he again try to reach King William Island, or should he go back to Igloolik? Given the few months of good travel that he might expect, he could not do both. He made the decision easily: "Certainly I am bound at once for Igloolik and Fury and Hecla Strait. There is not a shadow of a doubt about my duty, which is to fly to the rescue of the probable survivors of the Franklin Expedition." At King William Island, all he could hope to find were relics and possibly a written account of the disaster; near Igloolik, he thought, he might find living men.

In late March, after a year of inaction, he set out north again, this time with Ebierbing, Tookoolito, some Igloolik Eskimos, and Frank Lailer, the sailor whom he most trusted of the five he had hired. He left the other four behind at Repulse Bay to mind his supplies and equipment.

In two weeks, his party reached the Ooglit Islands, some fifty miles south of Igloolik, and there fell in with some natives. Hall stayed in the islands for ten days, asking questions about koblunas who had been seen near Fury and Hecla Strait. One Eskimo, Koolooa, told him that about thirteen years before he had been hunting with a friend, Kia; he said that he was leaning over a little pool of water to take a drink, when suddenly he heard a loud crack some distance away. A few hours later he and Kia found tracks, larger than most Eskimo tracks but undoubtedly human, and they de-

cided to move their camp out of the immediate area. After
they moved, Kia went out to hunt alone. He was hunting with
bow and arrow and had never seen a gun.

> By and by Kia saw a man coming up the hill on which he
> (Kia) was, coming directly toward him. Kia thought at first
> the man to be Koolooa, but on looking longer and more
> observingly, Kia saw his mistake, for it was not Koolooa,
> but a strange man having a cap on his head that was dis-
> tinct from his coat. He saw that he (the stranger) had
> strange clothes on and carried something strange in a
> strange way on his shoulder. Kia could not, from his posi-
> tion behind a rock, see much of the stranger's face; the
> clothes not black nor white; coat on that came down to or
> almost to his knees; the make of clothes altogether dif-
> ferent from Innuits. The stranger had something across
> his shoulder running diagonally; this something was long
> and wide at one end and narrow at the other. He was
> walking rather fast. Kia followed the stranger up for some
> time and looked sharp at him. Kia kept himself hid among
> the rocks all the time.

Kia and Koolooa moved out of the area altogether, frightened
by the stranger. Some years later, after Kia was killed by a
walrus, Koolooa returned there. He found a strange inukshuk
and a stone cache that had been broken into; he said that he
was certain they had not been made by Innuits.

There were several other stories. When Hall asked if
Etkerlins (Indians) had ever been seen in northern Melville
Peninsula, he was told that one night many years before, some
natives' dogs began to bark. When the men peered out of their
tents, they saw four or five Etkerlins filing silently by in the
gray light, carrying what looked to be rifles. They were not
seen again, but a few days later gunshots were heard nearby.
Another story concerned a dog. Only a few years before, an
Eskimo had been out hunting when suddenly a caribou had
come bounding out from behind a hillock; a few seconds

later, a large short-haired dog had appeared in pursuit. The Eskimo was so startled that he did nothing, and soon they were both out of sight. And there were other stories about relics of various kinds and strange buildings that had been found near Fury and Hecla Strait.

Hall left the Ooglit Islands on April 16. Wanting to reach the west coast of the peninsula, where Kia had seen the stranger hunting and Koolooa had seen the inukshuk, he cut directly west, following stream beds through the Parry Mountains instead of going north to Igloolik. He reached his destination on April 24. "Koolooa requested today that I would take a look with my spy-glass in a certain direction, after we had tramped four hours over hill, lake, ravine, and through deep snow. I looked, and sighted a monument above the snow." After examining the inukshuk and listening to Koolooa's repeated insistence that it could not have been built by Innuits, he looked about for the supposed cache, but deep snow and ice covered the place where Koolooa said he had seen it. Hall was beginning to lose faith in Koolooa when Ebierbing found something that convinced him the Eskimo had been telling the truth: an oblong tenting place, with heavy stones placed in the four corners and smaller stones marking where the tent walls had been. No Eskimo would have left such a shape, for Eskimo tents were always circular at the base. With good reason, Hall decided that white men had definitely been in the vicinity. In the week that followed he searched the northwest coast of the peninsula as thoroughly as he could, finding no more signs of koblunas but remaining convinced that he had found one more piece of evidence that survivors of the Franklin Expedition had spent some time on the upper Melville Peninsula.

This trip and the cluster of Eskimo stories that caused it is a good example of the problems Hall ignored when he accepted Eskimo reminiscences at face value. In this particular case, false chronology and dating misled him. Although Koolooa said that Kia had seen the lone stranger thirteen

years before—that is, in 1855—there is now convincing
evidence that the stranger was actually John Rae and that the
year was 1847. In 1880, when Rae read an account of Hall's
findings, he wrote a long letter to the *New York Herald,*
explaining that Kia's description of the stranger exactly fitted
him and his dress when he was near Fury and Hecla Strait on
his first expedition, adding that he had often hunted in the
area.[1] As for the Etkerlins, the Indians that Hall had heard
about, according to Rae they must have been the half-breeds
that he had with him on his expedition, the only Indians
known to have been that far north of Hudson's Bay. Richard
Cyriax, the Arctic historian, has accounted for the large dog
that so startled the Eskimo: it probably was Parry's grey-
hound (he had one with him aboard the *Fury*), even though
Hall was told that it had been seen only a few years before.[2]
The oblong tent markings and the inukshuk could have
been Parry's, or Lyon's, or Rae's. In spite of Hall's attempts
to consider other interpretations, he usually allowed most
of what he heard to fall into a preconceived pattern: Crozier
and some other survivors from the *Erebus* and *Terror* went
east from King William Island and continued to survive for
many years near Fury and Hecla Strait. That was the way he
wanted it to be.

After spending three more weeks at Igloolik and the Ooglit
Islands, Hall returned again to Repulse Bay for the summer.
The whalers had all left the bay in the fall so he and his
party had it to themselves. He hoped to spend a quiet summer there, and for several months he had what he wanted,
peace and rest, but late in July something happened that
shattered both.

The event remains somewhat cloudy and mysterious. Hall's
notes of June and July 1868 record the easy hunting and
fishing trips that he made with Eskimos and the five whaling
men whom he had hired. Although in his journal he occasionally mocked some of the white men for their lack of Arctic
skills ("I sent Pat and Sam out deer hunting, though with

but a pinpoint of confidence that they could succeed in killing a deer"), he did not seem to have any serious difficulties with them; in fact, he seemed glad to have them with him, and most of his complaints were, as usual, aimed at the Eskimos ("Any white man is better off living upon his own efforts & resources than to fall into the presence of Savage Innuits"). On July 30 he recorded the undramatic events of the day as usual: some Eskimos killed several seals out in the bay, and Peter Bayne, one of the sailors, also succeeded in killing one. In the evening he sent Bayne, Patrick Coleman, and Antoine with the dogs to a place where a caribou had been killed. After the dogs had fed on the caribou, Bayne and the other men returned with them. Hall complained mildly that they had not allowed the dogs enough time to digest the meat before the return run. He noted that the day was very hot.

Then there is a three-week gap in his journal—a series of empty pages. On August 21 he began to write entries again, making no reference to the blank period, as if nothing had happened during it. But something had happened: on July 31 he had shot Patrick Coleman, and it had taken the poor man two weeks to die.

In the *Narrative of the Second Arctic Expedition Made by Charles F. Hall,* published by the government after Hall's death, J. E. Nourse quotes a long passage of Hall's writing as if it were a normal journal entry under the date of July 31, but there is no such entry in the journal and it cannot be found among the other Hall manuscripts at the Smithsonian. Possibly it is a post factum account written by Hall after he returned to the United States; the style is like Hall's, and there is no reason to doubt its authenticity. Here is the passage:

> July 31—Gave Peter his order to take my rifle and go on a deer-hunt, and to take along Antoine and Pat, and show them where a certain deer he had killed and deposited was,

and to have them bring it in. The party started off at 10 a.m.
A short time after, sent Sam out to get a deer-skin and the
buck-meat my Joe had left on his way home yesterday. At
7 p.m., Sam returned, having been unsuccessful in finding
my Joe's bundle, and at 8 p.m. Antoine and Pat returned,
and a few minutes later Peter came in, having seen no
deer. Asked Antoine how far he should think it was to
where he and Pat got the deer they brought in? Answer,
ten or twelve miles. When Peter came in, I asked him how
far it was to the deer-deposit Antoine and Pat brought in,
and he said about the same as the musk-ox deposit, six
and a half miles, to where we went directly on the 23d.
I asked him if he did not think that Pat and Antoine
could have performed the service I sent them on in a little
more than half the time of ten hours? Answer, that he
thought they could. I proceeded to the men's tent, and
asked Antoine and Pat if they could not have made better
time in the work they performed to-day? They, with much
temper, replied they could not. I told them what Peter
had told me, and said that it became them to be as expedi-
tious as possible whenever I had work for them to do,
reminding them of their spending a whole day a short time
since in going out only some two miles after a couple of
deer, when they might have done the same in one-fourth
of the time. This was followed by a burst of real mutinous
conduct on the part of Pat and Antoine, to which demon-
stration Sam and Peter seemed to be a party. Pat was the
leader, and I felt for my own safety that something must
be done to meet so terrible a blow as seemed ready to fall.
I appealed to Pat especially to stop his mutinous talk and
conduct. I was alone, though a small distance off were all
the Innuits of the tent-village looking upon the scene. Pat
was standing in the door of the tent (he and Antoine, when
I first went into the tent, were seated in it, but as their
rage increased they worked themselves out to be in a circle
of the other two), where he was delivering himself of the
most rebellious language possible. I made an approach to
him, putting my hand up before him, motioning for him

to stop. He at once squared himself, doubling up his fists and drawing back in position, as it were, to jump upon and fight me. Failing to make him desist without forcible means, I thought at first to give him a good drubbing, but knowing Pat to be of a powerful frame and muscle, and that if I did make an attempt I should at once have a party of four upon me, I demanded of Peter my rifle, which he gave me. I hastened to my tent, laid down the rifle, and seized my Baylie revolver, and went back and faced the leader of the mutinous crowd, and demanded of Pat to know if he would desist in his mutinous conduct? His reply being still more threatening, I pulled trigger, and he staggered and fell. I walked directly, but more as a man then suddenly dreaming, to the front of <u>Papa's</u> tent, where was a crowd of frightened natives, passed the pistol to the hand of <u>Armou</u>, which still had four undischarged loads in it, and then ran back and assisted in getting Pat to my tent. I supposed he could not live five minutes, but a Mightier hand than mine had stayed the ball from a vital part.

Coleman survived until August 14. Nourse states: "Every effort was made by Hall to save his life by the use of all remedies at his command and by the most careful nursing, in which his other men took their full share." Nourse also adds that Antoine "made a full confession of his having done wrong" and that the Eskimos told Hall that they believed the sailors might have murdered him; then he drops the subject altogether.[3]

When Hall returned to the United States, he asked Henry Grinnell for help in this grim affair. Grinnell checked carefully to find out who would have jurisdiction in the case and discovered that no one wanted it. The British Minister in Washington wrote him that because the shooting took place beyond the borders of the Dominion of Canada, neither the British nor the Canadians would have anything to do with it; authorities in the United States apparently preferred to pretend that the whole thing had not happened. Hall was never held legally liable in any way for Coleman's death.

But was the shooting justified? Probably not. There is no evidence that a mutiny had been planned; whatever Coleman did was on the spur of the moment. Many years after the event Frank Lailer, the one sailor whom Hall entirely trusted, told a newspaper reporter that he had not been present when Coleman was shot, but that if he had been, he "could have fixed the matter up."[4] He stressed the fact that all of the sailors were young, and that Hall could have controlled them without using a gun. Even Hall's own description of the shooting seems to deny him a plea of self-defense: he had taken a rifle from Peter Bayne, and Coleman was unarmed.

In later years Peter Bayne himself was to give a reason for the shooting that is different from the one offered by Hall. While Hall was away in Igloolik, Bayne and Coleman apparently had many long conversations with the Eskimos about the Franklin Expedition, and from a native of Boothia they learned something new. The Eskimo told the sailors that he remembered the two ships that had been iced in near Neitchille, and had seen much of their men. He said that one man who had died aboard the ships had been buried ashore with great ceremony—and that his grave had been covered over with some substance that turned to stone. Bayne and Coleman decided that only Sir John Franklin himself would have merited such a ceremony and burial in what apparently was a cement vault. Excited by what they heard, they reported it to Hall when he returned from Igloolik. According to Bayne, Hall was angry, objecting to what he considered to be their interference in his business. Bayne said that thereafter Hall's relations with the sailors deteriorated, and that he shot Coleman partly out of resentment at his meddling.[5]

Although it is plausible that the fiercely possessive Hall resented the sailors' assumption of what he considered his prerogative, the questioning of Eskimos, it is inconceivable that he would have killed one of them for that reason alone.

On the other hand, such resentment may have been one of many irritants that put him into a state of mind in which he was capable of murder. The journals of his first and second expeditions show that he had often been on the verge of violence—that he had often felt so threatened by other men that he anticipated the necessity of defending himself in a fight to the death. He had been in the Arctic four years straight, his plans constantly frustrated by Eskimos, whaling men, weather, and sickness; and the inactive summer of 1868 had allowed him time to brood about these frustrations and his failure to reach King William Island. Coleman undoubtedly threatened him, but the explanation of Coleman's death probably lies less in the threat than in the intensely suspicious nature of Hall's mind and the psychological ordeal that he was undergoing.

Only a few days after Coleman's death, two whaling ships arrived at Repulse Bay. The four surviving sailors immediately deserted Hall to sign aboard them, but Hall himself was determined to stay on for another year. He had come north to reach King William Island, and reach King William Island he would, with or without the assistance of other white men. When the whalers left after only a brief stay, Hall once again found himself alone with Eskimos, facing yet another winter of waiting.

The winter of 1868–9 passed quickly and easily. Hall's health was excellent, and his relations with the Eskimos remained surprisingly good; everyone kept busy doing more surveys of the Repulse Bay area and preparing for the spring sledge journey. Hall made painstaking preparations. Throughout the winter, he supervised the drying of caribou meat over blubber lamps; beginning with almost seven hundred pounds of fresh meat, by March he had one hundred seventy pounds of jerky, which he mixed with fat to make pemmican. He took his sledges on frequent trial runs, making whatever repairs and adjustments he thought necessary. Remembering the rumors about the hostility of the Pelly

Bay and Boothia Eskimos, he also prepared arms: shotguns,
rifles, pistols, bayonets, spears, and knives. He molded nearly
six hundred bullets.

On March 21 he made the following entry in one of his
small "traveling" notebooks:

> Now for King Williams Land. My party consists of:
> "Joe" and "Hannah" [Ebierbing and Tookoolito] my In-
> terpreters
> Punny their adopted daughter [They had adopted her sev-
> eral months after the death of King William.]
> Ouela
> "Jack" (Nukerzhoo) & his wife, who is the mother of Punny
> "Jerry" & his wife, having an infant in the Hood
> 11 souls in all including myself.

On the first leg he followed the route that he had taken
twice before to Cape Weynton, which, in spite of heavily
laden sledges and the usual foot-dragging of Eskimos, he
reached in only ten days. From Cape Weynton he cut northwest across Simpson Peninsula, reaching Pelly Bay on April
10. On its bleak shores, the Eskimos became nervous and,
anticipating their first meeting with the infamous Pelly Bay
natives, began to fondle their knives and guns. The next day,
far out on the bay ice, they came on an igloo, deserted but
recently inhabited; on the following afternoon they saw foot-
prints in the snow, then a small igloo village. One Eskimo
went ahead to make the first contact with the men in the
village while the rest of the party tensely waited.

Their fears were groundless. The few Pelly Bay natives who
were in the village greeted them warmly and welcomed them
into the igloos. As soon as they entered, Hall noticed various
objects lying about that were obviously from white men's
ships, including the broken point of a sword. When he asked
about these things, he was told that they were from Kikertak—King William Island. None of the natives in the village

had been there, but they all knew men who had been, including Tooshooarthario, the man who had helped Crozier and his two companions. Hall was told that he might find Tooshooarthario at King William Island, where the Eskimo was hunting.

After a few days Hall continued his journey across the bay and soon reached its west coast. He did not pause there, but pushed westward into the tundra of Boothia Peninsula. In spite of frequent stops for musk-ox hunting, he and his party made their way across eighty miles of tundra in ten days. On April 30 they reached the shores of the Polar Sea at Rae Strait. All that lay between Hall and King William Island was forty miles of sea ice; the journey that he had half dreaded, anticipating a terrible ordeal, had turned out to be easy, and the fulfillment of ten years of work lay ahead of him, just out of sight over the horizon.

As they were preparing to set out across the strait Ebierbing sighted another cluster of igloos. Nervous though the Eskimos were, Hall insisted on approaching it: living there would be natives who knew King William Island well. Probably some of them would have firsthand knowledge of the Franklin Expedition, and perhaps Tooshooarthario himself would be among them. Once again his party made a cautious approach; once again their fears proved groundless. Out of the igloos came men who, far from showing hostility, immediately mingled with Hall's Eskimos, greeting them boisterously. Tooshooarthario was not there (he was far away at Coronation Gulf), but within minutes Hall was shown a large silver spoon bearing Franklin's crest, and in the hours that followed he saw many other objects that had belonged to the Franklin Expedition. He noticed that when the inhabitants of the village helped his men build igloos, they used white men's knives. Several of the sledges in the village had runners made from the masts of a ship that, he was told, had sunk not far away. He was shown part of a mahogany writing desk that had been taken from the same ship before it had sunk. Scat-

tered around the area were other relics: pieces of copper
stamped with the broad arrow of the British Navy, the planks
and ribs of a boat, a pickle jar, the shreds of a handker-
chief.

That evening Innoopoozheejook, the leader of the village,
made a sketch map of King William Island and the surrounding area; in the days that followed, he pointed out
places where his people had found relics, and told stories
about them. He pointed out Keeweewoo (O'Reilly Island),
where the ship, either the *Erebus* or the *Terror,* had sunk
after drifting down with the ice from northern King William
Island. He told Hall that when the Eskimos had boarded it
for plunder, they had found the body of a very large kobluna
in one of the cabins. Ashore, near the place where the ship
had sunk, they had seen the tracks of other koblunas, apparently four of them, and of a dog. He also told Hall about
a large tent on the western shore of King William Island,
fifty miles to the north of where the ship had sunk:

> Three men first saw the tent. It had blankets, bedding & a
> great many skeleton bones—the flesh all off, nothing
> except sinews attached to them—the appearance as though
> foxes and wolves had gnawed the flesh off the bones. Some
> bones had been severed with a saw. Some skulls with holes
> in them. Besides the blankets, were tin cups, spoons, forks,
> knives, two double-barrel guns, pistols, lead balls, a great
> many powder flasks, and both books and papers written
> upon. As these last were good for nothing for Innuits, the
> men threw them away.

On the beach near the tent was a ship's boat. In it were more
skeletons and more papers. ("These papers are all trash to
Innuits. . . . The Innuits would trample them under feet as
if grass.")

On the mainland just to the south of King William Island,
Innoopoozheejook said, some Eskimos found another boat,
and near it a keg of gunpowder. They did not know what

gunpowder was at the time (McClintock and Rae had not yet paid their visits to the area), and two Eskimo boys soon succeeded in blowing up their family's igloo, terrifying every Eskimo in the area but miraculously not killing anyone.

Not far from the place where Innoopoozheejook and Hall talked, across the strait and just off the coast of King William Island, was Keeuna, one of the Todd Islands, on which Eskimos had found the remains of five koblunas. Four of them had been mutilated—their limbs sawed from their bodies, their flesh torn from their bones—but one, wrapped in a blanket, was untouched. Inexplicably, considering the obvious signs of cannibalism, an unopened tin of meat lay beside the unharmed body. On the mainland, close to the Islands, were other bodies.

Hearing all of this, Hall was eager to spend the summer on King William Island looking for other relics and possible documents. He had heard, either from Peter Bayne or firsthand from the Boothia Eskimo who had talked to Bayne, that near Point Victory was not only a cement vault supposedly containing the body of Sir John Franklin, but also another vault containing documents. Above all, now that he had virtually given up hope of finding survivors, Hall wanted to locate such documents. When he talked to his party about his plans, however, he was met with sullen refusal even from Ebierbing and Tookoolito. They said that they would cross over to King William Island with him, but would stay no longer than a week; the time for sledging was growing short, and they wanted to start back to Repulse Bay by mid-May. Hall argued with them. In a week he could accomplish almost nothing, and he certainly could not reach Point Victory, which was far away on the northwest side of the island. His party stubbornly insisted that they would desert him after a week. Hall was furious but he finally gave in to them, knowing that if he stayed there for the summer, he would not be able to return to Repulse Bay until the spring.

Innoopoozheejook accompanied them across the frozen

strait to the Todd Islands, which they reached on May 11. Hall immediately set everyone to work looking for bodies and relics, but the snow lay too deep. After hours of searching, all they found was part of a human thigh bone. The next day they made the short crossing to King William Island itself, where they searched an area in which Innoopoozheejook said there had been bodies. Late in the afternoon, at a place where the snow had been blown thin, they found a skeleton. Hall built a stone monument there and had his little group fire a salute as he raised an American flag on a pole. After wrestling with his conscience, he decided that it would be proper for him to take the bones and the skull back with him to civilization. More than a year later, in England, they were identified by a plug in one of the teeth: the skeleton was that of Lieutenant Le Vesconte of the *Erebus*.

For a week Hall wandered the dreary southeast coast of King William Island, a forlorn and discouraged man. At several places where the Eskimos said they had seen relics or bodies, he held ceremonies and built little monuments on the deep snow. It was all he could do. This was the conclusion of the great quest to which he had dedicated ten years of his life—a caretaking for the unfound dead.

On May 20, when Hall left the King William Island area to begin his long return journey to Repulse Bay, he was more than discouraged: he was embittered. During his three weeks with the Boothia Eskimos, he had discovered several things that appalled him. He finally faced the fact that not only had the Eskimos gathered relics from the ground at the various sites of the Franklin disaster, but they also had plundered the bodies of the dead men, on several occasions disinterring them to do so. Far worse than this, however, was his realization that they had given the lost and starving men from the *Erebus* and *Terror* almost no help. Two of the Eskimos in Innoopoozheejook's village, Tutkeeta and Owwer, had actually seen Crozier and many other men near Cape Herschel, on the southwest coast of King William Island.

The elusive Tooshooarthario and another Eskimo were with them at the time of the encounter. When Tutkeeta and Owwer first told Hall their story, he had the impression that the four Eskimo families had given the starving koblunas much food, "all the seal meat they had." They were, he noted in his pocket journal at the time, "noble, generous men." Just before he started on his return journey, he made them repeat the story several times, questioning them more closely than he had previously. The first part of the story was the same: when they first met the koblunas on the beach, they were approached by an officer, probably Crozier, who by gestures asked them to open their packs. They did, and the officer took out some seal meat, ate it, and waved his hands in the direction of the other koblunas. The Eskimos then passed out more meat to the starving men. They spent that night camped near the koblunas. It was when Hall questioned Tutkeeta and Owwer about what happened in the morning that he discovered something new. At daybreak, the Eskimos deliberately packed up and began to move out of the area. As they were leaving, the kobluna officer tried to stop them; he kept putting his hand in and out of his mouth, repeating the word "seal" over and over again. The Eskimos moved on past him, ignoring his pleas. Hall wrote in his journal:

> These 4 families could have saved Crozier's life & that of his company had they been so disposed. They could have led them to their stores of freshly deposited seals that were along the coast of K. W. Island—& could have sent word to the natives to contribute aid toward saving the starving men. But no, though noble Crozier pleaded with them, they would not stop even a day to try & catch seals—but early in the morning abandoned what they knew to be a large starving Company of white men.

Hall was in no mood to see that precisely because it was large, the company of starving koblunas constituted a danger to the Eskimos, who, themselves often on the verge of starvation, could not afford to feed many others. He persisted in his interrogation of Tutkeeta and Owwer—and the bottom dropped out. For several years he had depended, above all, on the stories that he had heard about Tooshooarthario's helping Crozier and two others: they had been his main evidence that there might possibly be survivors. He asked the two Eskimos if Tooshooarthario had ever seen the koblunas again after leaving them on the beach. They said that he had not. Hall was certain that they spoke the truth, and that all the other stories he had heard were legend. He knew then that his mission was ended. Also ended was whatever admiration he still had for the Eskimos as a race. That part of him that was flexible and understanding about "the noble children of the icy North" disappeared, and he became an inflexible missionary: "CIVILIZE, ENLIGHTEN & CHRISTIANIZE them & their race," he wrote bitterly in his journal. "Then we shall have no more such sad history to hear & write."

He retreated from King William Island in haste, as if from some crushing military defeat. With Innoopoozheejook as a guide, he did not even bother to keep careful track of his return route. The weather was fine, and the country they traveled through was rich with game; although this made the journey easy, Hall found irony in it: twenty years before, more than a hundred men had died of starvation and scurvy not far from where he was seeing herds of fat musk-ox and caribou. The return took exactly a month, and as the days passed his incurable optimism began to reassert itself. In spite of his bitter conclusions after hearing Tutkeeta and Owwer's story, he found himself again admiring the Eskimos' ability to live and travel in their land and enjoying their capacity for laughter, their moments of kindness. By the time they reached Repulse Bay, he was himself again, finding some good in what he had done and planning ahead for what he would do.

During the remaining six weeks that he spent in Repulse Bay, he joined the Eskimos in hunting and whaling, and he talked more to Innoopoozheejook about what had happened on King William Island. He began to prepare a report on his accomplishments for Henry Grinnell; he had, after all, learned new details about what had happened to the Franklin Expedition, and, the more he thought about it, the more fascinating that vault with documents in it appeared.* But, he decided, he would not return to King William Island on his next voyage; he would go all the way north—to the Pole itself.

On August 5 the *Ansell Gibbs,* out of New Bedford, arrived at Repulse Bay. On August 13, she sailed for home. Aboard were Hall, Ebierbing, and Tookoolito.

* King William Island has been visited occasionally by other expeditions since Hall left it in 1869, some of them looking for written records of the Franklin Expedition. Two expeditions in particular were able to conduct careful searches. In 1878 Lieutenant Frederick Schwatka led an expedition that examined the entire western coastline of the island, although concentrating on the area near Point Victory. (It should be noted that Schwatka was guided by Ebierbing, who, in spite of a vow that he would not go north again after Hall's death, apparently could not resist the temptation of one final expedition.) In 1967, under the name Project Franklin, members of Canada's armed forces, with the support of helicopters and other aircraft, thoroughly searched all areas of historical interest in King William Island and its environs. Neither expedition found any written records—or any cement vaults. Project Franklin's operation included diving off O'Reilly Island: no signs of a ship were found under the water, but on the northern beach of the island the diving team found copper sheeting, tin cans, a belaying pin, and other signs that a ship might have been wrecked nearby.

chapter six

Interim

Although by 1869 the public had lost much of its interest in the Franklin Expedition, Lady Franklin was still haunted by a need to know more about what had happened on King William Island in 1847–8. She knew from the Point Victory message found by McClintock that her husband had died on June 11, 1847, but that was all she knew about his fate. She had not given up hope that somewhere in a cairn were documents, which, for better or worse, would fill in unknown details. In newspapers she had read Hall's occasional dispatches from the barrens, and she had heard rumors spread by whalers returning from northern Hudson's Bay that he was making extraordinary discoveries. She hoped that when he returned he would have not only new information, but possibly papers as well.

In August 1869 she wrote to Henry Grinnell from London, asking if there was any news from Hall. Grinnell replied that there was none and added that Mrs. Hall was in financial need. Lady Franklin replied immediately, offering fifteen pounds to Mrs. Hall as a gift. In mid-September Grinnell wrote to say that Mrs. Hall had refused the money, and that they had little hope that Hall would return that year, because whaling ships still in the Arctic would probably be wintered in. Much to Grinnell's surprise, Hall landed in New Bedford on September 26, only a few days after he had written this letter. Soon Lady Franklin also knew of his return and wired Grinnell to ask if he had found any journals or cairn messages. Grinnell replied with a one-word cable: "None."[1]

By the time Grinnell sent this discouraging wire to Lady Franklin, he knew that Hall had formed new plans and no longer would devote himself to solving the mystery of the Franklin Expedition. For several years Hall had confided his ambition to reach the North Pole only to his journal; now, with his beloved patron as an audience, he poured out his hopes with characteristic intensity and energy. The rhetoric that he used on Grinnell can be inferred from a letter that he wrote in November accepting an invitation to lecture in Cincinnati:

> There is a great, sad blot upon the present age which ought to be wiped out, & this is the blank on our maps & artificial globes from about the parallel of 80° North up to the North Pole. I, for one, hang my head in shame when I think how many thousands of years ago it was that God gave to man this beautiful world—the whole of it—to subdue, & yet that part of it that must be most interesting and glorious—at least so to me—remains as unknown to us as though it had never been created. Having now completed my Arctic Collegiate education, I feel to spend my life in extending our knowledge of the earth up to that spot which is directly under Polaris—the crowning jewel of the Arctic dome.

Although Grinnell apparently listened sympathetically, he must have thought to himself, "Here we go again."

This time Hall's ambitions knew no bounds. The war was over, and he seemed to believe that the government was obligated to spend massive sums of money on Arctic exploration. He planned to raise funds himself as he had in the past, lecturing and perhaps writing another book, but, as he told Grinnell, he also expected that the government would be eager to support a north polar expedition. He would go to Cincinnati to see his wife and children and to deliver some lectures, then return East and as soon as possible go to Washington. There he would buttonhole Representatives, Sen-

ators, members of the Cabinet, the President himself. He
would lobby relentlessly for a north polar expedition.

Early in November Hall traveled to Cincinnati as he had
planned, taking Ebierbing, Tookoolito, and little Punnie
with him. There he stayed for a month and a half, presumably
with his wife and his children, although he did not mention
them in his letters. Cincinnati welcomed her now-famous son
enthusiastically, making him the subject of innumerable
newspaper articles and crowding his many lectures. The
only untoward event of his stay seems to have been the loss
of one of his priceless Franklin relics during one of the
lectures—a knife that he had found on King William Island.

While he was in Cincinnati, Lady Franklin, through the
Grinnells, began applying pressure on him to postpone his
north polar venture. Before leaving New York Hall had written a special report for her on his findings, which Henry
Grinnell had sent to London. In reply, she wrote Grinnell a
long letter, in which she expressed her discontent with the
incompleteness of the report and also her hopes that Hall
could be persuaded to go back to King William Island in
the summer of 1870. Her letter was full of questions:

> My own impression is that Hall has done his best with the
> means that he had at his command; but his statement is
> full of omissions, and so devoid of order and dates as to
> leave much confusion and perplexity in the mind. He
> makes no distinction between the places he visited him-
> self & what he saw himself, and what he only heard of.
> What are the places he really set foot on in K. W. Land,
> and the dates on which he did so? Did he merely touch
> the Eastern Shore, or did he go along the Southern Coast
> by Cape Herschel and visit the other places where he says
> they finally perished?

In particular, her attention had been caught by Hall's reference to a vault containing documents:

Who was his authority for saying that the records are
buried in a vault (that is, I suppose, a hole dug for the
purpose) near Point Victory? Could the Esquimaux point
out the exact spot, and if so can we believe that they have
not opened or rifled it? Was this question put to them,
and is there reason to suppose that these documents may
yet exist in part in their possession?

She concluded with the crucial question:

I would ask you to ascertain from him whether he would
postpone his efforts to reach the Pole for one more season
(he may be quite sure there is no danger of anybody getting
there before him) and devote a whole summer to the recovery of the precious documents on King William Island
and the several adjoining places on the mainland where he
believes the last of our poor people perished.

In passing, she implied that a British officer might go as well
and hoped that "Mr. Hall would be willing to forgo the
chief command in order to act as co-adjutor."

Grinnell forwarded her letter to Cincinnati, but Hall did
not respond for several weeks. Then, on December 14 he
scrawled a rapid note:

Mr. Grinnell
Dear Sir:
Time & again have I taken in hand the subject matter of
Lady Franklin's letter for the object of giving full answer
to it, but in vain. I can say in truth that ever since my
arrival in this country . . . I have not had two (2) hours to
myself by which I could sit down & not be interrupted
many times. I despair at present of getting the time to
answer (as I would like) the letter referred to, for I am
busily flying here and there on Lecture tours. Lecturing
is a curse to my soul. . . .

He was determined to push for his north polar venture, he
wrote, but if Congress did not cooperate and he had trouble

getting money, then he should "do whatever I could to favor personally the noble aspirations of Lady Franklin." He had noted her implication that a British officer might be involved as well, however, and his response was characteristic:

> Let it be said here that no one should ask of me to accept a subordinate position in an ARCTIC EXPEDITION. If McClintock & myself be Lady Franklin's chosen ones, we could be CO-COMMANDERS & nothing less.

Lady Franklin had obviously intended to suggest such a co-command, and she had not specified McClintock (although she had mentioned him in the letter in an entirely different context), but Hall was touchy on the subject and was going to take no chances that his position might be misunderstood: he would serve under no one.

Although Hall left open the possibility that he might go back to King William Island in 1870, his heart was set on the North Pole. Late in December he returned to the East Coast. His destination was Washington, but before going there he paid a visit to Sidney and Sarah Budington in Groton, apparently wanting to renew his friendship with them. He had exchanged conciliatory letters with Mrs. Budington before leaving for Hudson's Bay, but now he made a greater effort to repair the damages of the quarrel, perhaps because Ebierbing and Tookoolito admired the Budingtons and wanted to see them again. On October 3 he wrote to Mrs. Budington:

> Long—long indeed has it been since you & your husband have heard direct from myself, Joe & Hannah, but this has not been because we have at any time forgotten you, for not many days have passed during our long absence in the North but we have thought and spoken of Capt. Sidney O. Budington & his wife. So far as my poor heart is concerned, I let by-gones be by-gones, & therefore I keep in mind only that Capt. Budington & I have been strong friends & hope that the same still continues.

His visit to the Budingtons was a success. As in the past, Ebierbing and Tookoolito stayed on with them when he left for New York early in January; considering that his quarrel with Budington had started over the Eskimos, Hall's leaving them in Groton was a significant act of trust, probably intended to be a symbol of his renewed friendship. In mid-January Ebierbing and Tookoolito rejoined him to make their always popular appearances at some lectures that he delivered in Pennsylvania and Ohio. Then they went with him to Washington.

When Hall arrived in Washington on January 30, he wasted no time. Immediately he began to hustle about the city, seeing old friends and meeting men who might take up his cause. Colonel James Lupton, one of his early backers in Cincinnati, was now working in the Patent Office; Lupton greeted him warmly, promised assistance, and introduced him to Senator Sherman and Congressman Stevenson of Ohio. The legislators agreed to help in a most important way: they would promote a bill in Congress. Then, only four days after his arrival in the capital, he and the Eskimos called on President Grant. Grant seemed interested in Hall's project and surprised him by displaying a considerable knowledge of Arctic exploration. Short as the interview was, Hall was very much encouraged. "So far as I know," he wrote Grinnell on the evening after he had met Grant, "my prospects are fair for my North Pole Expedition. This month will settle the point whether I am to get Congressional aid or not."

Inexperienced in the mills of government, Hall underestimated their slowness. More than a month would pass before his project was even introduced to Congress—and many months before it worked its way through the mazes of the legislature to the President's desk. In the meantime, all he could do was promote himself and his plans by any means at his disposal. Using letters from his old friends in New York and Cincinnati, he continued to meet members of Congress and the administration, and aroused enough interest to be asked to deliver a lecture at Lincoln Hall. Many Washington dignitaries, including President Grant himself, would be there.

During February, while he prepared the lecture, Mrs. Hall and young Charles (now about ten years old) went to Washington from Cincinnati to see him. Hall seldom mentioned his wife and children in letters or journals, so his relatively lengthy reference to them in a letter to Grinnell is surprising, especially because it implied an unexpected respect for Mrs. Hall's opinions:

> Your kind letter of the 16th inst. came at hand the same day Mrs. Hall & Charley arrived here. I am glad to say that on canvassing the whole matter in relation to my proposed North Pole Expedition with Mrs. H., she concluded that it is best for me to fulfill the mission to which my whole soul is so warmly attached, if I am satisfied that I cannot settle down here in the States until I make the geographical discovery from the 80° par. up the N. Pole. I thank her for this and am sure all lovers of Arctic discovery will too—for it shows that she is willing to make great sacrifices—indeed the greatest of all—for the cause of Geography and Science. Mrs. H & Charley leave here tonight for N.Y. thence they go to Cincinnati O.

One wonders what would have happened if, when "canvassed," Mrs. Hall had had the temerity to suggest that her husband stay at home for a change. Little Charley had seen his father a total of three months in ten years.

The lecture at Lincoln Hall, delivered on March 7, was popular. Hall wrote to Grinnell that the house was crowded and that he received many congratulations. President Grant and Vice-President Colfax sat directly in front of the podium, smiling and nodding their approval. "When I expressed my wish that the $100,000 I was about to ask from Congress, by which to fit out an Arctic Exploring party, should be placed in the hands of the President for disbursement, the house came down with great good cheers."

At this time, Hall hoped for a hundred thousand dollars because he planned to have two ships. His plan was to sail north in Baffin Bay to Jones Sound, a narrow waterway that cut westward just north of and parallel to Lancaster Sound. He had decided against trying to retrace the route of Kane and Hayes up Smith Sound, apparently because of their final failure. He was determined to make his try for the Pole even if Congress did not vote an appropriation, and told Grinnell that if worst came to worst, he would ask the Navy simply to drop him ashore on Ellesmere Island (or Ellesmere Land, as it was then known) as far north as they could get him, a suicidal plan.

On March 8 Congressman Stevenson read a joint resolution before the House:

JOINT RESOLUTION
Relative to a voyage to the Arctic Regions

Whereas Captain C. F. Hall is an enterprising and experienced explorer who has made two successful voyages in the Arctic regions, and whereas he desires in the interest of science and for the material advantage of his country to make a voyage of exploration and discovery under the authority and for the benefit of the United States: Therefore,

Be it resolved by the Senate and House of Representatives of the United States of America in Congress assembled, That the President be, and he is hereby, authorized to furnish a naval or other steamer and, if necessary, a tender for a voyage into the Arctic regions under the control of Captain C. F. Hall.

And be it further resolved, That the sum of one hundred thousand dollars be, and the same is hereby, appropriated out of any funds in the treasury not otherwise appropriated by law, which sum, or so much thereof as may be requisite, shall be paid out on the order and expended under the direction of the President in paying the proper and necessary expenses of said journey.

Hall had no claim to the title of "Captain"; it was at best honorific, but it was to stick, and thenceforth he was known by it.

The resolution was referred to the Committee on Appropriations. On March 25 Senator Sherman read the same resolution before the Senate, and there it was referred to the Committee on Foreign Relations. Hall's proposal had entered the mills, but by now he knew that the grinding was just beginning. He asked Grinnell, Brevoort, Lupton, Budington, anyone he could talk or write to, to help him apply the pressures that could be effective in Washington. He was becoming wise in the ways of the capital.

Hall arranged to meet the chairmen of the Appropriations Committee and the Committee on Foreign Relations, as well as the secretaries of the Interior and the Navy. He wangled "memorials," statements backing him and his plans, out of the governors of Massachusetts and Ohio and out of many rich and powerful citizens. He haunted the anterooms of Congress, talking and listening. "I heard yesterday," he wrote Grinnell on March 15, "that a prominent Democrat (one of the leaders of the House) had said to a friend of the Enterprise that the Democrats were all going in favor of it." (From this rumor he drew a political moral: "This then shows that Republicans & Democrats can join hands in one cause at least—that of an Expedition for Arctic discovery & science.")

He marshaled arguments for his cause in a long letter to the Senate Committee on Foreign Relations. First, he outlined his own career as an explorer, concluding, "Neither glory nor money has caused me to devote my very life and soul to Arctic Exploration. My desire is to promote the welfare of mankind in general under this glorious ensign—the stars and stripes." He referred to previous American ventures in

the Arctic, bemoaned how few they had been, and appealed
to the patriotism of the Senators on the committee by outlining the past dependence of the United States on knowledge of the Arctic gleaned by other countries, England in
particular:

> The English and other governments of the Old World,
> time and time again had sent out Expeditions for discovery,
> for enriching science, and for the promotion of Commerce.
> The only charts of the known world in the hands of our
> navigators were all foreign. We were reaping the benefits,
> and are now, of charts that cost treasure, toil, exposure,
> life on life, without so much as giving a thought of or a
> thanks to the authors in the Old World. The whole
> Arctic coast of the Continent of North America from
> Bering Strait to Labrador, has been discovered, explored
> and surveyed by the English Government, except the little
> that remained for me to complete, which I did in 1868.

While on the theme of patriotism, he made the transition to his main practical argument, the commercial. "To
whom are we indebted for all our Arctic whaling grounds,
from which our country is getting millions of dollars worth
of whalebone and oil every year?" he asked. "The answer is
TO THE ENGLISH!" His explorations on his next voyage
would open up new whaling grounds, and whaling was a
most lucrative business. He quoted from a Senate report
of 1852 to show how lucrative it had been. The report
concluded that the English, during the search for Franklin,
had opened up waters north of the Bering Strait which
yielded American whalers more than eight million dollars
in two years. Hall then narrowed his focus in a clever argument:

> In 1867 Capt. J. B. Winslow in the Bark *Tamerlane* cap-
> tured a whale in the Arctic sea that yielded three hundred
> and ten barrels and nineteen gallons. The value of the
> whale (oil and bone) was not far from twenty thousand

dollars. Surely Dr. Franklin was sagacious when he wrote, "He who draws a fish out of the sea, draws out a piece of silver." It would take seven whales like that of Capt. Winslow to pay the whole expense of my proposed five years' Arctic voyage.

Wisely, Hall decided against using an argument that he toyed with in the rough notes he made while preparing his letter, an argument apparently too farfetched to convince even himself. In these notes, he speculated that a colony might be established at the North Pole—even that the North Pole might become a second Australia.

Just as Hall was becoming confident that the way ahead was smooth and open, an obstacle loomed up. Out of his past emerged one of his *bêtes noires*, the antagonist who had almost aborted his first expedition by stealing his ship's captain. Doctor Isaac Hayes suddenly arrived in Washington and appeared before the Committee on Foreign Relations to argue that an expedition he was planning deserved government backing more than Hall's. Momentarily transfixed with outraged disbelief, Hall soon set furiously to work, all his combative instincts reawakened: he would fight and overcome this imposter, this Anti-Christ.

He went to the Library of Congress, where he found Hayes's book on his expedition of 1860–1, *The Open Polar Sea*. (This was the expedition that Hall, then still unknown and inexperienced, had volunteered to join before beginning to work on his own first expedition.) Hall combed through the book, checking the navigational data, looking for discrepancies. He was unable to find evidence of cheating, but, using the time-distance figures in the book, he was able to prove, at least to his own satisfaction, that Hayes was an inexcusably slow sledge traveler. He also spent hours taking notes on other arguments that he would use against Hayes in the Committee on Foreign Affairs. Except for a brief cruise to Baffin Bay with the painter William Bradford, Hayes had not been in the Arctic for ten years. Hall had announced his intention to mount a north polar expedition as soon as he had returned from an arduous five-year stay in the Arctic. Hayes, who had had available ten free years to work on an expedition, was simply jumping on a bandwagon that Hall had started moving by his own hard labor.

On April 14 Hall, knowing that Hayes had appeared a few weeks before him, appeared before the Committee on Foreign Relations. Hall used all the arguments he could muster to defend his qualifications and to assert the priority of his expedition over Hayes's. By innuendo, Hayes had attacked his most vulnerable weakness, his lack of formal scientific training. Hall first tried to deflect the attack with heavy sarcasm: "I confess I am not a 'scientific' man. Who will dispute the presumption that Dr. Hayes is? Let us all bow to his presumption that he is the savan of the world." Far more convincing was his argument based on his considerable knowledge of the history of Arctic exploration:

> No, I am not a scientific man. Discoverers seldom have been. Arctic discoverers—all except Dr. Hayes—have not been scientific men. Neither Sir John Franklin nor Sir Edward Parry were of this class & yet they loved science & did much to enlarge her fruitful fields. Frobisher, Davis, Baffin, Bylot, Hudson, Fox, James, Kane, Back, McClintock, Osborn, Dease and Simpson, Rae, Ross and a host of other Arctic explorers were not scientific men.

Although his argument was basically sound, one name on his list could have been used against him: his idol Elisha Kent Kane had been very much a "scientific man."

The three months that followed Hall's appearance before the committee were agonizing for him. Hayes had succeeded in persuading the committee to strike Hall's name from the resolution, leaving the commander nameless. Hall was assured that in fact he was still the prime candidate, but a seed of doubt had been planted; although he continued to act on the assumption that he would be the man chosen, he knew that the assumption could be wrong. Hayes also had delayed action on the bill. Hall persisted in his belief that if the legislators would act with even moderate speed, he could set sail that summer, but as the weeks passed they did not act. Hall's letters to Grinnell and Budington vacillated between hope and despair. Years later, Senator J. W. Patterson of New Hampshire, who had helped him from the beginning, described him during this period: "While the appropriation was pending and under discussion, the Captain seemed like one watching with a sick friend who hangs between life and death."

On May 16, confident that action was imminent, he requested Grinnell to inquire about the availability of steamers in New York and New London. His confidence seemed justified when the Committee on Foreign Relations reported the Arctic Resolution and introduced it to the Senate as an amendment to the general appropriations bill. Hall was to describe what followed as a "triumph," but the word was perhaps a little strong. The Senate indeed passed the bill, but the vote was a tie broken only when Vice President Colfax voted in favor.

The Senate having acted, the Committee on Appropriations and the House remained between Hall and the fulfillment of his desires. He was still confident because, as he wrote Grinnell, the chairman of the Appropriations Committee, Daws of Massachusetts, "is a warm friend of my enterprise." As far as Hall was concerned, all national politics boiled down to one thing, the Arctic. "Although Mr. Daws is a Republican & you a Democrat," he wrote Grinnell, "yet because he is so true & strong a friend to the Arctic cause to which you have been so many years devoted, you ought in fact to agree with me in thinking that he ought to be our next President."

Friendly as Daws was to the "cause," he alone could not push Hall's resolution through the committee. June passed, and no action was taken. Hall called the delay "vexatious" for more reasons than one. Some of the plans that he had carefully laid were being undermined as time passed, and his hopes that he would be able to set out in the summer of 1870 were fast withering. Trouble was in the air. In the spring Ebierbing and Tookoolito had gone to Groton to stay with the Budingtons. Early in June Budington notified Hall that one of the whaling captains in the area was trying to persuade Ebierbing to join him on a cruise. Hall rushed to Groton and managed to argue the Eskimos out of going with the whaler, but, not trusting their capacity to resist further temptation, he took them to New York to stay with the Grinnells for a time. New York offered only another kind of temptation: Ebierbing began to drink heavily. Clearly the Eskimos, yearning for the Arctic, would cause further trouble unless he could get them north quickly.

Even more serious was the bad news that he received from Budington in mid-June. Their friendship renewed, Hall had offered him command of the expedition ship, which Budington had accepted with enthusiasm. As the Committee on Appropriations continued to delay, however, Budington, if not Hall, had to face the probability that the expedition would not leave that summer. He had a living to make, and when he was offered command of a whaler for a July cruise, he accepted. Instead of blowing up with rage as he would have done in the past, Hall seemed to understand why Budington had made his decision, although he did try to persuade him to change his mind. He wrote him a letter one hot day while sitting on a "fanciful cast iron settee bench" under the shade of a tree in East Capitol Park. His hotel room, he explained in the letter, was unbearable during the day, and he returned to it only late at night when it had cooled. He spent all of his days wandering in and around the Capitol Building, nervously waiting for action on his resolution. "I long to have you with me on my North Pole Expedition," he wrote, coming to the point:

If in all honor, right & justice it could be so arranged that
you could be released so as to go with me, I should be delighted. WE ARE BROTHERS, having seen storm as well as
sunshine together, & therefore we should go to that part
of the world together that no white man has ever been
able to reach, to the North Pole.

At the end of the letter, he added a postscript: "God bless
you, Capt. B. May we meet many times yet on earth, but at
least a final meeting in Heaven may we have."

When Budington persisted in his decision, Hall still was
not offended, sign of a growing maturity and self-control
that were to be evident in the short remainder of his life.
As his dream-expedition approached reality, he seemed to
know that his driving energy would no longer suffice for
success—that he had to learn to deal patiently with other
men.

On July 2 the Appropriations Committee acted. Hall had
been in the corridors all day. Late in the afternoon he saw
the clerk of the committee, Mr. Stevens, leaving the conference room, and he approached him. The clerk said nothing
but passed him a note that simply read: "North Pole $50,000."
It was one half the sum passed by the Senate, but Hall had
been prepared to expect such a cut. He was overjoyed and
that evening wrote:

> Never shall I forget you, Mr. Stevens, & this moment.
> Months, years of anxiety now ended at the instant my eyes
> caught the underscored words. My hand seized Mr. S's hand
> & I think it quite likely not only his hand but his whole
> living temple got a grand shaking up.

Hall immediately left the Capitol Building to send a
wire to Grinnell. Then he went around Washington in a
happy daze, breaking the news to everyone he could find
who had helped. All of the scenes were as operatic as the
one that he had with Lupton:

As I entered with my arm raised vertical over my head, finger pointed to the zenith & my eyes directed in the same way, I said NORTH STAR! Instantly friend Lupton caught the significance, seized my hand & was like myself filled with inexpressible joy.

The final passage of the bill by the Senate and House was an anticlimax. When it went into the Conference Committee, all agreed on the sum of fifty thousand dollars; on July 9 the Senate and House finally confirmed the decision. One sour note was briefly sounded for Hall. After the bill passed, Congressman Daws told him that some friends of Isaac Hayes were passing around a petition that Hayes be put in command of the expedition. But Daws assured him that the petition would fail, and it did.

The act was approved by President Grant on July 12. Eight days later, Lupton sent Hall his official appointment as commander:

EXECUTIVE MANSION
Washington, D.C., July 20, 1870

DEAR SIR: You are hereby appointed to command the expedition towards the North Pole, to be organized and sent out pursuant to an act of Congress approved July 12, 1870, and will report to the Secretary of the Navy and the Secretary of the Interior for detailed instructions.

U. S. GRANT

Even in the joy of his accomplishment, Hall finally realized that he could not mount his expedition in time to leave that summer. Impatient as he was, he knew that he would have to bear almost a year of slow, complicated preparation, so he decided that he would pay a brief visit to his family in Cincinnati before setting to work. In mid-July, he went home.

During Hall's stay in Washington Lady Franklin had been maintaining correspondence with the Grinnells, not only in an endeavor to gain more information from Hall, but also in the continued hope that she could persuade him to postpone his North Pole expedition. An inveterate traveler, she had decided that she would go on a tour of the United States in the spring and summer of 1870, with the main practical purpose of seeing Hall and talking to him personally. Francis Leopold McClintock did not encourage her; he distrusted Hall's exuberance and his facts. "I do not see what Lady F. can want to see Hall for," he wrote to her niece, Sophia Cracroft. "His report has been moderate for *him* [McClintock's italics] & I think he is better left alone."[2] She was determined to see him, however, and after a long trip through western United States she finally met him late in July, in Cincinnati.

The city was enthusiastic about her visit. The *Daily Gazette* ran a large headline over its story: THE MOST DISTINGUISHED WOMAN OF HER TIME." Quibblers might submit the name of Queen Victoria for the title, but Cincinnati was too pleased to quibble. Lady Franklin certainly was *one* of the most distinguished women of her time, and she had come to see one of Cincinnati's residents—not one of its rich industrialists or powerful political figures, but one of its common folk who had become famous. Flattered for Hall, the city also was delighted with Lady Franklin herself. She was old, but she was still energetic and clearheaded. The *Gazette* noted that she was "a woman who had hoped when others sunk discouraged, who, with unwearying energy and unflagging devotion with her means and influence for twenty years, sought for her lost husband, encouraging enterprise in Europe and America, in search of tidings of the missing explorer, with her voice, pen and purse." It praised her "full, kindly English face, sprightly, cheery manner and freedom in conversation."[3]

She stayed at the elegant Burnet House, and one day she held a reception there for anyone who wished to see her. The *Gazette* pointed out that this was unusual: "This she has refused to do everywhere else, though frequently solicited, but consents here as a recognition of the services of our fellow townsman, Capt. C. F. Hall."[4] The next day she and Hall went across the river to Covington, where they paid a visit to President Grant's aged parents. During most of her stay, however, she and Hall were closeted alone, talking about his discoveries and the possibility of other discoveries yet to come. Unfortunately, there is no record of the conversations; Lady Franklin herself did not describe them in her letters, and Hall kept no journal during this period. Apparently Hall assured her that he would make another journey to King William Island, but only after completing his expedition to the Pole. His assurances could not have been very satisfying for Lady Franklin; she was almost eighty.

She left Cincinnati for the East after a stay of four days, and Hall himself followed her a week after she left: he not only had to begin organizing his expedition, but because the government would not begin paying him for some time, he also had to arrange more lectures. Already in debt to Grinnell, who had been sending him frequent one-hundred-dollar checks, he was forced to borrow more from him in order to keep going. By this time in his career, accustomed to living hand-to-mouth, Hall borrowed without any sense of shame—in fact, he borrowed for others as well as for himself. When Frank Lailer asked Hall for money, Hall simply borrowed from Grinnell to lend to Lailer; when Ebierbing and Tookoolito decided to buy some land in Groton, he again borrowed from Grinnell to get the money. The fifty-thousand-dollar appropriation seemed to have little effect on Hall's way of life.

His most important initial task in organizing his expedition was to find and hire the best available officers. The government, the Navy Department in particular, helped in the search, but Hall insisted that he be consulted and have the right of veto. He also reserved the right to make the most important appointment of all—that of ship's captain.

Budington would have been his first choice, but Budington was off on what was supposed to be a year's whaling cruise, so apparently sometime in the autumn Hall went to Groton and offered the command of his ship to Captain George Tyson. In view of later events, it is interesting to note that we have only Tyson's word for this, and in none of Hall's letters or notes does he mention making him the offer. But it is plausible that he did so, because Tyson was almost as experienced in Arctic navigation as Budington, and Hall had known Tyson as long as he had known Budington, if not as well. He had met Tyson on his first visit to Groton in 1859, then had seen him at Frobisher Bay, when Tyson had arrived with the *Georgiana,* and then again, frequently, in northern Hudson's Bay during his second expedition. He knew the man to be reliable and resourceful. According to Tyson, when Hall offered him the captaincy, he was forced to refuse it because he had committed himself to a whaling cruise for the summer of 1871.

Hall's problem was solved when Budington unexpectedly arrived back at New London, his cruise cut short by un- usually heavy ice in Davis Strait. After brief consultation with him, Hall offered him the post, and he accepted. Pleased as Hall was at Budington's return, however, he also took note of its ominous cause. Other whalers also reported that the ice in the North was the worst in years, and Hall knew Arctic history well enough to realize that luck would be an important element in his expedition, especially luck with weather and ice.

Another important post to be filled was that of Chief Scien- tist. Although the primary purpose of the expedition was to reach the North Pole, close scientific observations were to be made along the way for the National Academy of Sciences and the Smithsonian Institution. From the begin- ning Hall was uneasy about this aspect of his venture, per- haps because his lack of training in the sciences had been used against him by Hayes and he had become self-conscious about it. The Smithsonian and the National Academy of Sciences had been given virtual charge of scientific matters, including the appointment of scientific personnel, but Hall, wishing to keep all aspects of the expedition under his control, soon began to interfere. During Lady Franklin's conversations with him in Cincinnati, she mentioned that Doctor David Walker, who had been Surgeon-Naturalist aboard the *Fox* (McClintock's ship) in 1857–8, and who was living in San Francisco, had told her that he wanted to go north again. Hall asked Lady Franklin to write to Walker suggesting that Walker write to him, and in late August he received a letter. Walker was eager to join the expedition, so eager that he wrote his letter on the very day that he received Lady Franklin's note. He summarized his experience in the Arctic, concluding that "no one on this Continent has made Arctic Research, in its scientific branches, a deeper study than I have."[5] He had been serving in the United States Army with units engaged in Indian fighting, and so was in excellent physical condition. His credentials were well known, he said, as Hall would discover if he asked at the Smithsonian.

Hall wrote to Secretary Spencer Baird of the Smithsonian, enclosing Walker's letter and urging his appointment as Chief Scientist. Hall was becoming shrewd in argument, and he noted that Walker's appointment might well save money. Because the doctor was still in the Army, the President could simply detail him to the expedition, and his regular Army pay would be his salary, not a penny being drawn from the appropriation. In this letter, Hall also seemed to try a little bribery: he mentioned that he was thinking of giving his Franklin and Frobisher relics to the Smithsonian, dangling them in front of Baird like so much bait. Probably the bait was not needed. Walker was highly qualified, and Hall's idea of using his Army pay as salary was appealing; apparently Baird began negotiations with Walker soon after hearing from Hall.

Hall had been away from Washington for almost three

months, and by early November he knew that it was time to
return. He had to consult with the Navy Department about
his ship and crew, and with the Academy of Sciences and the
Smithsonian about their plans for scientific activity. He also
was worried about his budget; the fifty thousand dollars that
at first had seemed a huge sum seemed much smaller as he
began to brood about expenses.

Soon after Hall arrived in Washington, he saw his ship for
the first time. The Navy had selected the *Periwinkle*, a steam
tug of 387 tons burden. She was as yet entirely unprepared for
Arctic navigation, and was at best an unprepossessing scow,
but to Hall she was beautiful. He saw her in the Washington
Navy Yard, where rebuilding work was about to begin.
Winter and spring would be spent preparing the ship for the
ordeal by ice that she would have to endure. She was to be
virtually dismembered; new timbers were to be installed
inside and out; she was to be calked and coppered, replanked
and rerigged. The shaft, the propeller well, the propeller itself, all particularly vulnerable in Arctic waters, were to be
strengthened, and special cabin heating was to be supplied.
After seeing her awaiting transformation, Hall decided to
change her name to the *Polar World*—then, on further
thought, simply to the *Polaris*.

Seeing his ship was pure pleasure; less pleasurable was the
task of solving the problem of the budget. The Secretary of
the Navy, George Robeson, already was requesting that funds
be supplied from the appropriation to pay for the work on the
Polaris. Hall hoped to persuade the President to insist that
the Navy rebuild and even outfit the ship at its own expense,
but, much to his surprise, another, better solution to the problem was found. Quietly, almost covertly, the Committee on
Appropriations informed him that it would guarantee work
on the ship up to the sum of fifty thousand dollars beyond the
amount already authorized. Unofficially the appropriation was
back to one hundred thousand dollars, although he was told
that it behooved him not to spend the full amount.

On February 9 Hall wrote an exuberant letter to Budington. All was well. "A triumph, I trust, awaits the U. S. Polar Expedition!" He described the work on the ship for its future captain:

> A full force of hands are at work on her. It would make your ears tingle prettily to hear the busy, varied hum of a hundred or so of mechanics working like bees on and about the vessel. Mr. Delano, U. S. Naval Constructor of the Brooklyn Navy Yard, comes here every two weeks to see that everything is going right about the vessel & to lay out work. He has furnished me complete plans of the vessel as he proposes to have her when done. I am very much in love with it.

He described the rigging, the auxiliary engine, the spare propeller screw, the "ponderous Ice-chisel—of cast metal— to extend from keel up to a considerable way above the water line," the watertight compartment to be installed behind the bow. "There is a determination to have everything done right. There is no desire in Uncle Sam to give bad material or poor work to his Arctic devoted Sons."

Another reason for delight, Hall told Budington, was that negotiations with Doctor Walker were going well. Joseph Henry of the Academy of Sciences, Baird of the Smithsonian, the Secretary of the Navy, and the Surgeon-General of the Army all thought that Walker was probably the right man to be Chief Scientist. The Surgeon-General had arranged to have Walker ordered from San Francisco to Washington. "Of course this is a job well done," wrote Hall. The man, after all, was his own candidate.

A minor triumph Hall described for Budington was a meeting with President Grant:

> Yesterday I had the delight to shake hands with the President. The meeting was altogether unexpected. I was standing in the midst of a great crowd in the vestibule of the Execu-

tive Mansion looking intently at the passing company of
Washington Policemen. The President as it were was re-
viewing them. When through, his eye happened to spy me
in the midst of the crowd about him, when he instantly
with bowing head said, "Captain," & soon after, when
distance and human beings between us became less, the
President & this humble writer shook hands, he saying,
"I believe the Arctic Expedition is getting along well." Of
course, I said yes to this.

Finally, Hall looked ahead to the summer, treating Budington to a preview of their departure: "The whole Expedition
will be fitted out here—& will sail from here, the National
Capital—so you can prepare yourself for having a <u>high</u> time
—taking the President & all Washington aboard the North
Polar vessel & steaming down the Potomac—bound for the
far North."

At some time during the winter, Hall had his photograph
taken with three men who had helped him in Washington
from the beginning: Colonel James Lupton, Penn Clarke,
who was chief clerk of the Department of the Interior, and
Paymaster of the Army T. H. Stanton. Long afterward,
Clarke wrote a letter describing Hall and discussing the
photograph:

> Hall was heart and soul devoted to the Arctic. It formed
> his conversation by day, and, I doubt not, was the substance
> of his dreams by night. He appeared to me to have been
> specially created for the work and was sanguine of success.
> If ever a man had a mission upon earth, it was Hall's to go
> in pursuit of the North Pole, and if his life had been
> spared, I have little doubt he would have accomplished
> his work.

Clarke went on to call Hall "a singularly modest man" who
"had a great aversion to seeing his likeness in the papers."[6]
Clarke believed that he was destined for fame, however, and

insisted that he be photographed. Hall finally agreed, but only with the provision that Clarke, Lupton, and Stanton, his "council," also be in the photograph. The photograph shows the three men beside Hall, who sits in the center. Behind them hangs a picture of the *Polaris*. Hall's thick beard conceals his chinline and mouth, leaving only his eyes as an indication of his character; they are small and have an oddly humorous squint. Verbal descriptions of him all suggest that he was strong and stocky. He is seated and is shown only from the waist up in the photograph, but one can see that his shoulders are broad and powerful. His clothing is rumpled, careless. There is a bearlike quality in the image.

In his letter, Clarke gives another reason for his insistence that Hall be photographed, a reason that he did not give to Hall. "I was early impressed with the idea that Hall would fall a victim to his zeal and not live to return," Clarke wrote. "Feeling a presentiment that he would never return, I pressed the matter on him a number of times." It is well that Clarke pressed the matter: the picture of Hall is the only photograph that we have of him, and the engraved portrait that appeared in books after his death was taken from it.

In February Hall was informed by Joseph Henry and Spencer Baird that they had a new candidate for the position of Chief Scientist. Pleased with Walker as they were, they nevertheless had been screening men who had more impressive scientific qualifications than Walker, who was primarily a medical doctor. August Petermann, a distinguished German geographer, had written them to recommend one of his young disciples, Doctor Emil Bessels. Like Walker, Bessels was formally trained in medicine; born in Heidelberg, he had received his medical degree from its university. Unlike Walker, Bessels, who had money of his own, had been able to indulge his interest in the natural sciences; after receiving his medical degree he had gone on to study zoology at Jena and Stuttgart. In the summer of 1869 he had been a member of Petermann's expedition to the waters east of

Spitzbergen and had distinguished himself in his scientific activities. When Petermann wrote the recommendation, Bessels was serving as a military surgeon, but, Petermann said, he would be released from his duties if he were appointed to the American expedition.

Henry and Baird were enthusiastic about Bessels. He was only twenty-four years old, but already had proved himself an excellent naturalist. Although Walker's Arctic experience was greater than his, his scientific qualifications were more professional than Walker's, and Henry and Baird were above all interested in scientific qualifications. There is no evidence that Hall resisted their final decision to offer the appointment to the German, but he had been proud of the fact that he had found Walker himself, and the news must have been disappointing. Once the decision was made and Bessels had accepted the appointment, however, Hall acted with his customary initiative and energy. Transporting Bessels from Germany would be expensive, a drain on expedition funds; accustomed to asking favors, Hall set out to save some money. Composing a congratulatory wire to Bessels, he called on Cyrus Field himself to have it sent free of charge. Then he went to a German shipping firm, Oelrichs & Company, to ask if they would be willing to give Bessels free passage "in behalf of the cause of science & North Polar discoveries," as he phrased it in a letter to the company.[7] Apparently they agreed, and it was arranged that Bessels would take a ship that would get him to the United States by May.

In the spring one of Hall's most important tasks was to complete his roster of officers. Budington was already Ship's Master. As First Mate, Hall appointed another experienced whaling man, Hubbard C. Chester, whom he had known as Mate on the *Monticello*. He was particularly delighted with his choice of Second Mate, William Morton, a Navy yeoman of thirty years' service, because Morton had been with Kane on both his Arctic expeditions. On the second, almost twenty years before, Morton had distinguished himself with a fine sledge journey. He and an Eskimo, Hans Hendrick, had struck north along the shore of Greenland from the wintered in *Advance*; having succeeded in passing the Humboldt Glacier, they finally had been stopped by open water and rough terrain just short of Cape Constitution. On returning to the *Advance*, Morton had reported that the water north of the cape was open, thereby unintentionally perpetuating the myth of the Open Polar Sea. Seven years later, when Isaac Hayes found ice where Morton's open water had been, some men blamed Morton for his report (as if Arctic waters were unchanging), and a British commentator criticized Kane for allowing an enlisted man to make such an important mission alone. Kane had praised Morton, however, and Hall knew that he was still a good man, old though he was.

The Navy also had been recruiting. They had appointed as Engineer a German, Emil Schumann. The United States Navy and Merchant Marine both drew heavily from immigrants during this period, when adventuresome native Americans were moving west rather than going to sea. Of the ten common seamen who were to be crew of the *Polaris*, one was a Swede, one a Dane, and seven were German—only one, Noah Hayes, was American-born. Two of the scientific staff of three were to be German. There were to be as many Germans aboard the ship as native Americans, an interesting and, in the light of later events, an ominous statistic.

Emil Bessels arrived in the United States some time in May. We have no record of where or when he and Hall met, or of what the two men first thought of one another. Soon after Bessels's arrival, Joseph Henry, as President of the National Academy of Sciences, created a committee to prepare scientific instructions for the expedition, appointing some of the most distinguished scientists of the time—himself, Spencer Baird, J. E. Hilgard, Louis Agassiz, and others. The instructions that resulted were so elaborate and detailed, covering the fields of astronomy, meteorology, geology, glaciology, oceanography, botany, ornithology, and zoology, that Hall apparently felt threatened, worried that the scientific aspects of the expedition would become so important that he would lose control of its operations. One paragraph of the instructions begins: "Great difficulty was met with in obtaining men of the proper scientific acquirements to embark in an enterprise which must necessarily be attended with much privation, and in which, in a measure, science must be subordinate." In his copy of the instructions, Hall carefully underlined the last four words of this sentence: "science must be subordinate." In his correspondence with Henry, both men fenced with words, each eager not to offend the other. Henry took care to admit that the main purpose of the expedition was to reach the Pole; Hall, to insist that he would allow scientific observations to be made whenever possible. But while they bent over backward, each occasionally made his own interests clear. "From the fact that the National Academy was mentioned in the law, in connection with scientific instructions," wrote Henry to Hall, "it is evident Congress did not intend that scientific operations should be neglected." Wrote Hall to Henry: "I understand that the primary object of our Expedition is Geographical discovery, and to this, as the main end, our energies will be bent."

Although we have no clear indication that Hall and Bessels disliked one another from the outset, trouble is suggested in the Hall–Henry correspondence. Some time after Hall had met Bessels, Henry wrote to him: "I doubt not that you will give every facility and render every assistance in your power to Dr. Bessels, who, though a sensitive man, is of a very kind heart." Henry saw fit to repeat one phrase later in the letter, and to issue something like a warning: "As I have said, Dr. Bessels is a sensitive man; I beg, therefore, you will deal gently with him." To this part of the letter, Hall replied, "I appreciate the spirit with which Dr. Emil Bessels has entered into our enterprize and I shall give him my sympathy and cooperation in all his labors."[8]

There is one other piece of evidence that shows Hall was

uneasy about these arrangements. In May he paid a last visit to Cincinnati, and there he talked freely about his hopes and fears with some of his old friends. According to Judge Joseph Cox, Hall was "exceedingly sanguine that he should succeed," but also expressed fears of insubordination among some of his officers and men. He was more specific when he spoke to Doctor Robert Newton. Some years later Newton wrote a letter to J. E. Nourse, who was preparing a book on Hall for the government, saying that Hall had complained to him about the scientific organization of the expedition: "He said to me that he never would consent to this organization but for the fact that he had been told by parties that if he did not carry out the arrangements which were made, he would not be allowed to command the expedition."[9] This is the only evidence we have that such a threat was made. Was it actually made, or was Hall's suspicious nature surfacing again, after being dormant for a long time? The question cannot be answered.

In spite of his doubts and fears, he must have been excited as his dream approached reality. For ten years he had tried to mount a large expedition; now, at last, he had succeeded. Late in May he entertained President Grant, Secretary of the Navy Robeson, and other officials aboard the *Polaris* as it lay in the Washington Navy Yard, rebuilt from stem to stern. The Chaplain of Congress, the Reverend Doctor Newman, whom Hall had seen frequently in Washington, led a brief service for the occasion. He later was to go north with the tender *Congress* and give his final benediction to the expedition in Greenland.

On June 10 Hall sailed down the Potomac with Budington and a partial crew, bound for the Brooklyn Navy Yard and a layover of several weeks. Just before sailing, he had been given his official orders by the Secretary of the Navy. His copy of these orders still survives in the Smithsonian, bearing his scrawled notes and underlinings. The orders begin: "SIR: Having been appointed, by the President of the United

States, commander of the expedition toward the North Pole,
and the steamer *Polaris* having been fitted, equipped, pro-
visioned, and assigned for the purpose, you are placed in
command of the said vessel, her officers and crew, for the
purpose of the said expedition." He underlined the words
"commander of the expedition toward the North Pole."

The orders are concise but complete. They allow Hall the
right to decide precisely what route to follow once the expedition left the Greenland settlements. Although he originally
had thought to sail west through Jones Sound, he also had
the alternative plan of following the route that had been
taken by Kane and Hayes, north through Davis Strait into
Kane Basin. And once he arrived in Greenland he met a
scientist, Baron Von Otter, who informed him that ice conditions in northern Baffin Bay were extraordinarily good;
Von Otter's report clinched his decision to sail straight north.

The orders state that the expedition was equipped for two
and a half years, but that Hall could either extend it if he felt
that he had enough provisions, or cut it short if there was an
emergency or he achieved early success. The orders also detail relatively minor matters: all the literate men on the expedition were to keep journals, and those journals were to
be collected by Hall at the conclusion of the expedition, to
be used in preparing his final report; containers with notes
on the expedition's progress sealed within were to be thrown
overboard at regular intervals; cairns containing such notes
were to be built ashore whenever possible.

The orders carefully discuss the chain of command, allowing for the contingency of Hall either becoming disabled or
dying:

> Mr. Budington shall, in case of your death or disability,
> continue as the sailing and ice-master, and control and
> direct the movements of the vessel; and Dr. Bessels shall, in
> such case, continue as chief of the scientific department,
> directing all sledge-journeys and scientific operations. In the
> possible contingency of their non-agreement as to the course

to be pursued, then Mr. Budington shall assume sole charge and command, and return with the expedition to the United States with all possible dispatch.

As for the scientific aspects of the expedition, the Navy orders refer to the instructions that had been prepared by Henry's committee, and then state: "The charge and direction of the scientific operations will be intrusted, under your command, to Dr. Emil Bessels; and you will render Dr. Bessels and his assistants all such facilities and aids as may be in your power." Significantly, in Hall's copy of the orders, the words "under your command" are underscored.

While the *Polaris* lay in the Brooklyn Navy Yard undergoing final alterations, Hall was busy. His staff of officers and his crew had yet to be completed. Frederick Meyer, a German-born technician who was in the Signal Corps, had been appointed Meteorologist under Bessels. The third member of the scientific staff, who was to serve as Astronomer and Chaplain, was a recent graduate of Lafayette College, R. W. D. Bryan; he was not to join the expedition until later, sailing to Greenland aboard the tender *Congress*, which was to meet the *Polaris* at Disco. There were the usual last-minute changes to be made: the Assistant Engineer, a fireman, a seaman, and the cook all deserted and had to be replaced. Finally, there was a special appointment to be made. George Tyson's whaling cruise had been canceled, and Hall very much wanted him to be a member of the expedition. By special arrangement with Secretary Robeson, he created the position of Assistant Navigator for Tyson at the last minute. The completed roster listed twenty-five men:

C. F. Hall .... Commander
Sidney O. Budington .... Sailing Master
George E. Tyson .... Assistant Navigator
H. C. Chester .... First Mate
William Morton .... Second Mate
Emil Schumann .... Engineer

Alvin Odell .... Assistant Engineer
Walter Campbell .... Fireman
John Booth .... Fireman
John Herron .... Steward
William Jackson .... Cook
Nathaniel Coffin .... Carpenter

SEAMEN

Herman Sieman	Joseph Mauch
Frederick Anthing	G. W. Lindquist
J. W. C. Kruger	Peter Johnson
Henry Hobby	Frederick Jamka
William Nindemann	Noah Hayes

SCIENTIFIC STAFF

Emil Bessels .... Surgeon and Chief of Staff
R. W. D. Bryan .... Astronomer and Chaplain
Frederick Meyer.............. Meteorologist

In addition, there were Ebierbing, Tookoolito, and little Punny. In Greenland Hans Hendrick, his wife, and their three children would join the expedition, bringing the total number aboard to thirty-three when the *Polaris* finally sailed into unknown waters.

Shortly before the *Polaris* sailed from New York, the American Geographical Society held a reception for Hall, Ebierbing, Tookoolito, and some of the officers of the expedition. Grizzled old William Morton spoke, pleasing his audience with a few words of remembrance for his former commander, Elisha Kent Kane ("It was my sad fortune to lose as brave a man as ever lived. He has passed from among us into a world where martyrs receive their reward."). Emil Bessels also spoke, beginning by apologizing for his unfamiliarity with English. He briefly praised Hall's enthusiasm, saying that it was the stimulus that would drive them to success, then concluded with a reference to the scientific aspects of the expedition: "If anything could be an additional stimulus to us during our trip, I think it will arise from the fact that such eminent men of science, such as compose this Society, are watching with interest the actions of our expedition."* Hall spoke at greater length than Morton or Bessels, not only because he was the commander of the expedition, but also because he was in familiar surroundings. From the beginning of Hall's career as an explorer, he had received encouragement and help from the American Geographical Society, and by now many of its members were old friends. After Judge Daly introduced him, emphasizing his "indomitable energy," Hall spoke informally, apologizing for having been so busy that he had been unable to write a speech. He thanked the government for its generosity, praising Secretary Robeson in particular ("I almost worship him"). He asserted his faith in his men: "I have chosen my own men; men that will stand by me through thick and thin. Though we may be surrounded by innumerable icebergs, and though our vessel may be crushed like an egg-shell, I believe they will stand by me to the last." At the high point of his speech, denying that he was as adventuresome as some persons believed, he sang praises of the Arctic:

> Many who have written to me, or who have appeared to me personally, think that I am an adventurous spirit and of bold heart to attempt to go to the North Pole. Not so. It does not require that heart which they suppose I have got. The Arctic Region is my home. I love it dearly, its storms, its winds, its glaciers, its icebergs; and when I am there among them, it seems as if I were in an earthly heaven or a heavenly earth.[10]

* Another scientist who had trouble with English was present at the reception and addressed the gathering through an interpreter. He was Doctor Octave Pavy, and his presence was an irony that will strike readers familiar with the history of Arctic exploration. Pavy was one of those who died on the Greely Expedition twelve years later. The irony lies in the fact that Pavy was to play Bessels to Greely's Hall. The two men had trouble with each other from the outset: the elegant, European-educated Pavy condescended to his commander, a professional soldier rather than an intellectual; Greely, in turn, found Pavy uncooperative and disobedient.

Three days after the reception the *Polaris* sailed from the Brooklyn Navy Yard. After a run of seventeen hours she put into New London, where she picked up replacements for the men who had deserted. Then, on July 3, she weighed anchor again. At the American Geographical Society reception there had been a brief ceremony in which Henry Grinnell had presented Hall with a flag that had been to Antarctica on the Wilkes Expedition of 1838–40. In accomplishments, the Wilkes Expedition had been a fair success, but it also had been torn by insubordination and dissension, and it had concluded with the court martial of its commander, Charles Wilkes. As a symbol, the flag was at best of ambiguous significance. Flying this rather ill-omened ensign, the *Polaris* sailed out of New London harbor toward the Arctic.

chapter seven

Greenland—
the Expedition

The Polaris Expedition was doomed to failure. The ship achieved a record farthest north; the expedition explored and charted unknown areas of the High Arctic and pioneered a route to the Polar Sea later followed by such explorers as George Nares, Adolphus Greely, and Robert Peary; its members, even in conditions of extreme hardship, made scientific observations of value to geographers and naturalists. Nevertheless, it was a failure— a failure made bitter by fierce animosities and dissensions among those who participated in it. Charles Francis Hall's career as an explorer began in the shadow of tragedy, the disappearance of the Franklin Expedition; it was to end in the shadow of mystery and controversy.

Hall's first two expeditions must be reconstructed from his own journals. Because his writing is our only source of information, the events that occurred during those journeys are inseparable from the intense man who not only lived them but also recorded them in his highly subjective manner. Because we must see Hall's lonely wanderings on Baffin Island and in the barrens through his eyes, we can only guess what Sidney Budington thought, or Ebierbing and Tookoolito, or Patrick Coleman. On the Polaris Expedition, however, Hall became the object of other men's journalizing and reminiscence, and the events of the expedition can be seen only through their eyes. Hall's journals are gone, mysteriously lost after his death.

Events during the Polaris Expedition must be reconstructed from documents that often disagree with one another. There is the actual log of the *Polaris*, kept by Hall and, after his death, by Captain Budington and First Mate Hubbard Chester, but in the manner of most logs, it is spare and factual, dealing mainly with winds, temperatures, and navigational data. A more fruitful source is the journals kept by some of the men. Most of these—the journals of Herman Sieman, John Herron, Hubbard Chester, and William Morton—are laconic and loglike, their writers suppressing personal thoughts to record only natural conditions. Two, however, are remarkably detailed and vivid. The journals of the common seamen Noah Hayes and Joseph Mauch are extraordinary not for literary merit, but for honesty and immediacy. Far more than most journals, they show the impact of Arctic life on the minds of ordinary men. The gradual degeneration of Hayes's and Mauch's personalities as revealed in their writing suggests what happened to every man aboard the ship as discipline and solidarity began to crumble.

Another journal presents a problem. George Tyson apparently kept a record of his responses to events aboard the *Polaris*, but it was lost when he was separated from the ship. During his long ordeal before he was rescued, he began another journal, and this one survived. On his return to civilization, he was urged by a professional editor, E. Vale Blake, to cooperate in writing a book colorfully entitled *Arctic Experiences: Containing Captain George E. Tyson's Wonderful Drift on the Ice Floe*. The book is made up largely of long quotations from Tyson's "journal," but one is aware of the rather heavy hand of the editor throughout, and those sections which deal with life aboard the ship are reconstructions of the notes that Tyson lost. Tyson possibly did not make any major revisions, but his point of view was not unbiased and he must have taken advantage of the opportunity to rewrite in the light of later events. The early part of Tyson's "journal," then, is actually more a memoir than a journal.

There is one other important source of information about the Polaris Expedition, in some ways even more immediate and vivid than the journals, although it is a post-factum report. It is the Navy Department's report to the President on its investigation of the expedition. It is largely a verbatim transcription of the interrogations of members of the expedition, and it is immediate and vivid because the interrogations were held while memories were still fresh, emotions still hot. Many of the men who were inhibited as they wrote their journals became uninhibited under the prodding questions of the examining board and gave vent to their frustrations and grudges.

From these documents and others like them, the story of the Polaris Expedition must be reconstructed, and Hall, as the subject of other men's talk and writing, becomes an unwontedly silent and somewhat cryptic figure. What survives of the writing he did during the expedition is dry and official: log entries, written orders, dispatches to Washington. We can only guess what he wrote in his personal journal, but when one knows the man's quickness to take offense and his capacity for suspicion, it is not difficult to imagine the mood of what he wrote during his moments of privacy as the atmosphere aboard the *Polaris* grew electric, and as he brooded on the movement of events that were to culminate in his death.

"July 27—At Sea—At daylight this morning, 3 o'clock, Greenland's icy mountains were visible, their snow-covered peaks just above the horizon." So begins the journal of Noah Hayes, an Indiana farmboy who moved east and went to sea at a time when many of his countrymen were moving to western farmlands. The Polaris Expedition was the twenty-six-year-old Hayes's first experience of the sea, and he had been in a state of wide-eyed excitement on the cruise from New

London to Newfoundland to Greenland. After the first sighting of Greenland on July 27, his excitement increased as the
Polaris coasted northward, with huge icebergs spawned from
High Arctic glaciers to port, Greenland's magnificent mountains and fiords to starboard. When she put into coastal
settlements, Hayes stared insatiably at the Eskimos and described them in colorful detail in his journal.

His excitement reached a peak when the commander of the
expedition asked him if he would like to go for a walk in the
mountains at Disco. Hayes was a young man after Hall's
heart, eager, ambitious, devout. He approached the expedition with an enthusiasm that overflows the early pages of his
journal, the style of which, sometimes self-consciously inflated, but always energetic, is similar to Hall's. Hayes, admiring Captain Hall's strength and piety, was flattered when
Hall asked him to go on a walk. Taking his specimen bag,
he left the harbor with his commander to climb the hills
above the settlement of Godhavn. While they walked Hall
told Hayes about the Franklin Expedition, pointing out from
the heights the Whalefish Islands, where the *Erebus* and
Terror had received supplies from their tender before disappearing forever. When the two men came down from the
mountains, they happened on one of those natural gardens
that emboss the Arctic landscape, and they shared a vision of
beauty. Hayes waxed eloquent in his journal:

> A little to the left of the bluff was a small portion of the
> valley in the form of a parallelogram, about forty-five yards
> in extent, enclosed on three sides by perpendicular high
> stone walls. At the upper end of the enclosure was a beauti-
> ful spring which emptied into a natural basin, forming an in-
> viting little pool of fresh pure water. Thence by a very
> circuitous route it found its way out and was lost in the
> distance on its way to the sea. Without parting the vegeta-
> tion an inch of ground could nowhere be seen, so thickly
> was it grown over with flowers, moss and grass. Encircling
> the little pool and lining the margin of the rivulet was a

compact sod of fine, velvety green and purple moss, thinly interspersed with variously colored harmonizing flowers. The moss retained in the form of globules the particles of water splashed upon it by the motion of the stream, and had the appearance of being thickly studded with pearls and gems, diamonds, rubies, emeralds, according to the tint reflected from the various colored moss. Never had my eyes beheld or my mind contemplated such unalloyed beauty as this little Eden was clothed in.

Hayes's walk with Hall confirmed his devotion to his commander and his enthusiasm for the expedition. Often in his journal he looked forward to that Sunday on which he and the other men of the *Polaris* would hold divine services at the North Pole.

In his enthusiasm Hayes saw only good in what was happening around him, but the more experienced and skeptical George Tyson watched with foreboding as signs of discontent and animosity appeared among the officers. Joining the expedition late in its preparations, he at first had been ignorant of Hall's suspicion of Emil Bessels, but soon after reaching St. John's, Newfoundland, he noted that Hall was beginning to have trouble with both Bessels and Frederick Meyer, the meteorologist. The two Germans seemed to be preparing to resist Hall's authority, although their resistance had not yet come to the surface. Tyson also noted that Captain Budington was surly about Hall's command. In his later testimony to the Board of Inquiry, Budington himself admitted that as early as St. John's he had trouble with Hall: "Captain Hall had a very slight difficulty with me about some of my—well, it was a very careless trick in me, and he gave me a reprimand on leaving St. John's." According to Tyson, Budington's "careless trick" had been to raid the store of provisions for a snack (not for liquor, Tyson suggestively insisted to the Board, just for food—this time).

Although Tyson was sharply critical of all those who fomented trouble, he himself was probably not entirely innocent. It is tempting to accept George Tyson's version of everything that occurred on the Polaris Expedition, because he wrote and spoke so extensively and plausibly about it, and because he was fundamentally a sound man, experienced and responsible. But Tyson was in an awkward position in the expedition hierarchy, and he was only human. According to him, he had been offered the captaincy of Hall's ship, but afterward had found himself in a vaguely defined, almost supernumerary position somewhere beneath his fellow whaling-captain, Budington. He did not always accept the situation gracefully. In his testimony and in his writing, Tyson was critical of almost everyone aboard the ship, his tone often revealing more personal disaffection than disinterested judgment, and Budington was his special target.

But Tyson's sense that things were going wrong early in the expedition was not unfounded. When the *Polaris* reached the island of Disco, men other than Tyson were forced to recognize that hostilities were developing. At the Disco settlement of Godhavn the *Polaris* made rendezvous with her supply ship, the *Congress*, and when Captain Davenport of the *Congress* and the Reverend Doctor Newman, who had come north to give the expedition his final benediction, went aboard the *Polaris*, they found themselves in a hornet's nest. The Scientific Corps, consisting of Doctor Bessels and Frederick Meyer (R. W. D. Bryan, the third scientist, had come up on the *Congress* to join the expedition at Disco), had openly refused to obey one of Hall's orders. Meyer had been keeping Hall's official journal for him, and had complained that it was interfering with his duties as meteorologist. Hall had ordered Meyer to stop making meteorological observations for a time in order to concentrate entirely on the journal and on assisting in the navigation of the ship. Meyer had refused. Doctor Bessels was present at the confrontation, and so, for a short time, was steward John Herron, who overheard the angry conversation and later testified: "Captain Hall told him [Meyer] that he was the officer of the vessel, and Mr.

Meyer said that he had his orders from headquarters. Captain Hall wished him to produce these orders, and then Dr. Bessels took the thing up and said that if Mr. Meyer wanted to go on shore, he could do so." Bessels later admitted that he went farther than this, announcing that if Meyer resigned from the expedition, so would he—and take the German crewmen with him.

Apparently Captain Davenport, to whom Hall appealed for help, brought some of his naval authority to bear on the situation. On the sixth page of Hall's own copy of his official orders from the Secretary of the Navy, a sentence is underlined in pencil: "All persons attached to the expedition are under your command, and shall, under every circumstance and condition, be subject to the rules, regulations, and laws governing the discipline of the Navy." In the margin, dated "God Haven Greenland, August 16, 1871," is a statement in Hall's hand: "As a member of the United States naval north polar expedition, I do hereby solemnly promise and agree to conform to all the orders and instructions as herein set forth by the Secretary of the United States Navy to the commander." The statement is signed by Frederick Meyer. Apparently Hall had agreed to a compromise, however, because Meyer was soon relieved of his duties as expedition journalist and replaced in that function by a young seaman, Joseph Mauch.

Bessels and Meyer were not the only trouble makers at Disco. Tyson said it was at Disco that he first discovered that Budington had broken into the expedition's stock of liquor. Hall kept some bottles of whiskey, cognac, and wine under lock and key, for use on holidays and special occasions during the expedition. At Disco, Tyson testified, Budington one day invited him to have a glass of wine, and he accepted. Budington furtively took him to an alleyway where he kept one of his personal sea chests, opened it, and revealed several bottles of wine, "claret, in bottles—a light wine," Tyson specified for the Board of Inquiry. Tyson asked Budington who had given him the wine, but the Captain evaded answer, saying, "Never mind who they were." Tyson admitted that he had no real evidence that Budington had stolen the wine from expedition supplies, but thought his behavior clearly indicated guilt.

On August 17 the *Polaris* left Disco to continue north. Before it weighed anchor Captain Davenport and Doctor Newman came aboard from the *Congress* for a final farewell. Captain Davenport, worried about what he had seen and heard, delivered a brief lecture on naval discipline to the assembled expedition, and Doctor Newman read a prayer. Most of the prayer was suitable for any naval expedition: "While on the mighty deep, be Thou our Father and our Friend; for they who go down to the sea in ships, that do business in the great waters, see the works of the Lord and His wonders of the deep. It is Thee who raiseth the stormy wind which lifteth up the waves; it is Thee who maketh the storm a calm, so that the waves thereof are still." One part of the prayer seemed designed for the Polaris Expedition in particular, however, possibly written by Doctor Newman after he had observed what was happening on the ship: "Give us noble thoughts, pure emotions, and generous sympathies for each other, while so far away from all human habitations. May we have for each other that charity that suffereth long and is kind, that envieth not, that vaunteth not itself, that is not puffed up, that seeketh not her own, that is not easily provoked, that thinketh no evil, but that beareth all things, hopeth all things, endureth all things; that charity that never faileth."[1]

The *Polaris* had several more ports of call on the Greenland coast before she left for the unknown. The first was Upernavik, where Hall hoped to enlist Hans Hendrick, a Greenland Eskimo famous among Arctic explorers. Hans had been north with Kane in 1853–5 and with Isaac Hayes in 1860–1. Although he had finally deserted Kane's expedition for a Polar Eskimo wife, he nevertheless had proved

invaluable to Kane and to Hayes; without his skills as a
hunter and his services in liaison with the Polar Eskimos,
their expeditions would have suffered greater losses than they
did. Hall believed that Tookoolito, Ebierbing, and Hans
would provide his expedition with as much native knowledge
and skill as could be hoped for. When the *Polaris* arrived at
Upernavik, Hans happened not to be there, but at Proven,
some fifty miles to the north. First Mate Hubbard Chester,
who had proved himself an excellent hand with small craft,
took an open boat to Proven and returned a day later, boat
loaded to the gunwale with Hans, his wife and three children,
his equipment, and a swarm of dogs and puppies: Hans had
refused to go on the expedition without his goods and chattels.
Second Mate William Morton stepped forward and extended
his hand as Hans came aboard. Seventeen years before, he and
Hans had left the rest of the Kane expedition behind and
with dog sledge had reached Cape Constitution, where they
had been allowed a fleeting glimpse of what they then
thought might be the Open Polar Sea. Morton had so aged in
seventeen years that Hans did not recognize him, but when
the old sailor pointed to scars on Hans's hands, the result of
a gunpowder explosion on the Kane expedition, the Eskimo
remembered and greeted him warmly.

The day before leaving Upernavik Hall decided to face
openly some of the hostilities simmering aboard the ship. It
was a Sunday, and he chose the moment after divine services
to stand up and address the assembled company. Noah Hayes
recorded the import of his speech: "After Service (at 11 AM)
Cap. Hall found it necessary to assert his determination to
maintain order and obedience to all lawful commands—that
he would summarily chastise all opposition to what he considered the interests of the Expedition and if necessary die
in the performance of his duty as a commander rather than
yield a letter." Hayes went on to express his own confidence
in his hero, losing control of his writing in the process: "And

I am sure that in nowise will he fall short of the ability confidently reposed in him by those who placed in his hands this
great responsibility of faithfully conducting this arduous
undertaking with various difficulties and exegiencies that
necessarily will arrise."

Joseph Mauch apparently heard the speech differently, perhaps because, being German-American, he was more aware of
what Tyson was to call "the German Party." Describing the
same speech in his journal, he wrote: "At 11 AM Divine
Services by Mr. Bryan, our astronomer and chaplain. After
divine services Capt. Hall made some remarks insulting
Dr. Bessels most severely, whether with right or not I can not
judge. He charged him of having tried to make disturbances
amongst the ship's company & told him that he should report
to the authorities at home on the Doctor's conduct."

After two more stops the *Polaris* was ready to make for
Smith Sound, the entrance to the unknown. At the small
island of Kingitoke Hall negotiated vainly for dogs; and at
Tasiussaq he vainly tried to enlist a Greenlander named
Jansen, a veteran of the Hayes Expedition. Although Jansen
refused to join the expedition, he did sell Hall some dogs
at an outrageously high price. As Hall prepared to leave
Tasiussaq, he wrote his last dispatch to Washington. At Holsteinborg he had met a Swedish expedition that had been
carrying out hydrographic surveys; its commander, Baron
Frederick Von Otter, had given Hall the very good news that
ice conditions to the north were extraordinarily favorable
for navigation, and Hall had decided definitely to head directly north through Smith Sound, following Kane's route,
instead of going westward through Jones Sound. The *Polaris* had sailed and steamed well up the coast of Greenland,
and she was crammed with coal, foodstuffs, and other supplies.
Her crew was complete; besides the crew, officers, and scientific staff of three, there were seven Eskimo men, women, and
children, and many dogs aboard. In spite of the troubles that

he had had with some of the officers, Hall apparently felt optimistic. On August 22 he began his last dispatch:

> The prospects of the expedition are fine; the weather beautiful, clear, and exceptionally warm. Every preparation has been made <u>to bid farewell to civilization for several years, if need be</u>, to accomplish our purpose. Our coal bunkers are not only full, but we have full ten tons yet on deck, besides wood, planks, and rosin in considerable quantities, that can be used for steaming purposes in any emergency. Never was an Arctic expedition more completely fitted out than this.

On the next day, just as the *Polaris* was about to steam out of the harbor, a thick fog settled on Tasiussaq. Hall impatiently waited twenty-four hours for it to lift, then decided to hire a good pilot and make his way out of Tasiussaq through the fog: the season for good sailing was growing late, and he could afford no more delays. On August 24, he added final notes to his last dispatch:

> *1:30* P.M.
>
> The anchor of the *Polaris* has just been weighed, and not again will it go down till, as I trust and pray, a higher, a far higher, latitude has been attained than ever before by civilized man. Governor Elberg [who had come with the expedition from Holsteinborg] is about accompanying us out of the harbor and seaward. He leaves us when the pilot does. Governor Lowertz Elberg has rendered to this expedition much service, and long will I remember him for his great kindness. I am sure you and my country will fully appreciate the hospitality and co-operation of the Danish officials in Greenland as relating to our North Polar expedition.
>
> *2:15* P.M.
>
> The *Polaris* bids adieu to the civilized world. Governor Elberg leaves us, promising to take these dispatches back to

Upernavik, to send them to our minister at Copenhagen by
the next ship, which opportunity may not be until next year.
God be with us.[2]

A very short time after Tasiussaq was out of sight astern,
George Tyson came upon Hall writing in his cabin. Knowing that Hall had brought his notes from his second expedition in order to work on a book during his spare time, Tyson
asked him about it:

> I asked him if he was writing up his Franklin search book,
> about which he had often talked to me. He said, 'No; I left
> all those papers at Disco!' I did not like to ask him, but I
> looked 'Why?' A sort of gloom seemed to spread over his
> face, as if the recollection of something with which they
> were associated made him uncomfortable, and presently,
> without raising his head, he added, 'I left them there for
> safety.' I saw the subject was not pleasant, and I made no
> further remark; but I could not help thinking it over."[3]

When the *Polaris* sailed from Tasiussaq, she sailed out
of contact with the civilized world. With the radio yet to be
invented, she might as well have been on the dark side of the
moon. Families of the men aboard, authorities in Washington, and the newspaper-reading public accepted such complete separation as an unavoidable part of Arctic exploration
and settled down to wait for so long as two years for any
word. They thought about the expedition occasionally,
during the winter in particular, appreciating their firesides
as they imagined the tiny ship dwarfed by icebergs, whipped
by Arctic storms. The fall and winter of 1871–2 passed, then
the spring, summer, and fall of 1872. During the winter of
1873 newspapers occasionally reminded their readers that the
Polaris was still in the North, but they could print no news
about her because there was none to print. During the early
spring of 1873 the men in the Department of Navy who had

taken part in organizing the expedition anticipated hearing from the *Polaris* in the summer. She was not supplied to stay North through another winter, and they knew that if they did not hear from her by August they might be facing a disaster. On May 9, far earlier than they expected, they received their first word—a brief, shocking wire from the United States Consul in St. John's:

ST. JOHNS, NEWFOUNDLAND

MAY 9, 1873

THE ENGLISH WHALING-SHIP WALRUS HAS JUST ARRIVED, AND RE-
PORTS THAT THE STEAMER TIGRESS PICKED UP ON THE ICE AT
GRADY HARBOR, LABRADOR ON THE 30TH OF APRIL LAST, FIFTEEN
OF THE CREW AND FIVE OF THE ESQUIMAUX OF THE STEAMER
POLARIS OF THE ARCTIC EXPEDITION. CAPTAIN HALL DIED LAST
SUMMER. THE TIGRESS IS HOURLY EXPECTED AT ST. JOHNS.[4]

On the morning of April 30 Captain Isaac Bartlett of the *Tigress* was piloting his sealer slowly through fog off the Labrador coast when he was startled to hear a voice shouting from the water below. He was even more startled when he looked down to see an Eskimo in a kayak, far from where any Eskimo should be. In broken English the Eskimo persuaded Captain Bartlett to follow him to an ice floe a quarter of a mile off, and there the crew of the *Tigress* was amazed to see a large group of men, women, and children, all waving their hats and cheering. Bartlett immediately lowered boats to bring these strange castaways to his ship. One of the *Tigress* crew addressed the man who appeared to be their leader as they clambered aboard: "How long have you been on the ice?"

"Since the fifteenth of last October."

More than half a year on the floe! The men of the *Tigress* goggled and one blurted, "And was you on it day and night?" As George Tyson later wrote, he could not stop himself from laughing: "The peculiar expression and tone, with the

absurdity of the question was too much for my politeness."
The tensions of a six-month, fifteen-hundred-mile drift on
sea ice burst with Tyson's laughter.[5]

Tyson and the others (Frederick Meyer, eight crewmen,
four adult Eskimos, and five children—nineteen persons
rather than the twenty mentioned in the wire to Washington) wanted nothing more than to get to land as fast as possible, but Bartlett insisted on remaining at the sealing
grounds until his hold was filled. Tyson and his exhausted
party had to wait a week before they reached Newfoundland,
and in the meantime the Department of Navy was agitated
and frustrated. The wire suggested a disaster but gave no
details. What had happened to the expedition that so many
of its members had been cast adrift on a floe? Where were the
Polaris and the rest of her men? How had Charles Francis
Hall died? Secretary Robeson and his department could have
no satisfactory answers to these questions until the castaways
were brought to Washington. In the meantime, Captain
Bartlett learned some of the story from George Tyson.

In the six days after leaving Tasiussaq, the *Polaris* had
made a remarkable cruise to the north under sail and steam.
In spite of fog and ice, she reached Cape Alexander and
the mouth of Smith Sound in three days. Ahead lay three
hundred miles of narrow waterway between Ellesmere Island
and Greenland, often clogged with ice and torn by gales that
could make the ice a crushing force, as Kane and Hayes had
learned to their regret. In 1853 Kane's *Advance* had rounded
Cape Alexander and entered Kane Basin only to be caught
in a gale that drove the ice before it and finally forced the
Advance to take refuge in Rensselaer Harbor, as far north
as she was to get on the expedition. In 1860 Hayes's schooner
United States did not even reach Rensselaer Harbor: she
was nipped by ice in a gale off Littleton Island and had to put
into Hartstene Bay, only a few miles north of Cape Alex-

ander. Both Kane and Hayes had been forced to leave their
ships and carry out their explorations to the north by sledge
and small boat.

Hall was more fortunate. The *Polaris* passed Hayes's Hartstene Bay at five p.m. on August 27, Kane's Rensselaer Harbor
at eight p.m. the same day. Less than twenty-four hours later,
she had steamed the length of Kane Basin and had before her
the narrows of Kennedy Channel. In hours she had achieved a
northing as high as that achieved in months of hard labor
by Kane and Hayes. Hall's good fortune continued. In less
than a day he was through Kennedy Channel and on his way
up what was to be called Hall Basin. This part of the cruise
was particularly exciting for Morton and Hans, as it brought
them into the waters they had only glimpsed from Cape
Jackson seventeen years before, the open waters they had
thought might be the Open Polar Sea.

At six a.m. on August 30, the *Polaris* reached her highest
point north, the northern mouth of Robeson Strait, at about
82° 11′. Before her was the impenetrable ice of the Lincoln
Sea. Hall was never to know it, but no land then lay between
him and the North Pole, only the constantly moving pack, the
immense pressure ridges and hummocks, and the treacherous
leads of the Polar Sea. Before him was the answer to those
optimists who believed that the Polar Sea was open.

Hall's fortune turned at the edge of the Lincoln Sea. The
floe directly north of the *Polaris* appeared massive and solid.
Fog settled in, followed by snow, and a relentless current
pushed the ship southward back toward Hall Basin. Hall
went ashore in a boat to examine a bight on the Greenland
shore which he thought might be a possible winter harbor,
but it turned out to be only a shallow indentation in the
coastline. Although he decided not to moor his ship there,
calling it "Repulse Harbor," he performed a little ceremony,
raising the American flag in the most northerly place it had
ever been raised and claiming the land for the United States.
Then he returned to the *Polaris,* which was moored to a floe,

and faced the decision that had to be made. After a conference with his officers, who gave him conflicting advice— some suggesting that he retreat southward, others that he find a winter harbor immediately, others that he persist in trying to go farther north—he decided to steam westward along the edge of the floes toward what he called "Grant Land" (the northern tip of Ellesmere Island), hoping to find a northward lead near its shores.

His decision to persist almost doomed the expedition. The *Polaris* made only a few miles westward before she was trapped in the floes. On the next day, a northeast wind pushed the ice against the ship with mounting pressure until it was obvious that she might be nipped and seriously damaged. The situation was so dangerous that Hall ordered provisions unloaded on the ice in case the ship had to be abandoned. At divine service that Sunday, September 3, he called on the men to pray with particular earnestness and intensity. Herman Sieman, a devout Lutheran crewman, heard Hall well and remarked in his journal, "Ship and crew appear to be ready prey to the ice. But there is a God, who aids and saves from death; to Him I trust, between these icebergs, although I do not deserve all the good He grants me."

The floe that had trapped the *Polaris* drove her southward. Most of the time the atmosphere was thick with fog or snow, and when it cleared at short intervals the officers desperately took sightings, trying to keep track of their location and bearing. Hour after hour the ship lost the northing that she had achieved, drifting back through Robeson Channel to Hall Basin. Finally, after four days at the mercy of the floe, the *Polaris* escaped into open water, and Hall had Budington bring her in close to the Greenland shore. There he found a small harbor that he thought might do for winter refuge, not cut as deeply into the land as he wished, but at least out of the main current with its deadly floes. To the north was a bluff that Hall named Cape Lupton, which he hoped would provide some protection from drifting ice. Budington maneuvered the ship just inshore of a huge grounded iceberg that would give them further protection, and there she dropped anchor. On Sunday, September 10, after Bryan had held services, Hall addressed the men. He told them that he had decided to call their refuge "Thank God Harbor," the huge berg that protected them "Providence Berg."

George Tyson told Captain Bartlett about the preparations that were made for the winter ahead. The ship, soon fixed in bay ice, was banked deep with snow and ice blocks, and her whole deck was covered with a canvas tent. In order to allow more room for the galley, Hall moved out of his private stateroom into a cabin that he shared with Bessels, Bryan, Meyer, Schumann, the cook, and the steward. Some provisions were brought across the three hundred yards of bay ice between the ship and the shore, and on the shore Emil Bessels began to erect his scientific observatory, a small prefabricated shed.

Whenever Hall had the chance, he led brief trips to explore the immediate area: Thank God Harbor was only a shallow scoop in a large, lowland plain twelve miles wide and thirty miles deep, enclosed by mountains to the north, east, and south. The plain was almost level, its flatness relieved only by slight rises in the land and by the cuts of small glacial streams. Underfoot was a moraine of silt, clay, shale, and limestone pebbles and cobbles—dead except for occasional growths of ground willow and clusters of alpine flowers set in beds of moss, tributes to the persistence of life. The mountains that contained the plain were not high, but they were abrupt and rugged, their flanks scarred by glacial runoffs, their peaks eroded by wind, riven by frost. On clear days the men of the *Polaris* could see the white glow of the Greenland icecap over-arching the mountains to the southeast.

Even on these brief trips the country sometimes took measure of the men. One day Meyer, Bryan, and Mauch went on what was planned to be an easy tramp across the bay ice to the southern mountains, which they thought were only a few hours away. Nine hours later they reached the foothills and immediately turned back, realizing that the return hike might be even more difficult. The wind had been blowing constantly and was moving the ice. As darkness came the men were forced to scale high hummocks and push through drifted snow; more serious, cracks were beginning to appear in the ice, sometimes concealed by the blowing snow. All three men fell through cracks, soaking themselves in the icy water of the bay. The ship was out of sight far ahead, and to take bearings they were forced to look back at the mountains: black against the darkening sky, they appeared as massive as when the men had been in their foothills, a discouraging sign of how short a distance they had come, how long a distance they yet had to travel. Wet, almost freezing, exhausted, they began to panic. Meyer and Bryan, wearing light Eskimo boots, began to leave Mauch, who wore heavy cowhide boots, far behind. Finally, in the early morning hours, Meyer and Bryan arrived back at the ship. Hall immediately sent out a group of men to find Mauch. They found him reeling like a drunkard and almost unconscious. Bryan passed out soon after boarding the *Polaris,* and was put limp into his bunk. Hall and others stood around him, waiting anxiously for his return to consciousness. After some time, his eyes fluttered. He saw the worried faces looking down at him and said very slowly: "Captain—traveling—in—this—country—is—very—discouraging."

No one knew better than Hall how discouraging travel in the Arctic could be, but he was determined to make an extensive sledge reconnaissance of the land and the sea to the north before winter set in, scouting the way for a push to the Pole in the spring. On October 10, accompanied by Chester, Ebierbing, and Hans, and using only one sledge, he set out northeastward along the edge of the mountains that bordered the plain, intending to get as far as possible on land before going out onto sea ice. The day after he left he sent Hans back for more dogs, another sledge, and various other equipment. Then the little exploring party disappeared for two weeks.

Tyson told Bartlett that when Hall was preparing for his trip, he had assured Tyson that he wished he could take him along. Then, according to Tyson, Hall paused for a moment, pointed at Budington, who was busy about the ship, and said: "But I do not trust that man. I want you to go with me, but I don't know how to leave him on the ship."[6]

Hall and his party returned on October 24. On their trip out they followed the edge of the mountains for three encampments, then cut northward, following the twists of a riverbed over the highlands to a large bay. When they reached the shores of the bay, Hall read a prayer written by Doctor Newman and named the bay after him. They sledged on the solid bay ice toward the mouth, which they reached in two days. There Hall and Chester climbed a high mountain and had a panoramic view of the area. Below them to the west was ice-jammed Robeson Strait, and across it rose the mountains of Ellesmere Island, which seemed to end at a cape some sixty miles north of them. Hall rightly conjectured that the land there turned abruptly westward and that what they were looking at was the northeast tip of an island. The coast on which they stood seemed to run northeast for about ten miles, then tended eastward, evidence of the insularity of Greenland.

If Hall had possessed the power of foresight, he probably would have lingered on the top of that mountain, for there he was given the most northerly vision he was ever to have. But he did not know what the future held for him and, always impatient to move on, he did not linger. He and Chester came down off the mountain. After some scouting they decided that they should return to the *Polaris;* conditions were not favorable for sledging, and they would have to wait until spring to go farther north. Regretful, they set out to retrace their route back to the *Polaris.*

Tyson told Bartlett that he was banking the ship when he saw Hall and his party coming across the plain on their return and went out to meet them. He said that Hall was exuberant about his little expedition and promised Tyson that he would take him along the next time. Then Tyson went back to banking the ship, and Hall went aboard. That afternoon, not long after his arrival, Hall was suddenly taken ill. When Tyson heard the news he went to the cabin that Hall shared with six other men and found the explorer in his bunk. Hall told Tyson that he had been taken violently sick to his stomach immediately after drinking a cup of coffee when he had come aboard; he said that he felt bilious but was hopeful that he would be better in the morning. In the morning, however, he was not better—he was worse, and in a few days he became delirious.

Tyson was tight-lipped and brief as he described to Bartlett the two weeks of horror that followed Hall's first seizure. For several days Hall's condition became steadily worse. He was partly paralyzed on his left side, was in considerable pain, and was sometimes apparently demented. Everyone on the cramped ship knew of his condition. Doctor Bessels went about darkly predicting his death, saying that he had suffered an "apoplectical insult," but the men would have known that Hall was desperately ill without the doctor's predictions. In order not to disturb him, musters and services were held as far away as possible from him, in the forecastle, and the men were told not to go into his cabin. But they could sometimes hear their commander moaning or shouting at night, in his dementia accusing some of the officers of murdering him.

The pall of sickness and death that fell upon the ship was thickened by a strange and ugly disease that struck the puppies one by one. A pup's bowels would protrude through its anus, and unless the creature was put out of its misery, it would die slowly or be torn to shreds by the other dogs. Some of the men were given the harsh job of killing the afflicted pups.

After a week Hall's condition began to improve. He appeared clear-headed and took more nourishment. He again concerned himself with the expedition, calling Joseph Mauch to his cabin to take dictation. One day, to the delight of Noah Hayes, he got out of his bunk and stayed up for most of the day. Hayes had been much concerned about Hall, but, like most of the crew, had not been allowed to see him. He had been convinced by rumors that even if Hall survived, he would be unfit for command; seeing Hall on deck gave the lie to the rumors, and Hayes rejoiced in his journal that Hall was apparently going to remain in command of the expedition. Then, just when Hall seemed on his way to full recovery, he suffered a relapse. On the morning of November 7 he became comatose. He lived through that day, but died in the early morning hours of November 8.

They buried Hall on November 10 at eleven in the morning. Because the long winter darkness was coming on, they had to find their way from the ship to the grave with lanterns, although there was some light in the sky above, where stars shone through an eerie boreal glow. Hall's corpse, clothed in a blue uniform and wrapped in an American flag, lay in a simple pine coffin, which they towed on a sledge across the bay ice to the land. Some of the crew had dug a grave a few hundred yards south of the observatory, shallow because two feet under the surface they had struck the adamant and permanent frost that underlies all Arctic soil. They put Hall into his grave with his face toward the East and Resurrection, his back toward the frozen waters of Thank God Harbor. Noah Hayes, shivering with cold, kept his eyes fixed on the lanterns during the service; they flickered and dimmed in a strong northeast wind while Bryan read a few prayers over the grave. Then the coffin was covered with silt and stones and snow, and the men returned to the *Polaris*.

For George Tyson as he told Captain Bartlett his story, the events that followed Hall's death must have seemed to conspire against himself, all pointing in one direction: toward his separation from the expedition and his ordeal on the ice floe. Only a week after Hall was buried, a furious three-day gale struck Thank God Harbor. The wind blew at fifty miles an hour for two days, and on the third day the men of the *Polaris* heard the ice around them grinding and cracking. Soon the ship began to rock; then suddenly the wall of snow that had been laboriously banked against her side dropped through the ice, and the ship was adrift. To the horror of all aboard, she began to float out of her refuge toward the maelstrom of ice and water that churned beyond. She could not be steered—the men were helpless. Suddenly the *Polaris* came up against the huge iceberg that Hall had named Providence, which had remained grounded and stable during the gale. One of the German sailors, William Nindemann, crawled through a forward porthole out onto the berg and, the storm still raging around him, scaled its side to a small ledge. An ice anchor and a pan containing a rope soaked in kerosene were passed out to him. By the light of the burning rope, Nindemann planted the anchor in the berg and attached a hawser from the ship to the anchor. Soon two more anchors with hawsers attached were planted, and the *Polaris,* for the time being at least, was safe from the ice outside Thank God Harbor.

Providence Berg, which saved the *Polaris* from one storm, almost destroyed her in another. As soon as the first storm abated, Budington moved the ship fifty feet away from the berg. Within four days, new bay ice formed around her and once again she seemed secure for the winter. Then, on November 28, another gale blew up, driving floe ice against the berg with increasing pressure until suddenly it split in half. While the men looked on, again helpless, one of the halves, fifty feet high and almost two hundred feet broad, was ungrounded and began to move toward the ship, bearing down with awesome stateliness. Just as it seemed inevitable that the ship would be crushed, an underwater spur of the berg scooped under her, lifting her bow slightly. The berg continued its drift toward the shore, half carrying, half pushing the *Polaris* ahead of it, until finally it was grounded again.

The ship had been saved once more, but her situation was far from secure. Her bow still rested on the underwater spur, held solidly there by the bits and pieces of floe that had jammed against it. At high tide, when the stern came up to the level of the bow, the *Polaris* would be almost even keel, but at low tide the stern dropped and she would heel sharply to port. So uncomfortable was her situation that the Eskimos, never entirely happy on board a ship in any case, insisted on leaving and setting up camp ashore. The others, who all stayed aboard, had to live with nerve-racking sounds and motions as the tides ebbed and flowed. Insecure as the position of the ship was, nothing could be done, and she remained cradled in ice for the entire winter, the hull weakened by constant strain.

Tyson told Bartlett that the winter and spring of 1862 could only be endured. Little could be done to further the cause of the expedition even if the men wanted to do anything, and Tyson implied most of them were content to forget about the North Pole. Hall's death had left the expedition with an ambiguous command. Budington was in charge of the vessel and of all things concerned with her; Bessels was in charge of scientific activities and of all things concerned with them, including, he maintained, the dogs and sledges. The two men held their tempers, but officers and men could sense the strains developing between them as each tried to exert his authority. To Bessels, Budington was a boor, uneducated in science, uninterested in the higher purposes of the expedition; to Budington, Bessels was an intellectual snob, arrogant in his lack of practical experience of the Arctic.

The strains between the two ranking officers were not unique aboard the ship. As the winter and spring dragged on, most of the men became self-concerned, withdrawn, and

highly critical of others. Tyson himself liked neither Budington nor Bessels, and for some reason he also had a grudge
against Hubbard Chester, who returned his ill feelings. Schumann did not like Tyson, and Budington did not like
Schumann. Meyer sided with Bessels against Budington, but
also had quarrels with Bessels. The taciturn old sea dog
Morton was suspicious of both Bessels and Meyer, as was
Chester. Of the officers, only Bryan—hearing no evil, seeing
no evil, speaking no evil—seemed out of this round robin
of hostility.

If the thoughts of Hayes and Mauch are any indication,
things were no better in the forecastle. Judged by his journal,
Joseph Mauch was a cool young man, not given to emotion
and usually very much in control of himself. During the
winter, however, Mauch built up an intense dislike of Emil
Bessels, venting his spleen in journal entries full of invective
and sarcasm. Among other things, Mauch doubted Bessels's
integrity as a scientist, calling him a "d——d imposter" and
claiming that he frequently falsified data on observations that
he was too lazy to make. At other times, Mauch's dislike became more generalized; he reveled in self-pity, feeling that
he was much abused—an educated man whose abilities
were wasted on the common seamen with whom he had to
live. At such times everyone was Mauch's enemy; he stood
alone.

Even more striking was the radical change in the personality of Noah Hayes. On the cruise from Tasiussaq Hall had
assigned Hayes to the fireroom as an assistant to Schumann.
Hayes believed that the assignment had been only temporary,
and that, if Hall had lived, he would have been promoted.
As it was, during the winter he found himself working under
a rather truculent fireman named Walter Campbell, who
apparently had little sympathy with Hayes's youthful enthusiasm. In spite of that, Hayes remained steadfastly cheerful and optimistic until March 5, when suddenly a dam
broke somewhere within him and all his good cheer and

optimism were washed away in a flood of self-pity and rage. On that day, Hayes filled fourteen large pages of his journal with three thousand words of bitter accusation against Schumann and Campbell. Everything before this entry was sweetness and light—everything after it was bitterness and gloom.

Nathaniel Coffin, the carpenter, had periodic fits of insanity during the winter and spring. A sensitive man, a convert to Catholicism who had, in Hayes's words, "seen better days," Coffin from the beginning had been nervous with the rough sailors of the forecastle; taking their banter seriously, he had become convinced that they disliked, even hated him. Perhaps Hall's ravings about murder set him off, but whatever the cause, not long after Hall's death Coffin became prey to a delusion that the crew was trying to murder him. He believed that one night while he slept, someone would bore a hole through the wall beside his bunk and spray carbonic acid on him, freezing him to death. He took to changing his sleeping place often, furtively moving out of one cabin into another late at night, sometimes curling up in an alleyway or a corner of the galley, terrified of everyone around him. When these fits were on him Coffin was a ghostly embodiment of the suspicions and fears that were at work in the minds of all the men aboard the *Polaris*.

Some of the psychological problems may have been caused by prolonged inactivity. Budington believed in leaving his men free of organized exercise and recreation or make-work chores—an apparently humane but perhaps a debilitating policy. Because there was little actual work to be done, the men soon became profoundly bored, slipping into a state of dangerous lassitude. When spring came some excursions were made from the ship, but they were halfhearted and ill-organized. Occasional musk-ox-hunting expeditions went out for a few days at a time, and Bessels led a small sledge team on a fifteen-day exploration to the south in March, but little of value was accomplished by anyone until summer, when there was a sudden burst of activity.

Early in June, under Budington's direction, a series of
haphazard boat expeditions began, having the grandiose
purpose of reaching the North Pole. In spite of the ice that
had blocked the *Polaris* in the fall, some of the officers still
believed that they could reach the Pole, or at least approach
it, by boat. Budington organized two separate boat crews,
one commanded by Hubbard Chester, the other by George
Tyson. On June 7 Chester's boat set out northward; Tyson's
prepared to follow soon after. Chester and his men returned
only two days later, to report that their boat had been
crushed in the floes and lost with all of her equipment. Perhaps some of the mutual dislike between Chester and Tyson
can be traced to Tyson's reaction to Chester's story. He called
the cape near which they lost the boat "Cape Disaster" and
the bay in which the boat was crushed "Folly Bay," which,
he later commented, "I believe was rather displeasing to
Mr. Chester."[7] The accident had almost been fatal to the
whole party, and the men barely reached the shore, but
Chester was determined to go north, and Budington allowed
him to rig the portable canvas folding boat intended for
emergency use by sledge parties. While Chester's crew prepared for their next voyage, Tyson's crew, including Bessels,
managed to find enough leads through the ice to round Cape
Lupton. They were followed on the next day by Chester
and his crew in their canvas boat. The two parties met at
Newman Bay, where they set up a camp and remained for
more than a month, accomplishing little but apparently determined not to return to the ship until it was absolutely
necessary.

While Chester's and Tyson's parties—most of the expedition's able-bodied men—camped at Newman Bay, there was
activity aboard the *Polaris*. Budington had been constantly
alert to changes in ice conditions, wanting to get his ship
free of Providence Berg at the first opportunity. On June 20
a gale cleared away the outer floes, but the ship remained
fixed in ice between the berg and the shore, with open

water only ten yards away. Budington set his skeleton crew
to work sawing and blasting the ice around the ship. They
worked furiously for three days; then suddenly the ice opened
and the *Polaris* slid off the spur of Providence Berg, afloat
for the first time in six months. Budington soon discovered
the damage that had been wrought during the winter. In
clear water he could at last see the spur jutting out from the
berg, and he could also see where it had wrenched the hull
of the *Polaris*. Below decks he could hear the ship leaking
steadily, dangerously in the holds, and he immediately had
the mechanical pump started. His plan, he later said, was
to sail north to Newman Bay, pick up the boat crews, and
try to reach a new high latitude, but more probably he intended to get the crews aboard and head south as fast as
possible. In the two weeks that followed the freeing of the
ship he made several attempts to round Cape Lupton, but,
frustrated each time by ice, he returned to the relative safety
of Thank God Harbor. He sent messengers afoot to Newman
Bay, demanding that Chester and Tyson return to the ship
immediately.

At Newman Bay, Tyson and Chester were at loggerheads.
Tyson told Bartlett that he had tried to persuade Chester
to leave the boats behind and join him in an overland
trek to the north, but Chester had refused even to consider
the proposition. When Budington's demand that they return to the ship reached them, they again disagreed. Tyson,
worried that Budington would sail south without them,
decided to return to the ship, but Chester stubbornly refused to move. Several of Chester's men admitted that Budington might desert them, but they maintained that they
could make their way south by boat if he did. Angry at what
he thought their stupid optimism, Tyson returned to the
Polaris, leaving Chester and his crew behind. Chester held
out for two more weeks; then, in mid-July, he too returned
to the ship with his men.

The *Polaris* fully manned again, Budington was prepared

to sail south as soon as conditions would permit, and he kept a constant ice-watch mounted on a bluff above the harbor. As days went by and the outer channel remained clogged with floes, the men aboard the ship were haunted by the prospect of being locked in ice again. They all were willing to risk their lives rather than spend another winter in Thank God Harbor. During the wait Hubbard Chester whiled away time by carving a headboard for Hall's grave. A few months before, Emil Schumann had put up a board with a simple inscription written on it in pencil, but Chester felt that Hall deserved something better. He carved deep into a piece of pine:

In Memory of
CHARLES FRANCIS HALL,
late commander of
U.S. Steamer Polaris, North Pole Expedition.
Died
Nov. 8th, 1871 — Aged 50 years.
"I am the resurrection and the life; he that believeth
on me, though he were dead, yet shall he live."

When Chester mounted the headboard, he noticed that some ground willow that had been transplanted to the grave-site in the fall had taken root; its gnarled, tough little branches were beginning to spread out among the rocks.

On August 12 Budington decided to force his ship through the nearby floes to the outer channel, where some open water had at last been sighted. Early that morning, as if in anticipation of their escape from Thank God Harbor, Hans's wife gave birth to a boy. Her loose Eskimo clothing had concealed her condition, and the event was a complete surprise to almost everyone aboard, but the men looked on it as a good omen. They called the baby "Charles Polaris" and celebrated his birth with cheers as steam was being built up for the voyage ahead. Late in the afternoon the *Polaris* slowly eased out of Thank God Harbor, weaving her way between the floes, bound for the open water beyond. The open water, however, turned out to be only a lead. After a few exhilarating hours of free sailing, the *Polaris* was again hemmed in by ice, and Budington had no choice: he tied her to a floe. This was to be her situation most of the time during the two months that followed; tied to the floe, she drifted passively southward with the ice. In her drift she remained near the center of the channel between Ellesmere Island and Greenland, so land was usually at least twenty miles away. If the ship should sink—and she was still leaking badly—the men would have little chance of making it across the broken ice to the shore. The sound of the pumps, burning nine hundred pounds of coal a day, was a constant reminder of their plight to everyone aboard. And so the ship drifted through August and September, her pumps working, making steady but agonizingly slow progress southward through Kennedy Channel and Kane Basin. Distances that it had traveled in hours on the outward cruise took days or even weeks on the return drift.

On the evening of October 12, as the *Polaris* was drifting through Smith Sound, George Tyson's hour of destiny arrived with a violent gale blowing from the southwest. The wind had increased during the day, driving a blinding snow, and by evening it was obvious that the ship was in immediate danger. In the gloom the appalled men could see huge bergs, pushed by the wind, smashing through floes past the ship and driving the sea ice against her hull. At seven-thirty p.m. the pressure from the ice suddenly raised the *Polaris* up and threw her to port; the men could hear the sound of cracking timber even above the grinding of ice and the shriek of wind. Schumann ran from his engineroom, where he was trying to get up steam, to report that water was rushing into the ship below decks. According to Schumann, Budington immediately shouted, "Shove everything overboard." Then there was panic.

Some of the crew jumped from the ship out onto the

floe while others began to throw supplies and equipment overboard, grabbing whatever came to hand. Tyson shouted at Budington that the two surviving boats were on the ice and asked if they should be brought aboard, but Budington ordered him to forget the boats and haul the provisions on the floe farther away from the ship. Ebierbing and Hans had put their wives and children on the floe. As Tyson frantically moved supplies back from the edge of the water, he was aware of Tookoolito beside him, working as hard as the crew. There was little light, but at intervals the moon showed through scudding clouds, and then he could see a scene of hellish confusion: the ship lurching against her hawsers in the newly opened water, waves smashing against the floe and filling the air with freezing spume, bergs bearing downwind in the murk like monstrous sails. At one point, he noticed some musk-ox hides lying across a spreading crack in the ice and grabbed to save them from dropping through; then he saw, wrapped in one of the hides, three of Hans's children asleep. He had barely saved them from being drowned or crushed.

At about ten o'clock, according to the later testimony, the floe seemed to explode. Nineteen men, women, and children were on the ice at the time, fourteen men aboard the ship. The ice that held the stern anchors broke free of the floe, and the ship swung around rapidly on her forward hawser. Then the hawser somehow pulled out of its anchor, and with incredible speed the *Polaris* was driven away from the floe. As she disappeared into the storm, the steward John Herron, who had tried to reach the ship when she broke free of its moorings, shouted after her, "Good-bye, *Polaris!*" Some of the men aboard the ship could hear his voice even over the scream of the wind.

Tyson told Bartlett that his first action when the *Polaris* disappeared was to gather together the party that had been left behind. He had to go out in a boat to pick up some of the men, who were adrift on small pieces of ice that had been dislodged from the main floe. Then, exhausted, they had huddled together to wait out the stormy night. Early in the morning, when the storm had blown over, Tyson scouted the floe. It was nearly circular, about four miles in circumference; like most sea ice, it was not smooth, its surface broken up by hillocks of ice as high as thirty feet and pitted by small ponds made by the summer thaw. From one of the hillocks Tyson could see that there was enough open water for them to reach the shore by boat, but he also saw that more ice was drifting down from the north and would soon be on them. He immediately went back to rouse his sleeping party.

His troubles with the men, he told Bartlett, began then. They saw no reason to hurry. They believed that the *Polaris* would soon return to rescue them, and they said that even if she did not, they could reach the shore later. With a deliberate slowness that infuriated Tyson, they prepared breakfast, lighting a fire to cook and making themselves as comfortable as possible while they ate. Finally Tyson persuaded them to load the boats, and they set off toward the Greenland shore. Tyson had been right. The ice that he had seen to the north had drifted down and blocked the leads. The ice jam was too solid to navigate even in a small boat, but not solid enough to walk on. Discouraged, they hauled the boats back up on the floe.

Only a few minutes later they saw something that would haunt and frustrate them for many months to come: the *Polaris* under both sail and steam a few miles to the southeast, close against the Greenland shore. Quickly Tyson and his men spread out a large piece of rubber cloth on the side of a hillock, hoping that its blackness would be seen against the white of the ice. Tyson could make out the ship plainly through his telescope; he told Bartlett that although he could see no one on her decks, she was in full motion, like a ghost ship. The anguished men on the floe watched helplessly while she moved farther and farther away from them, finally disappearing behind an island.

All of the men, women, and children suffered privation and fear in the months that followed. Within a few days of their separation from the ship, the floe had drifted from the relatively narrow Smith Sound into the open waters of northern Baffin Bay. As the land receded from them on both sides, they knew that their chances of gaining the shore diminished every hour, yet ice conditions prohibited them from trying to reach it. Reluctantly they built shelters, Tyson a wooden hut, the Eskimos igloos. Although they had large quantities of tinned meats and other supplies, Tyson realized that unless the food was carefully rationed it would not last long. After he and Frederick Meyer made a pair of scales, the careful allotting of food became a daily break in the monotony of the drift—a break far too often charged with jealous suspicion as each man compared his portion with the others'. They began by rationing eleven ounces of food for each adult, half that amount for each child, but as the supplies dwindled, so did the rations. It was not long before the Eskimos began to kill the dogs for food, and soon there were no more dogs. The shortage of fuel was as serious as the shortage of food. When the Eskimos killed a seal they had blubber, but much of the time there were no seals and no blubber. Early in the ordeal they chopped up one of their boats for wood, but, cold as they were, they knew that it would be fatal to destroy the other one.

"We survive through God's mercy and Joe's [Ebierbing's] ability as a hunter," Tyson wrote. Time after time, just as they verged on death by starvation, Ebierbing would kill a seal or, on two occasions of celebration, a polar bear. Like the Eskimos themselves, the men would gorge on the raw meat and drink the blood. Then, within days, they would be starving again.

According to Tyson, their constant hunger and cold had one virtue: it distracted them from the fear that otherwise might have driven them to madness. Their original floe was four miles in circumference, but when it was reduced to a tenth of that size, they moved to another. During the winter, when there was plenty of sea ice around them, they knew that they would be able to make such moves when necessary, but as they drifted southward and winter passed into spring, the chances increased that they would be trapped on one steadily diminishing floe. In March violent gales swept Baffin Bay, breaking up the ice and separating them from the main pack. When their floe was reduced so much that Tyson counted only twenty paces between the shelters and open water, they piled into the boat and moved to another. A few weeks later it too broke up in a gale, and one stormy night they found themselves so restricted that they could not all lie down. The sea broke on their ice island, washing over it, soaking them, and sweeping away some of their precious supplies. They barely escaped to another floe.

By late April they were often moving from floe to floe, finding momentary security, then losing it in a gale. They had no idea how far away land was, but they knew that if a gale caught them in open water in their overloaded boat, they surely would be killed. They also knew that soon they would have to take that chance. On the day before the *Tigress* rescued them, they were on a tiny floe endangered by bergs. If the ship had not appeared, they probably would have had to make the desperate gamble of heading for shore.

The hunger, cold, and fear were shared by all, but George Tyson suffered most. Before their separation from the ship, all the men and women on the floe except Tyson had taken personal equipment with them onto the ice, including spare clothing. Tyson had only the clothes he wore, and in the winter he was forced to cover himself with whatever was available, odd pieces of cloth and canvas that gave him little protection from the cold. The constant psychological strain was no less an ordeal than were his physical sufferings. As Frederick Meyer was the only other officer present, Tyson was the ranking officer on the floe. He felt the responsibilities of his position, but soon discovered that it was virtually impossible to fulfill them. From the first day of the drift, when the men refused to try to reach shore, they resisted Tyson's authority. He was to testify before the Board of Inquiry:

> I endeavored to maintain the discipline of the party as well as I could; but there was little or nothing that could be called discipline. Every man was armed with pistols but myself; I was on the ice without anything, and they did as they pleased. I could merely advise them.

The Germans formed a clique, often speaking only their native language to one another. According to Tyson, Meyer established himself as leader of these men, ignored Tyson, and issued his own orders. As Tyson told the Board of Inquiry, they were armed and he was not; he knew that if he insisted on his authority too persistently, he might jeopardize what little power he had over them. Supplies were pilfered, but Tyson could do nothing about it. Meyer misled the men about their position, giving them false hopes of reaching land, but Tyson could not correct him. When the Eskimos killed a seal, the men would seize the meat and take it into their own igloo, and Tyson was unable to stop them. Always surly, they never laughed or even smiled. One day, in an apparent test of Tyson's will, Kruger stalked into his hut and abused him foully. When Tyson sat silent, refusing to respond, Kruger seemed frustrated; Tyson believed that the German was trying to bait him into a fight, and that if he had responded, the other men would have attacked like a pack of wolves. Later, during the darkest hours of near-starvation, Tyson was haunted by another fear—cannibalism. He worried about the Eskimo children in particular, and Ebierbing shared his worry. "I don't like the look out of the men's eyes," the Eskimo muttered to him one day and handed him a pistol. Tyson took the gun gratefully, fully expecting that the time would come when he would have to use it.

But the time never came. Perhaps if the *Tigress* had not rescued them from their last tiny bit of floe, Tyson's fears would have been realized in a dreadful burst of violence. As it was, they were saved just when they all faced death—from each other if not from sea or ice.

George Tyson told his story to Isaac Bartlett during the week that the *Tigress* remained on the sealing grounds. Bartlett remembered vividly what he had heard from the emaciated and exhausted Tyson, and many years later he repeated it to his nephew Bob Bartlett, a boy who was to grow into one of the great Arctic navigators—repeated it with such tedious regularity that young Bob tried to sneak out of the house whenever his uncle Isaac paid a visit.

The *Tigress* put into St. John's on May 12. The American Consul immediately went aboard to inform Tyson that the Secretary of the Navy would probably send a ship to pick up his party and carry it to Washington. In the meantime, Tyson was told, he was to be in charge of all its members, to watch over their behavior and see to their comfort and safety. Tyson must have been bitterly aware of the irony of this sudden authority given him from on high, but he soon realized that his party did indeed need to be watched. They had become famous. They were stopped in the streets of St. John's and asked about their experiences. The women of St. John's so fussed over the Eskimo women and children that Tyson had to protect them by prohibiting visitors. The day after their arrival he received a wire from Harper & Brothers requesting that his party have a group photograph taken for publication in Harper's *Illustrated Weekly*. Tyson knew that there would be an official investigation of the expedition and that the Department of the Navy would frown on too much exposure before the investigation began, but he allowed the photograph to be taken.

Tyson also committed a serious indiscretion. While talking to one of the partners of the firm that owned the *Tigress*, he angrily charged Budington with a plot to scuttle the *Polaris* and the expedition. During the spring after Hall's death, Tyson said, Budington approached him with "an astonishing proposition." In his book, *Arctic Experiences*, Tyson was to refer to such a proposition but he avoided saying what precisely it was. However, he told the partner of Harvey and Company that Budington proposed that they take the *Polaris* south to waters frequented by whalers, scuttle her, go ashore in boats, and wait through the winter to be "rescued" by a whaler in the spring. In that way, Budington reasoned, they would collect pay yet take few risks. The partner immediately informed the American Consulate of Tyson's charge, but was requested by the Consul to keep secret what he had heard. He did until fifty years later, when he told his family the story.[8] If indeed Tyson made such a charge, he did not repeat it to the Board of Inquiry, although he was to make cryptic reference to it in his book; and if the Board had heard of the charge, it chose to ignore it.

On May 27 Tyson and his party boarded the USS *Frolic*, which had been sent from Washington to pick them up. They left behind them a St. John's still excited by their stay; they had before them a Washington tense with expectation. Newspapers had carried the story of their rescue, creating a sensation, but many persons suspected that more sensation was yet to come when the full story could be heard.

chapter eight

Washington—
the Inquiry

Within hours after George Tyson and his party arrived in Washington on June 5, 1873, they appeared before a hastily convened Board of Inquiry presided over by Secretary of the Navy George Robeson. After two days of intensive interrogation, Robeson set about organizing a search for the *Polaris,* his department chartering the *Tigress* from her Newfoundland owners and preparing a small naval vessel, the *Juniata,* to accompany it. The *Juniata* sailed for Greenland on June 24, followed by the *Tigress* on July 14. Aboard the *Tigress* as ice-master and acting lieutenant was George Tyson, who had volunteered to return to the Arctic to help in the search, and also Ebierbing, who was to serve as Eskimo interpreter.

After meeting at Upernavik, the two ships carried out independent cruises, the larger and better equipped *Tigress* making for the site of Tyson's separation from the *Polaris.* Commander Greer of the *Tigress* landed near the place where Tyson had last seen the ship, and there he found evidence that Budington, Bessels, and the other lost men had wintered ashore: a wooden hut, bunks and mattresses, manuscripts, pieces of ship's equipment. No cairn was found, no message, no ship, but Eskimos living in the area told Greer that the *Polaris* indeed had been driven aground there and that her men had set up quarters ashore. Accord-

ing to the Eskimos, they had spent the winter there, and in
the spring had set out southward in two boats fabricated
from the wood of their ship. One of the Eskimos told Greer
that Budington, before his departure, had made them a
present of the hull of the *Polaris,* but that soon afterwards
a gale had driven it from the shore and sunk it. Greer took
a boat to the place where the ship had gone down, which
the Eskimos said was shallow, but the water was covered by
floe and he was unable to see the *Polaris* in her grave.

Greer sailed southward, staying as close to the Greenland
coast as he dared in the hope that he might see some signal
ashore. He hoped that when he reached the Danish settlements he would find whalers who might have picked up
the survivors, but the season was late and the whalers had all
left the grounds. Greer discovered that there had been many
whalers in the area, however, and even as he continued his
search across the bay along the shores of Baffin Island, he
felt confident that the men had been rescued. When he put
into St. John's, he was relieved to learn that Scottish whalers
had indeed picked up all the officers and men of the *Polaris*
and taken them to Great Britain. Even as Greer heard the
news, they were on their way home from Dundee.

Most of the men who were aboard the *Polaris* when she
broke loose from the floe testified before the Board of Inquiry
that when they were carried away on the ship they had
wished they were on the floe rather than on the ship. "Those
who were on the ice were very glad to get there," Hubbard
Chester said. "They considered themselves in the safest
place there; everybody thought that the safest place." The
men on the *Polaris* knew that the ship was leaking badly
and that, once free of the ice, she might sink. As the floe
disappeared in the storm, they were acutely aware of the
fact that the boats were on the ice and that if the ship did
sink, they might well go down with her. At their interrogation the men of Tyson's party had complained bitterly that

the *Polaris* did not try to rescue them; they had seen the ship only a few miles away, but she had not come to take them off the ice. In the later interrogation of the *Polaris* party, Budington and others testified that even if they had seen the men (and they all swore that they had not), the ship was so badly damaged that they would not have been able to reach the floe. Indeed, only hours after Tyson's party were tormented by the sight of the ship and what they considered to be safety, Budington had run her aground and her men had deserted for the shore.

Luckily for the *Polaris* party, they had landed near the Polar Eskimo settlement of Etah. The Eskimos of the area were familiar with white men, remembering Kane and Hayes, and they gladly helped the men of the *Polaris* not only in setting up their winter camp but also in stocking it with meat during the months that followed. Largely because of the Etah Eskimos, the party ashore did not suffer the privations that were endured by the party on the floe: their ordeal consisted mainly of boredom, for all they could do was wait for spring. In April they started building two boats, and early in June there was enough open water for them to head south. Several weeks later they were picked up by the Scottish whaler *Ravenscraig,* and shortly thereafter they were carried to Scotland.

Most of the *Polaris* party arrived in New York aboard a British steamer on October 7 and were immediately transferred to the USS *Talapoosa,* which was waiting for them at the Brooklyn Navy Yard. A few of the men did not return to the United States until later, but the *Talapoosa* did not delay: she sailed immediately for Washington, where Secretary Robeson and his Board of Inquiry awaited her. The earlier interrogation of Tyson's party had brought up many questions that remained unanswered. With the return of Budington, Bessels, and the others, Robeson hoped he could learn the answers to some of those questions and stifle the

rumors that were beginning to spread—rumors darkly suggesting that criminal prosecution might be necessary in the
Polaris case.

The inquiry began aboard the *Talapoosa* soon after she
arrived at the Washington Navy Yard. At eleven-thirty a.m.
on October 11, the Secretary of the Navy started the pro-
ceedings by calling Sidney Budington as the first witness.
Secretary Robeson explained the purposes of the investigation to Budington in his opening address:

> Captain, you are aware that, when the party from the *Polaris*
> who were on the ice-floe arrived, we thought it proper to
> examine them and obtain their full statements with a view
> to preserving everything, not only that the Government may
> be informed of what has been done and what has been
> omitted, but that whatever there was of value to history or
> science might be secured at once; it seems also proper that we
> should go on with your party in the same way, so that we
> may have the statements of everybody freely and fully made
> from their own recollection of what occurred. We have sent
> for you first as the commander of the expedition after the
> death of Captain Hall, and we desire you to give a state-
> ment, so far as you can, of everything which seems to have
> any reference to the subject-matter.

Gentle as Robeson was in mentioning the positive aspects
of the Board's inquiry—the gathering of information for
"history and science"—Budington well knew that he was
unofficially on trial. George Tyson, in testimony to the
Board four months before, had been sharply critical of Budington's behavior throughout the expedition, venting con-
tempt in vicious little jabs:

> *Question:* Did you know of any difficulty between anybody
>   left on board and Captain Budington?
> *Answer:* Nothing more than that feeling that will always

be between an incompetent man and a subordinate who thinks him so.

One specific charge that Tyson had initiated was that of drinking. Tyson reported that Budington had stolen alcohol from Doctor Bessels's supply and that he was drunk on the day that the ship had first been beset by ice in her southward voyage:

> *Question:* Was Captain Budington drunk at the time you were beset?
> *Answer:* Yes, sir; he was drunk; not on rum, but on alcohol.
> *Question:* How do you know that?
> *Answer:* The doctor caught him at it, and they had quite a tussle together; I was not present; I was on deck.
> *Question:* Tell all you know about that.
> *Answer:* Captain Budington was drunk, and the doctor said he was going to catch him. He went into the pantry, where the natives were, and secreted himself there. Captain Budington came down to take his nip, and the doctor came out of his hiding place and took hold of him. The doctor did not keep his alcohol there, but Captain Budington had secreted some there, and he would go down and take his nip. There was no liquor on board, except this alcohol, at that time.

Tyson's charge that Budington drank was substantiated by some of the other men. The steward John Herron, when asked if Budington ever drank, replied, "You want the truth; I must answer you when you ask me. He did, both before and after Captain Hall's death. . . . Captain Budington, if he drinks at all, must get drunk." Frederick Jamka simply said, "Captain Budington was drunk very often," and Hubbard Chester, in an obvious understatement, testified, "I have seen him once or twice in a condition that we would call 'boozy.'. . . I have seen him boozy when I thought that there was nothing else on board."

Budington admitted to the Board that twice on the ex-

pedition he had been drunk, and he also admitted that
Bessels had caught him drinking some of the alcohol that
the doctor used to preserve specimens: "I went to the aft
hatch to get something to drink. He was down there at the
time and made some remarks about it. I just took him by
the collar and told him to mind his own business." Robeson
bore in on the subject, not allowing Budington to dismiss
it too easily:

> *Question:* Was not the alcohol put on board for scientific
> purposes?
> *Answer:* Yes, sir.
> *Question:* What did you drink it for?
> *Answer:* I was sick and down-hearted, and had a bad cold,
> and I wanted some stimulant—that is, I thought
> I did; I do not suppose I really did.
> *Question:* Were you in the habit of drinking alcohol?
> *Answer:* I make it a practice to drink but very little.

In the course of its investigations the Board soon discovered
that Budington was not the only man aboard the *Polaris*
who had been drinking. According to Emil Schumann,
George Tyson was also an offender: "I saw Captain Tyson
drunk like old mischief. I saw Captain Tyson when he could
scarcely move along." Another man said that Schumann
himself had made a key to open Bessels's supply of alcohol
and had used it often. The carpenter, Nathaniel Coffin, although asserting that he never saw anyone drunk on duty,
admitted that he had seen Hubbard Chester "under the
influence of alcohol." Clean-cut Richard Bryan blew the
lid off the subject of drinking. Although probably not intending to, Bryan gave the impression that the expedition
had been an extended Arctic bacchanal. Especially after
Hall's death, Bryan testified, the officers drank and, like
Budington, stole alcohol from Bessels's supply. "Of course
when the officers did go and take the liquor and did get
drunk," Bryan said, "all that could be done was to accept

the fact, and keep them quiet and get them to bed as soon
as possible." The officers were not alone in availing themselves of the alcohol; Bryan testified that some of the crew
had discovered that they could crawl through the engine
shaft to a place where some was stored. When the Board
asked Bryan if anyone had tried to stop the drinking, the
young officer replied: "The only way it could have been
stopped . . . was by taking all the liquor aboard the vessel
and throwing it overboard."

The fact that Budington not only was drinking but also
was obviously blinding himself to drinking by others brought
up the question of discipline aboard the ship. In dealing
with this subject, as in dealing with any other, the Board
soon found that in matters of fact and in matters of opinion
the survivors of the *Polaris* expedition were frequently at
odds. Asked about discipline after Hall's death, Budington
stated, "The discipline of the ship was very good." Some of
the other men supported this affirmation, but most disagreed.
"I think it was lax," Noah Hayes said. (Hayes, vociferous in
his complaints in his journal, was curiously quiet-spoken
before the Board.) According to Frederick Jamka, "everything went backward" after Hall's death, and Gustavus
Lindquist reported that there was good discipline so long
as Hall was alive, "but we put discipline along with him in
his grave." Immediately after Hall's death Budington had
canceled the required morning muster and prayer, a small
but significant action. The sense of communal purpose that
must underlie all discipline rapidly disappeared and, as
many of the men testified, each man did what he pleased.
"We made ourselves as comfortable as possible," one of the
crew admitted. "We did not do much of anything."

It was all too evident that Budington had had little enthusiasm for the main purpose of the expedition, the attack
on the North Pole. Hubbard Chester told the Board, "His
idea was, as it struck me, that the enterprise was all 'damn
nonsense.'" He was not inspired by the drive that must

vitalize an explorer, and George Tyson told a story that
seemed to characterize his attitude. On the day after the
Polaris first put into Thank God Harbor, Hall had called
a conference of his officers to discuss the question of whether
or not they should try to take the ship farther north. According to Tyson, he and Chester urged Hall to try for a higher
northing, but "Captain Budington, with an oath, said that
he would be damned if she should move from there." Tyson
went on to comment, "The man had neither heart nor
soul in the expedition. It was not his intention to go north if
he could help it." Undisciplined by a sense of purpose himself, Budington could not, or would not, impose discipline
on others. Chester commented, "As a whaling commander
Captain Budington, I think, does very well, but not so good
for a north-pole expedition."

In his testimony, Budington was on the defensive. He
knew that Tyson's party had already prejudiced the Board,
and that George Tyson in particular had been critical of
his command. He vehemently protested some of the charges
that had been made against him:

> No conversation occurred in which Chester and Tyson ex-
> pressed a desire to go north while I expressed a disinclina-
> tion to do so. I never so expressed myself. I have seen that
> report printed in the papers, but it is not correct. No man
> in the ship would ever so express himself to Captain Hall
> and get along with him. . . . I did my very best to get the
> ship north. I never said anything about never going any
> further north.

Given the opportunity, he jabbed back at Tyson. Secretary
Robeson asked him if he had reason to complain about anyone on the expedition:

> *Answer:* Yes, sir; somewhat.
> *Question:* Let us hear all about it.
> *Answer:* Captain Tyson. He was a man that was rather

useless aboard, and complained bitterly about
the management generally. He did not appear
to be satisfied with anything that was done. I
would consult him on a subject and he would
perhaps agree to it, and then afterward would
say that he thought it was no use to do anything
of that kind; that he knew it was of no use. He
generally acted that way. I got so that after a
while I did not pay much attention to him.

Tyson had made one charge against Budington that Budington was unable to answer because the Board did not con-
front him with it. From the beginning of the expedition,
Tyson said, Budington circulated among the men as an equal.
This would partly explain the weak discipline when Budington took command of the expedition, but Tyson made more
of the subject than Budington's lack of authority. He said
that Budington had used his familiarity with the men to
subvert Hall's command. "I must say that he was a disorganizer from the very commencement," Tyson testified.

> *Question:* How do you mean? how did he disorganize?
> *Answer:* By associating himself with the crew, and slander-
> ing his commander, and in other ways that I
> might mention.
> *Question:* Let us have the whole of it.
> *Answer:* Well, sir, he associated himself with crew very
> much, cursing his commander, and blaming him,
> and speaking slightingly of him.
> *Question:* Was it Captain Hall of whom he so spoke?
> *Answer:* Yes, sir.
> *Question:* In what way, particularly?
> *Answer:* In his own way; I could not describe it to you.
> *Question:* What seemed to be the ground of complaint, if
> any?
> *Answer:* His ground of complaint was that the captain
> was not a seaman. On the most frivolous things
> he would be among the crew and complaining
> of Captain Hall.

Question: Was he insubordinate to the captain in any way?
Answer: O, no, sir; he was very subordinate to the captain in his presence.

Chester confirmed Tyson's testimony, saying that Budington "at times rather depreciated Captain Hall, using language
around the main-deck that should not have been used by
a man in his capacity." Chester went on to clarify what he
meant: "When I say 'main-deck,' I mean among the seamen.
He did this when he was sober. He did not speak very respectfully of the commander, or of the expedition." One
of the seamen later admitted that Budington "made fun of
Captain Hall a good many times. Captain Budington was
very friendly to Captain Hall till his back was turned."

At one point in his testimony, Budington seemed to confirm the charge. He told the Board that just before Hall's last
sledge trip, he, Budington, had argued fiercely with Chester,
Morton, and Tyson about the value of such trips. At the time,
Noah Hayes was sweeping the deck. Hall had instructed Budington to save all deck sweepings because anything that
could be used as fuel was of value. Excited by the argument,
Budington had stormed up to Hayes. "Save all those shavings
and put them in a barrel," he snarled at the startled youth.
"They will do for the devilish fools on the sledge-journey."
He admitted that he did not want Hall to hear his remark—
"it was about the worst thing I could have said in his case,
as he was very much in favor of sledge-journeys"—but Hall
had overheard and had roundly castigated his ship's master.

The charge of being a "disorganizer" was serious. It was
one thing for Budington to be accused of laxness and inefficiency, another for him to be accused of subverting a
commanding officer. For some reason, the Board did not press
the matter, even avoiding the subject during most of the
interrogations. It probably recognized the awkwardness of
the situation. Although under Navy orders during the expedition, Budington was actually a civilian whaling captain.

A Navy officer could have been court-martialed, but the legal problems of punishing a civilian would have been knotty, and the case undoubtedly would have become a *cause célèbre,* the last thing in the world that Secretary Robeson wanted. The Board came to the conclusion, contained in its *Report to the President,* that Budington, "though he was perhaps wanting in enthusiasm for the grand objects of the expedition, and at times grossly lax in discipline," was "an experienced and careful navigator, and, when not affected by liquor, a competent and safe commander."

The Board members had first heard the story of the expedition and the separation of the party on the ice floe from George Tyson. Tyson's often-bitter testimony also revealed that the expedition had been crippled by hostility among its officers and, after the death of Hall, by ineffective leadership. Sidney Budington's testimony had, if anything, confirmed Tyson's. Although Budington sometimes tried to deny his fellow whaler's direct charges against himself, his tone throughout the interrogation was one of defeat, of weary resignation snapped by outbursts of indignant denial.

The Board knew that Budington, as commander of the expedition after Hall's death, was partly a scapegoat. Budington's drinking, his lack of authority in command, his apathy, even his occasional subversion of Hall—all these had obviously contributed to the failure of the expedition, but they also obviously were not the only cause of it. As the Board progressed in its inquiry, it must have realized that darker forces were at work than drinking, weak discipline, apathy, or even the kind of subversion of which Budington was culpable. His subversion, perhaps his most serious fault, consisted mainly of sarcastic remarks made to crewmen about Hall—a serious breach of naval discipline, but under most civilian law very hard to prosecute. For Budington himself, however, legal prosecution was perhaps unnecessary. What

had led him to those sneaky attacks on his commander? Was
his apathy, his indifference to the purposes of the expedition,
merely indifference? Or was it a spiteful refusal to share his
former friend's enthusiasm and submit to his former pupil's
authority? (Hall had been Budington's pupil aboard the
George Henry.) Had Budington tried to stop himself from
undercutting Hall, failed, and loathed himself for failing?
Why had he suddenly become a heavy drinker? The Board
did not ask such questions, but perhaps Budington asked them
of himself—and prosecuted himself. At his interrogation, he
was almost stupid in his lethargy, acting psychologically
crippled. His career was over. One of the finest whaling captains of his time, there is no record to indicate he ever went
to sea again.

Budington was not the only witness to show ravages of a
psychological ordeal. Tyson himself, while charging some of
the officers and men with almost criminal shortcomings, was
too generally bitter to be entirely convincing, and Budington's remark that he "did not appear to be satisfied with anything that was done" rings true. Removed from a position of
direct responsibility, Tyson was hypercritical. He had little
good to say about anyone but Hall, and Hall was dead; one
wonders if Tyson would have praised Hall as warmly as he
sometimes did had Hall lived and continued in command.
All in all, Tyson acted too much like a hurt man looking for
trouble.

Dark undercurrents that the Board could not plumb ran
through most of the interrogations, showing only when signs
of bitterness or guilt welled up to the surface of a testimony.
Even when the undercurrents did not show, they were there,
running still and deep. Reading Noah Hayes's testimony,
a toneless recitation of facts, one would believe that Hayes
had been unaffected by his experiences. But Hayes's journals
show that he had been profoundly affected. Eager and innocent at the outset, he had later become almost paranoid in

his distrust of his fellows, filling pages of his notebooks with tantrum. Then there was a third phase in Hayes's psychological ordeal, as painful as the second and probably shared by most members of the expedition. For many months Hayes had been filled with a volatile mixture of fear, spite, hatred, and self-loathing. After he was rescued, when immediate physical hardships and dangers ceased, he experienced a backwash of guilt. For Hayes this experience was particularly painful because he had written down so many of his thoughts and feelings, recording his mental aberrations in humiliating detail. It had been ruled that all private journals would be collected and examined, and when Hayes's journal was called for, he sat down to conclude with what he called a "preface," an anguished summary of his experiences and of his disillusion with the Arctic:

> I have just closed my journal and now I will bundle them up for transportation, hoping that the Captain will yet decide not to take them. I am utterly disgusted with writing and with what I have written, as I am with myself, the country, everything in it, and everybody that has a fancied interest in it.

At places in his "preface," Hayes regretted some of his criticism of individuals (of Hubbard Chester, for example, who infuriated Hayes by his refusal to return to the ship from Newman Bay), but as he approached his conclusion he seemed overwhelmed by the vividness of his memories, and again lashed out at individuals and at the expedition as a whole. He introduced a new charge, one not brought by himself or by any other man before or after: he claimed that many of the medical supplies—"chloroform, quinine, and all other drugs enough to last the entire Navy five years"—had been stolen during the expedition.

Only Hall remained unscathed to the very end of Hayes's

journal. Mentioning Hall for the last time, the youth re-affirmed his faith in him: "He alone perhaps really meant to do something worthy of the munificence of the government which sent him." But Hall had not succeeded in communicating his love of the North to his admirer, and as Hayes wrote his "preface," brooding over his own and other men's behavior during the Arctic winter, he reached a bitter conclusion, one that could serve as an epigraph to the story of the Polaris Expedition:

> I believe that no man can retain the use of his faculties during one long night to such a degree as to be morally responsible. . . .

The question of whether some of the men on the *Polaris* were morally responsible became increasingly important at the inquiry. So long as the Board was dealing only with the failure of a large expedition, the loss of an expensive ship, and charges and counter charges of command negligence, it could attempt to measure moral responsibility in terms of naval tradition, asking questions designed only to assess how much the officers and men did or did not do their duty. One senses that the members of the Board were almost happy to ask such questions—happy to be on such firm, familiar ground, where moral responsibility was something that they could understand and measure. When the Board focused on duty, it could partly blind itself to psychological causes, to the inner compulsions and inhibitions of individual men that might explain their actions.

But as Secretary Robeson and his fellow Board members well knew, the failure of the Polaris Expedition was not the only matter under investigation, and the question of moral responsibility went far deeper than duty. The specter of Charles Francis Hall haunted the inquiry. Much as the Board members might have wanted to ignore it or exorcise it, they could not. Hall had died charging that he was being murdered. George Tyson, as the first witness, introduced the grim subject:

> *Question:* Did he ever talk very rationally after he was taken ill?
> *Answer:* I think about the 3rd of November, after he had been sick seven or eight days, he got better; he talked rationally, and went to writing about his business. But he still appeared to be thinking on one subject; he thought someone was going to injure him; he was very suspicious; he seemed to think somebody was going to poison him. . . .
> *Question:* Did he accuse anybody when you were by?
> *Answer:* Yes, sir, almost everybody; and when I was absent he might accuse me for aught I know. He accused Captain Budington and the doctor of trying to do him an injury.

The later witnesses confirmed what Tyson had said: in his dementia, Hall had accused virtually all of the officers and some of the men of murdering him. He apparently had been out of his mind, but the Board could not simply dismiss his charges. Robeson knew that the circumstances surrounding his death would have to be investigated, distasteful and difficult as the investigation would be.

The investigation was difficult partly because Hall's own journals were lost. Early in the inquiry, knowing that Hall was an inveterate journal-keeper, the Board asked George Tyson what had been done with Hall's papers after his death:

> *Question:* Were they not certified and sealed up?
> *Answer:* No, sir.
> *Question:* Did not you mess with Captain Budington?
> *Answer:* Yes, sir; we messed with him.
> *Question:* Did not you know what he did with the papers?
> *Answer:* I did not know what he did; I saw some of them; I know many remarks were made about them; I understand some were burned.

Question: Did anybody suggest that the papers should be
    sealed up?
    Answer: I did myself; that they should be sealed, boxed,
    and screwed down, and suggested it to Captain
    Budington.
Question: What did he say?
    Answer: He did not make any remark whatever, or merely
    his usual "Damn his papers."

The Board, noting Tyson's passing remark that some of the
papers had been burned, asked more questions. Apparently
they had already heard something about the matter and knew
that Budington was involved:

Question: While he was delirious did Captain Budington
    get him to burn up some papers?
    Answer: He told me he was glad the papers were burned,
    because they were much against him; and he got
    him to burn them.
Question: Did nobody see him burning them?
    Answer: I do not know; I heard it talked of on board the
    ship, and I supposed it to be the truth.

Later witnesses confirmed Tyson's testimony. William Morton's journal, examined by the Board, contained an entry
made on November 11, the day after Hall's burial: "This
morning Captain B. took possession of all keys composing of
ship's stores, and also of Captain Hall's effects, for which from
this date I will not consider myself responsible." Frederick
Meyer and others testified that Budington had taken charge of
Hall's papers and had put them into a large tin box; according to Meyer, there was no public examination of them,
although Budington himself read them. Tookoolito testified
that Hall had asked her to watch out for his letters and journals if he died: "He said to take care of his papers; get them
home, and give them to the Secretary [Robeson]." She went
on: "After his death I told Captain Budington of this charge

several times. He said he would give them to me by and by."
But, she said, he never did give them to her.

When Budington took the stand, he denied that he had
taken charge of Hall's papers. "The clerk [Mauch] had charge
of them and stored them in a box," he testified. The box, "a
large japanned tin box," was locked up and put in a cup-
board. He also contradicted Tookoolito, saying that she had
had access to the papers: "The key was among a lot of keys.
I think Hannah had the whole of them. She had control of
the keys and about everything Captain Hall had." Remembering Tyson's statement that Hall had burned some of his
papers at Budington's instigation, the Board also asked about
that episode, putting its question in a vague passive construction: "Were any of his papers burned?" Budington did
not hesitate to tell the story:

> At one time during his sickness we were having a talk to-
> gether about one thing and another. He said he had written
> a letter to me and took it out, and he thought I had better
> not see it; but if I insisted, he would show it to me. I told
> him it didn't make any odds. He then said he thought it
> ought to be burned, as he did not approve of it, and he
> held it to the candle and burned it.

The Board did not press Budington any farther on the episode.

Not until the very end of its inquiry did the Board discover anything definite about the final fate of the papers.
Early in the inquiry, before the *Polaris* party had returned
to Washington, Frederick Meyer testified that he had seen the
japanned box sitting on a table in Budington's cabin on the
night of the separation from the ice floe; Meyer said that he
assumed the papers were still aboard the *Polaris*. When Budington appeared before the Board months later, however, he
said that he believed the box had been put overboard onto
the floe:

> It was quite a heavy box, and it was quite full of books; the books of ship's accounts were all in there, all his private letters and all his journals of every kind. They were all missing that night; they were put out on the ice, I suppose. I did not see it done, but they were gone.

Later, Budington said he believed that Bryan had put the box overboard, but when Bryan testified, he denied it. Only when Joseph Mauch appeared, the next-to-last man to testify, was the matter at least partly cleared up. Mauch said that he had put the box overboard:

> At the time we got separated from the other party I had these papers. I took care of them because I wanted to save them. They were Captain Hall's papers, and I wanted to preserve them. I therefore put them out on the ice, and told the men to put them on a high point that was there. I put them out myself. I do not know whether they were put on the high point or not; but I told them to put them there. Everybody was in such a hurry that probably nobody heard me speaking about it.

Mauch, who remained aboard the ship, did not know what finally happened to the box—nor, apparently, did anyone on the floe. Probably, in the confusion of that terrible night, the box slipped off the ice into the open water and sank.

In spite of the lost journals, the Board was able to reconstruct in some detail the events leading to Hall's first sickness. Early in the afternoon on October 24, 1871, as most of the men were engaged in banking the ship with snow and ice, Hall, Chester, Ebierbing, and Hans appeared, coming across the plain on their return from the two-week journey to Newman Bay. Walter Campbell, the fireman, who was walking behind the observatory at the time, was the first to greet them. Hall did not look well to Campbell, who asked him if he felt ill."He said 'no, he was pretty tired, but quite well in health.'" Campbell accompanied them as they walked on toward the ship. When they passed the observatory Doctor Bessels emerged, shook hands with Hall, and strolled along with him, discussing his discoveries and his plans. Between the observatory and the ship, Frederick Meyer and Noah Hayes joined the group. Hayes thought that Hall looked "very much exhausted," but Hall insisted to everyone that he was in good health, and the men, with the exception of Hayes and Campbell, testified that he looked well.

Doctor Bessels, according to his own statement, left the group after a few minutes to return to the observatory. He said that he did not see Hall again until about an hour and a half later, when Frederick Meyer came to tell him that Hall had been suddenly taken sick and wanted to see him. Meyer confirmed that he had gone to the observatory after Hall was put to bed, but he said that he had gone because he was on duty. He did not mention seeing Bessels or telling him about Hall's illness. For some reason the Board made no effort to confirm Bessels's statement that he had returned to the observatory before Hall went aboard the ship—a serious oversight, because both William Morton and Joseph Mauch, who were aboard when Hall was stricken, stated that they believed the doctor was present at the time.

As Hall and his group approached the *Polaris*, other men joined them. Tyson, Budington, and Morton, who were supervising the banking of the ship, came across the ice to shake his hand. "He said he was never better in his life," Tyson reported. "He enjoyed the sledge journey amazingly, and was going right off on another journey, and wished me to go with him." When Budington asked if Hall thought the Pole could be approached along the shore just explored, Hall replied that it could.

Hall paused before going aboard the *Polaris*, greeting the men who were banking the ship and thanking them for their good behavior during his absence. "He looked first rate,"

Henry Hobby testified. When he went aboard most of the men who had walked with him returned to their chores, only Ebierbing, Chester, Campbell, and Morton going aboard with him. Steward John Herron and Bryan greeted him at the gangway. He stayed on deck a few minutes talking to Bryan, then went to his cabin. At the doorway he met Joseph Mauch, who told him that he had kept a full record of events during Hall's absence, as he had been ordered to do. Hall told him that he would read it as soon as possible. Then, entering the cabin, he spoke to the steward:

> He asked me if I had any coffee ready. I told him that there was always enough under way down stairs in the galley. I asked him if he would have anything else. He said that was all he wanted. I went down stairs and got a cup of coffee. I did not make the coffee. I told the cook it was for Captain Hall. He drank white lump-sugar in his coffee.

Some of the men disagreed about the coffee in their testimony. The cook, William Jackson, testified, "The coffee was taken from the galley the same as everybody else had." One might assume that in this matter the cook would be dependable, but Jackson's memory is in doubt because he also stated that the coffee had been left over from dinner, which, he said, he had served shortly before. Actually, dinner was served several hours after Hall arrived, at three p.m., and although Jackson denied that he had prepared the coffee specially for the sledge party, both Campbell (who was assistant steward) and Mauch said that the coffee *was* specially prepared for Hall and his party.

While the steward was below getting the coffee, Morton helped Hall remove his wet boots and went to get him a change of clothing. Bryan was in the cabin with Hall when the steward returned with the coffee. The Board did not ask Bryan who else was in the cabin at the time, and Bryan did not volunteer the information:

I remember Mr. Morton was seeing about getting his wet boots off, and I remember his drinking a cup of coffee. Then he got up to change his shirt, and he said 'I feel sick,' or 'something is the matter with me,' or something of that kind. He made some such remark as that he was very weak. . . .

The Board tried to make Bryan be more exact about time:

Question: Was this within half an hour of his coming into the cabin or coming on board the vessel?

Answer: Yes; I think it would be safe to say it was within that time.

Question: Did he then take the coffee?

Answer: Yes; I think I saw him then take the coffee, and almost immediately afterward——

Question: Within five minutes afterward?

Answer: I do not know about that, because he might have given the cup back, and he might have spoken a little while, and my attention being turned off to something else, I could not see whether he took it or not; but I associated the two facts in my mind, that just as soon as he took the coffee he complained of feeling sick and went to bed. It might have been more or less of an interval; I could not tell you exactly how long.

Morton, who had left before the coffee arrived, returned in about twenty minutes to find Hall vomiting. When the alarmed old sailor asked what was the matter, Hall insisted, "Nothing at all—a foul stomach." According to Bryan, Morton and "some one else" then assisted Hall into his bunk. Was that "some one else" Doctor Bessels? Morton said, "The doctor was there also, at the time he was vomiting and sick, and I believe while he was taking the coffee. He asked the doctor for an emetic, and, as far as I could understand, the doctor said 'No,' he was not strong enough, or it would weaken him too much, or something to that effect." If Mor-

ton was wrong about Bessels being present when Hall was
stricken, then he was sent for immediately, because others
testified that he was in attendance soon after Hall was in bed
and that he refused to give an emetic. Budington remembered coming into the cabin: "I went in, and he was then in
his bunk, and said that he felt a little sick coming in out of
the cold, and had been vomiting slightly." In spite of his
sickness, he told Budington that he planned to go north again
within a few days.

> He said he thought he had a bilious attack, and inquired of
> me if I didn't think he needed an emetic. I told him 'yes.'
> Dr. Bessels stood by, and said it would not do for him to
> take an emetic.

Bessels himself, testifying that he had been sent for at the
observatory, gave the Board a detailed account of Hall's symptoms and of his initial treatment:

> I found him in his bed. It was rather warm in the cabin, and
> the first thing I did was to open the door before I spoke to
> him. He told me he had been vomiting, and that he felt
> pain in his stomach and weakness in his legs. While I was
> speaking to him, he all at once became comatose. I tried
> to raise him up, but it was of little use. His pulse was
> irregular—from 6o to 8o. Sometimes it was full, and some-
> times it was weak, and he remained in this comatose con-
> dition for twenty-five minutes without showing signs of any
> convulsions. While he was in this comatose state I applied a
> mustard poultice to his legs and breast. Besides that, I made
> cold-water applications to his head and put blisters on his
> neck. In about twenty-five minutes he recovered conscious-
> ness. I found that he was taken by hemiplegia. His left arm
> and left side were paralyzed, including the face and tongue.
> I made him take purgatives. I gave him a cathartic consist-
> ing of castor-oil and three or four drops of croton oil.

Bessels said that he believed Hall had suffered what the
official journal of the expedition called "an apoplectical in-

sult" (apoplexy or a "stroke"), and the symptoms that Bessels described indeed could be those of apoplexy. When the Surgeon General of the Army, who had been asked to sit on the Board during Bessels's testimony, asked the doctor what might have been the immediate cause of the seizure, Bessels replied:

> My idea of the cause of the first attack is that he had been exposed to very low temperature during the time that he was on the sledge journey. He came back and entered a warm cabin without taking off his heavy fur clothing, and then took a warm cup of coffee, and anybody knows what the consequences of that would be. He had been exposed to temperatures as low as 20° below zero. His coming into this cabin, where the temperature was so different, produced a sudden reaction.

Four months before Bessels testified, the steward John Herron had mentioned to the Board that as Hall had entered his cabin "the heat seemed to affect him very much," giving credence to Bessels's theory.

But Hall himself, on the morning after he was taken ill and in moments of lucidity later, seemed obsessed by the coffee. Ebierbing went to visit him in the morning:

> Captain Hall did not eat supper, but only took cup of coffee. I did not see him that night. I saw him next morning. He remained abed. After breakfast he asked to speak to me. He says, "Very sick last night." I asked him what is the matter. He says, "I do not know. I took cup of coffee. In a little while very sick and vomiting."

When the Board asked if Hall had said anything about poisoning, Ebierbing replied, "Yes; something. I can't tell sure. He asked me, 'Now, Joe, did you drink bad coffee?'" According to Ebierbing, he later reverted to the subject. "Once, all alone, he tell me, 'Bad stuff in coffee; feel it after awhile; burn stomach.'" When Hall talked to Tookoolito also, he

mentioned the coffee—again, not when he was raving but
when he appeared clearheaded. "After he had been bad about
the head he began to get better," she testified. "Then he
talked about the coffee. He said the coffee made him sick.
Too sweet for him. 'It made me sick and vomit.' . . . I used
to make coffee for him and tea. He said he never saw anything like the coffee he took on coming aboard."

The course of Hall's illness, summarized mainly from the
testimony of Doctor Bessels:

> *October 25*: Hemiplegia (paralysis on one side), difficulty in
> swallowing and speaking, numbness in tongue. Bessels ad-
> ministered more purgatives (castor oil and croton oil, a
> powerful cathartic). Hall clearheaded all day. By evening
> paralysis partly gone, but had a restless night.
>
> *October 26*: Ate preserved fruit. Doctor Bessels: "He com-
> plained of chilliness, and indeed he had some very rapid
> changes of temperature—changes of temperature like you
> find in cases of intermittent fever. I tried the temperature
> by a thermometer. The temperature sometimes rose to 111°
> and fell to 83°. I applied it in his arm pit and sometimes his
> mouth." (Bessels's measurements must have been inaccurate,
> perhaps because he took many of them in the arm pit: at
> 111° Hall would have been dead.) Doctor Bessels adminis-
> tered injection of quinine, and Hall's temperature began
> to level off. Clearheaded all day.
>
> *October 27*: Appetite improved, but numbness in tongue re-
> turned. More quinine injected. Clearheaded all day.
>
> *October 28*: First signs of dementia: at three p.m. Hall
> jumped out of bed, shouting that Budington and Tyson
> were going to shoot him.
>
> *October 29–31*: On October 29 Hall refused medical treat-
> ment from Doctor Bessels and continued to refuse it until
> November 4. Apparently demented.
>
> *November 1–3*: According to the testimony of Joseph Mauch
> and others, Hall much improved, stronger in body, clearer
> in mind. Continued to refuse treatment from Bessels.
>
> *November 4*: Allowed Bessels to treat him again. According

to Bessels, great difficulty in speech, tongue numb, seemed
slow-witted, but few signs of paralysis. Ate heartily.
November 5–6: Treatment by Bessels. On November 6 up
and about, even going on deck. Ate heartily.
November 7: At one a.m. suffered relapse. Comatose through
the day until late afternoon, when there was a brief return
to consciousness.
November 8: Died three twenty-five a.m.

The initial paralysis on Hall's left side was evidence that
Bessels's diagnosis of apoplexy could be sound, such paralysis frequently resulting from a stroke. The Surgeon-General
took the trouble to inquire into this matter in some detail,
asking Bessels how he analyzed the paralysis:

Question: How did you know he was paralyzed? He was
lying on his berth?
Answer: Yes, sir.
Question: How did you ascertain he was paralyzed? Was it
a paralysis both of motion and sensation?
Answer: It was only paralysis of motion after the recovery.
His paralysis did not leave him until the next
day.
Question: Motion and sensation both?
Answer: Yes, sir.
Question: Did you try the sensation in the first attack?
Answer: Yes, sir; I tried it with a needle.
Question: How did you try the paralysis of motion?
Answer: I lifted his hand, and as soon as his hand was
lifted it would fall.
Question: You had no doubt, then, that it was a case of
this kind?
Answer: O, no, sir; there was not the least doubt about
that. As soon as the hand would be lifted it
would fall back again. He was not able to sup-
port it.

There was some disagreement about the paralysis among
the other witnesses, however. Emil Schumann, supporting

Bessels, said that even when Hall seemed on his way to recovery, he had trouble with his left arm: "I do not think he
had any trouble moving his left leg, but I always saw that arm
hanging down. When he got into bed he would take hold
himself of his left arm with his right and lift it up." But
William Morton, while allowing that Hall was "not smart in
his movements," did not notice that one side was affected
more than another, and Bryan testified, "I heard that he was
paralyzed all on one side, but I never noticed anything of the
kind." Bessels himself said that the paralysis was transient,
however, as is often the case with a stroke, and Hall possibly
could have been paralyzed briefly without Bryan's noticing it.

Some of Hall's other symptoms—his initial erratic pulse
and his temporary lapse into coma, for example—also could
indicate a stroke, but the changes in body temperatures mentioned by Bessels, setting aside the fact that they are impos-
sibly high and low, would not be symptomatic of a stroke.
Perhaps Hall was suffering from a secondary illness or in-
fection undiagnosed by Bessels. Whatever the cause of such
radical changes in temperature, if indeed they actually occurred, they were the reason given by Bessels for his most important medication, injections of sulphate of quinine. In the
nineteenth century quinine was often used to allay fever, and
Bessels testified that his first injection, early in Hall's illness,
was almost immediately effective in leveling his temperature. There remains the question of why Bessels continued
this treatment afterwards, when apparently Hall's temperature was normal. According to the standard American book of
pharmacology of the time, *The Dispensatory of the United
States of America* (1866 edition), quinine could "be employed
with benefit in all morbid conditions of the system," but the
same book warns against heavy or frequent doses, noting
that they could dangerously upset the stomach and bowels.
The Surgeon-General did not ask Bessels why he continued
the quinine treatment after Hall's temperature leveled, and
Bessels did not volunteer a reason.

Bryan, who once watched Bessels administer quinine, described the procedure for the Board: "He had little white crystals, and he heated them in a little glass bowl. It was given in the form of an injection under the skin in his leg." Perhaps the preparation of the quinine explains a strange part of the testimony of Henry Hobby. Hobby told the Board that Joseph Mauch, who had studied pharmacology, one day spoke to him about a smell in Hall's cabin:

> Joe Mauch, captain's clerk, came into the cabin in the morning and told us that there had been some poisoning around there. I asked Mauch about it, and he told me that there was "llousaure." I do not know what it is in English. He did not say any more about it. I do not know what it was used for, whether it was good or bad. He did not mean to say that Captain Hall had taken this, but that the smell was in the cabin—used there for some purpose or other.

The word transcribed as *llousaure* was perhaps the word that Hobby had used, but it is meaningless. Probably the word used by Mauch was *Blausaure,* German for "blue acid," designating prussic acid. Why Mauch believed that prussic acid was being used in Hall's cabin remains unexplained, but perhaps he misinterpreted Bessels's preparations of quinine. The Board, in another of its odd oversights, did not ask him about the matter, although he testified after Hobby. Prussic acid, a deadly poison, was sometimes used medicinally in the nineteenth century in a very diluted form, but Bessels at no point in his testimony mentioned using it, and there is no reason to believe that he did.

But if Mauch believed that prussic acid was being used, and if he confided his suspicions to Hall, that might explain a hallucination that sometimes terrified the dying man in his dementia. One night when Budington was alone with him, Hall suddenly lunged from his berth and seized him. Budington shouted to Chester and Tyson, who were just outside the cabin, but Hall, clutching Budington with one hand and holding onto the doorknob with the other, kept the two men out for several minutes. He told Budington that he saw a blue vapor around the kerosene lamp—then, that he saw a blue flame coming out of Budington's mouth. Later, after Tyson and Chester forced their way into the cabin and joined Budington in pacifying Hall, he said that the blue vapor was clinging to Chester's coat, and tried to brush it off. When he was safely back in his berth, he sat up and felt for Tyson's mouth, whispering, "What's that coming out of your mouth? It is something blue."

This particular hallucination repeatedly haunted Hall. If Mauch had spoken to Hall about the "Blausäure"—and, having access to him, he might well have done so—he probably would have translated the term into "blue acid" before going on to explain that it is a deadly poison. Mauch was very proud of his learning, as he constantly showed in his journal. Possibly the image of a dangerous blue substance impressed itself on Hall's mind, to return in a terrifying form when mania struck him.

Hall's visions of blue flames and vapors was only one form that his dementia took. He accused the cook of poisoning his food and made Chester and others taste it before he ate. For a time he kept his own tinned goods under lock and key, allowing only Morton or Tookoolito to prepare them for him. Once, when someone tried to put fresh socks on him, he resisted strongly, saying that they were poisoned. Sometimes he would be defiant in his fear. Accusing Chester of wanting to shoot him, he shouted, "I am not afraid of your powder." At other times his fear drove him to a cunning humility, and he would apologize for anything that he had done that might have offended anyone. Emil Schumann remembered, "He begged my pardon about ten times. He used to say to me, 'Mr. Schumann, if I ever did wrong to you, I beg your pardon; I am extremely sorry.' He said this to most everyone."

Although at one time or another Hall accused virtually everyone aboard of wanting to murder him, sometimes as individuals, sometimes as partners in a monstrous conspiracy, his suspicions and fears focused in particular on Doctor Bessels. When Bessels bathed his feet in warm water and mustard, Hall accused him of attempted poisoning. When Bessels refused to let him eat seal meat, Hall said he was being starved. When Bessels administered medicines, Hall often insisted that someone test them before he would take them. The Board asked Budington if Hall accused any one man more than others, and the captain replied, "Dr. Bessels. At times he thought everyone was at it. But he appeared to spit out his whole venom on him; that is, he appeared to think that the doctor was the proper one." Bryan, testifying to the most elaborate manifestation of the hallucination about blue vapor, said that Hall believed Bessels had "an infernal machine" that produced the vapor:

> He used to frequently remark to me that the doctor had some infernal machine there in the berth that emitted some blue vapor. He said he could see the blue vapor coiling all around in the atmosphere, and hanging alongside the edge of the berth; and he would call my attention to it, and ask me if I did not see it. He would say, "Now, it is there crawling along your nose." He said that the doctor had put that machine somewhere, and that he was pumping this blue vapor into his berth, and it was killing him.

Even when Hall believed that he was the victim of a conspiracy, he usually saw Bessels as the leader, the spider at the center of the web. Accusing others of joining in a plot with Bessels, he sneered at the doctor in his presence, calling him "that little German dancing-master."

To the men who witnessed Hall's madness, however, Bessels seemed only attentive and kind, quietly persisting in his treatments when Hall would allow him, ignoring the abuse that was often heaped on him. Apparently he was not offended during the period when his patient refused to see him, and later, when Hall relented and let him begin treatment again, he did so with no apparent grudge. Some nights he slept in a chair beside Hall's bunk, with a string tied to his own arm at one end and to Hall's at the other: if Hall needed anything he could pull the string without awakening the other men in the cabin. "There were very few hours that the doctor slept," Emil Schumann testified. "The doctor was especially kind to him and did everything he could."

In the two days before Hall suffered his fatal relapse, he was apparently well on his way to recovery, clearheaded and growing stronger every hour. He kept Joseph Mauch busy bringing journals up to date, and he talked eagerly about his plans to anyone who would listen. During that period one of the sailors who had not seen him since he had first been taken ill was carrying the meat of a freshly killed seal aboard and happened to glance through the cabin window. Hall had heard about the seal and was pleased. "I did not see him after he was taken sick until this once, when I saw him through the window, when I was carrying the seal aft. I could see him through the window, and I saw him laughing and rejoicing."

Because he had seemed to be improving so rapidly, his relapse came as a shock. He went to bed on the night of November 6 apparently in good spirits and health. That afternoon he had told Budington, "I shall be in to breakfast with you in the morning, and Mr. Chester and Mr. Morton need not sit up with me at night. I am as well as I ever was." In spite of Hall's insistence that he was well, Chester sat up beside him that night. At about midnight, Chester noticed that he was breathing with difficulty. Chester awoke Bessels:

> I asked the doctor about it. He said it was all right, and started out as quick as he could to the observatory. He had

not been gone but a few minutes before Captain Hall raised
up in his berth, and I saw he could not speak. His tongue
was swelled. He tried to mutter out something, and I ran
out on deck, and one of the men happened to be on the ice
taking the tide observations. I sent him right to the observatory for the doctor.

After Bessels returned, Chester also notified Budington, who
testified:

Shortly after 12 o'clock, I think it was, Chester aroused me
up and says, "Captain Hall is dying." I ran up as quick as
I could. He was sitting in the berth, with his feet hanging
over, his head going one way and the other, and eyes very
glassy, and looking like a corpse—frightful to look at. He
wanted to know how they would spell "murder." He spelled
it several different ways, and kept on for some time. At last
he straightened up and looked around, and recognized who
they were, and looked at the doctor. He says, "Doctor, I
know everything that's going on; you can't fool me," and he
called for some water. He undertook to swallow the water,
but couldn't. He heaved it up. They persuaded him to lie
down, and he did so, breathing very hard.

Bessels, who examined Hall more closely than the others,
later said that he noticed that his left eye was dilated and his
right contracted, a sign that he had suffered another attack of
apoplexy. "When I asked after the state of his health, he
said that he felt rather worse than he did the day before; that
he experienced more difficulty in speaking. He became comatose, and, at the same time, as soon as that happened, you
could hear gurgling or rale in his throat."

Hall remained comatose most of the next day, lying flat
on his stomach, breathing heavily. Hubbard Chester, sitting
beside him, noticed many sores around his mouth and at the
side of his nose. When Bessels examined him in the afternoon,

he could see "reflectory or spasmodic motions of his muscles on the left side, resembling Saint Vitus's dance on one side of his body." Early in the evening he regained consciousness briefly. As Bessels was preparing him for the night, tucking in his blankets, he looked up and said, "Doctor, you have been very kind to me, and I am obliged to you," then turned on his side and went to sleep. These were his last words, and the tone in which they were spoken can never be recaptured. Was he actually acknowledging the doctor's help—or was his voice edged with irony? The Board did not ask.

Only Morton was awake beside Hall when he died, and the old sailor described his end for the Board:

> He was in a heavy sleep as I thought, lying with the side of his face on the pillow, his mouth and side of his face down in the pillow. I sat by his side, and he breathed very heavy, and Mr. Chester remarked to me, "He is asleep, and I don't think he is any better; he is very bad." Chester turned in. After a while I spoke to him but he made me no answer. I raised his head with my hands, and I saw something about his mouth—saliva about his mouth. I then turned him partially on his back, and put his head a little more upright, wiped his mouth, and put a teaspoonful of some kind of drink between his lips, but he never noticed it.

Several more hours passed, with Morton quietly sitting, watching, listening. The other men in the tiny cabin all slept soundly as Hall's breathing became more labored.

> At about 20 or 25 minutes past 2 o'clock, when I was with him, he ceased breathing. I kept my cheek close to him, but I could not hear any breathing. While he was in these last moments his face was very placid. There were no contortions; nor was it red and flushed; it was pale, sallow-looking, as when he was alive.

Morton awoke Bessels first to tell him, then Budington and the other officers, that Hall was dead. Soon the cabin was crowded with whispering men looking at their dead commander.

Although the Board did not ask him to, Morton went on after describing Hall's death to a description of his burial:

> After he was dead we dressed him, and made him ready for burial. He was left in the cabin until a coffin was made in the fire-room below by the carpenter. When it was ready, we put him into it, took our last look at him, nailed the coffin-lid down, and put the coffin out on the poop-deck. During this time, we were making a grave. Tyson, Chester, myself, and several men were hard at work two days digging it out of the solid earth, which was just like flint, with crowbars and pickaxes. We finished it, and on the second day, the 11th, we carried him there and buried him on a flat piece of baleland on Polaris Bay, opposite the ship's winter quarters. Regular service for the dead was performed by Mr. Bryan. The service was read by the light of a lantern held for that purpose. It was dark then—the arctic night.

The Surgeon-Generals of the Army and the Navy had been present at the examination of Doctor Bessels, and the Board appended their brief statement to the end of its *Report to the President:*

Washington, D.C., December 26, 1873

SIR: We, the undersigned, were present by request of the honorable Secretary of the Navy, at the examination of Dr. Emil Bessels, in regard to the cruise of the *Polaris* and the circumstances connected with the illness and death of Captain Hall. We listened to his testimony with great care and put to him such questions as we deemed necessary.

From the circumstances and symptoms detailed by him, and comparing them with the medical testimony of all the witnesses, we are conclusively of the opinion that Captain Hall died from natural causes, viz, apoplexy; and that the

treatment of the case by Dr. Bessels was the best practicable
under the circumstances.

Respectfully, your obedient servants,

W. K. BARNES
Surgeon-General United States Army

J. BEALE
Surgeon-General United States Navy

The Board added nothing to the Surgeon-Generals' statement;
it accepted the conclusion that Hall died "of natural causes,
viz, apoplexy." It recommended no actions to be taken
against anyone, no further investigations to be made. So far
as the United States Government was concerned, the case was
closed.

At no time during or after its inquiry did the Board
express an opinion about Charles Francis Hall himself, his
capacities as an explorer and commander or his role in the
Polaris disaster, although in the course of its investigations
it had gathered enough evidence on which to base an opinion.

There was no doubt that Hall had trouble in dealing with
some of his officers, and which officers they were could be
deduced from their response to his death, even if no other
evidence were available. Predictably, Sidney Budington was
most tactlessly outspoken. Several of the crew reported that
Budington had said "There's a stone off my heart," but Budington denied using such an expression. He did not deny an
exchange that he had with Henry Hobby only a few hours
after Hall died. According to Hobby, he met Budington on
deck soon after hearing of Hall's death. Budington approached Hobby to confide, "We are all right now." Hobby,
who admired Hall, asked sharply, "How do you mean by
that?" and Budington replied, "You shan't be starved to death
now, I can tell you that." As Hobby left his new commander
to go below, he snapped back, "I never believed we would."

What Budington meant by saying that the men would not starve to death is not entirely clear, but probably he intended to imply that, with Hall's death, the expedition was concluded; under Budington's command, it would return to the comforts of civilization.

Soon after Hall's burial, according to one of the crew, Frederick Meyer complained loudly that Hall "had consulted with sailors and not with his officers," going so far as to say that "the sailors had command." With Hall's death, Meyer implied, naval hierarchy would return: the officers would assume their proper position, and the expedition would be better for it. Apparently the wounds of Meyer's early confrontation with Hall at Disco had never entirely healed.

The only other man reported to have expressed relief at Hall's death was Bessels. Several of the crew said that he acted relieved, and Noah Hayes heard him virtually celebrate the event:

> One day I was over at the observatory with Dr. Bessels. I was there a good part of the time about that time in the winter. He appeared to be very light-hearted, and said that Captain Hall's death was the best thing that could happen for the expedition; I think those were the words that he used. The next day he was laughing when he mentioned it. I was much hurt at the time, and told him I wished he would select somebody else as an auditor if he had such a thing to say.

These three—Budington, Meyer, and Bessels—were precisely the men who had openly criticized Hall while he was alive and even defied him. Hall himself may have been insecure and defensive in dealing with them, but the records show that they were the aggressors, each resisting Hall's command in one way or another. Budington, with some reason, believed himself more experienced in Arctic living than Hall, and better able to lead the expedition safely through the perils of sea ice. In their relationship to Hall, both Meyer and Bessels were intellectual snobs; so far as they were concerned, Hall was ignorant in the natural sciences and therefore ill-equipped to lead what to them was primarily a scientific expedition.

The records also show that these three men were exceptional in their attitude toward Hall, and that the rest of the officers and men admired him and respected his command. According to most of the testimony, Hall had been a strong leader. William Morton, who called himself "an old man-o'-wars man, familiar with discipline," praised Hall's firmness: "He was a very kind man, but strict. There was nothing tyrannical about him, still everybody appeared to dread him and respect him. That was my feeling toward him." He was exacting in the operations of his expedition, keeping watch over all its phases and allowing little margin for error. Bryan told the Board that Hall had "very much executive talent," and part of that talent showed itself in meticulous concern for detail. Before leaving on his last sledge journey, for example, he handed Budington detailed written orders on what should and should not be done during his absence. What follows is only a small selection of them:

> You will as soon as possible have the remainder of the stores and provisions that are on shore taken up on the plain by the observatory, and placed with the other stores and provisions in as complete order as possible. . . . Have the night watch kept up in accordance to my winter instructions of September 23d, with simply this change, that the watch is to be continued until the cook commences his morning work. Have every light in the ship extinguished at 9 p.m., except from this hour a candle-light is to be allowed forward, for the use of the watch. . . . You will see that no more coal is consumed in any stove of the ship than is actually necessary. I find by my thermometers placed in the men's quarters forward and both cabins aft, that the temperature of the air is kept far higher than it should be. . . . You will require no

more coal shall be consumed than is necessary to keep the thermometer, forward and aft, at 50°. . . . A very small fire to be allowed forward to be kept up from 9 p.m. . . . Have the dogs well cared for, feeding them every other day. Look out for some good warm place in the ship for the puppies. . . . You will have plank and boxes so placed under the poop that the dogs cannot get to the raw-hide wheel-ropes. . . . All the fuel, kindling, and coal, before being used, must pass through the hands of Noah Hayes. . . . No box, barrel, package, or anything else containing stores or provisions must be opened but by Mr. Morton. . . .

As Morton said, he was strict. He required attendance at a daily muster-and-prayer meeting. He forbade profanity. He made frequent and thorough inspections of the ship. If he believed that any man was laggard in duty, he reacted immediately and strongly. When the cook became slovenly, attending to your business," he threatened, "you shall not Hall was overheard castigating him. "If you are not down have a cent of pay when you get home."

But Morton's opinion that he also was kind was shared by the men. Robert Kruger (the sailor who threatened Tyson on the ice floe) was only one of many to express his sense of loss at Hall's death: "We were sorry when he died, because Captain Hall had been very kind to us." Hall had done what any decent and wise commander will do: he had tended to the needs of his men and had expressed his concern for their welfare by actions more than by words. Before the expedition left Washington Budington had told the crew that in regard to mess they should consult him, not Hall; then, apparently, he had proceeded to arrange that the officers should receive preferential treatment in mess. Some time later Hall happened to overhear one of the men complain about the food, and immediately investigated. The following day he announced at muster that thenceforth all differences between the officers' and enlisted men's messes would cease:

they were brothers in a common cause and would eat the
same food. The grateful men responded by writing him a
letter, their syntax tangled but their feelings made clear:

> The men forward desire publicly to tender their thanks to
> Capt. C. F. Hall for his late kindness, not, however, that we
> were suffering want, but for the fact that it manifests a dis-
> position to treat us as reasonable men, possessing intel-
> ligence to appreciate respect and yield it only where merited;
> and he need never fear but that it will be our greatest pleas-
> ure to so live that he can implicitly rely on our service in
> any duty or emergency.

Hall's strictness and his kindness, important as they were,
finally were of only secondary importance to his success as
a leader. What gave him the power to lead was his own drive.
In the past, that drive had hurt him in his relations with other
men; it had impelled him beyond patience and tolerance
with followers not so inspired as himself by the urge to explore. He had shot Patrick Coleman. On the *Polaris*, apparently he had learned to control his energies, to adapt himself
to working with other men, and to temper his impatience.
Independent as he was, he had made himself accept the conditions of a shipboard society. He had exerted control, as
much over himself as over his men.

But his drive was still there, controlled as it might have
been, and the men could sense it. So long as he lived, the
crew and most of the officers had no doubts about the purposes of the expedition or its value, nor did they have doubts
about their commander's capacity to do what he had set out
to do. He gave them confidence. Noah Hayes admired him
to the point of hero worship ("He was a hero," Hayes wrote
in his journal, "a moral God-fearing hero at that."), and
Hayes's attitude was shared by most of the crew. Almost a
year after Hall's death, Hayes wrote, "If the enterprising,
courageous, active, persevering part of the world ever owed
a man their profound sympathy and sorrow, Cap. Hall claims

this as his due." Hayes was dazzled by Hall's energy, and he saw him as a martyr to it, believing that "he broke his constitution by excessive labor." Other men were not so free with words as Hayes, but in their own ways they expressed their admiration of Hall. "Not only did the expedition lose a commander in him," said Robert Kruger, "but we were heavy losers in all regards." Herman Sieman echoed Kruger: "We lost everything when Captain Hall died. I mean the expedition died with Captain Hall. No ship ever had the privilege we had."

The testimony that most would have pleased Hall himself came from Ebierbing. Hall's relations with the Eskimo had been uneven: well as he knew him, at times in the barrens during the second expedition, seeing him as an utter stranger, he had loathed and feared him. But Ebierbing and Tookoolito had been his fast friends, perhaps the best friends he had in his life. For ten years they had stayed by him, giving him help and accepting his help in return. They had introduced him to the North, had taught him much of what he knew about it, and somehow they represented his link to the Arctic land and sea that had obsessed him.

After the Board finished asking Ebierbing questions about the expedition and Hall's death, they wanted to know about his plans:

> *Question:* Do you want to return North?
> *Answer:* I would not like to; Captain Hall my friend. With a man like him, I would go back.
> *Question:* Is there anything else you can think of, or that you would want to tell?
> *Answer:* Captain Hall good man. Very sorry when he die. No get North after that. Don't know nothing more.

epilogue

For five years after the *Polaris* weighed anchor and steamed through the ice of Thank God Harbor out into Hall Basin, Charles Francis Hall's grave was undisturbed by any human. Eskimos had once hunted the area, but the rings of stone that marked their camp sites were paleolithic; hunting parties had not ventured so far north for hundreds of years. Wind-driven snow and silt blasted the headboard of the grave, but it remained upright, and Hubbard Chester's deep-cut inscription remained sharp and clear. Lemmings burrowed into the mound of the grave, and foxes pawed at its surface, but the coffin beneath was untouched, and the ground willow above remained rooted among the rocks.

In May 1876 Hall's grave had its first human visitors since the departure of the *Polaris*. Members of the British North Polar Expedition led by Captain George Nares arrived with a brass tablet that they had brought from London, knowing they would pass by the gravesite. The tablet was inscribed:

SACRED TO THE MEMORY OF
CAPTAIN C. F. HALL
OF THE U.S. SHIP POLARIS,
WHO SACRIFICED HIS LIFE IN THE ADVANCEMENT OF SCIENCE
ON NOVʳ 8ᵗʰ 1871

———

THIS TABLET HAS BEEN ERECTED
BY THE BRITISH POLAR EXPEDITION OF 1875
WHO FOLLOWING IN HIS FOOTSTEPS HAVE PROFITED BY HIS EXPERIENCE

While twenty-five members of the expedition stood solemnly by, an American flag was hoisted and the tablet was erected at the foot of the grave. The Nares Expedition, like the Polaris Expedition, was not destined to reach the Pole; not long after the ceremony, two of its men, dead of scurvy, were buried only a few hundred yards away from Hall.

Six years later, the grave was visited again. The Greely Expedition, spending the winter thirty miles across Hall Basin at Lady Franklin Bay, came to check on supplies that the Polaris Expedition had cached and to see what was by then known as Hall's Rest. Sergeant William Cross, while rummaging in the wreckage of Bessels's observatory, which had been crudely dismantled before the *Polaris* left, carved his name on one of the boards that lay scattered about. A year later Cross was dead, the first of nineteen men to die in the terrible ordeal of the Greely Expedition. Between 1898 and 1909 Robert Peary passed Thank God Harbor several times aboard the *Roosevelt,* but, with a singlemindedness Hall himself would have admired, did not take time to go ashore. Knud Rasmussen, on his Thule Expedition, arrived in 1917. He found the original headboard lying face down on the ground, perhaps cuffed by the same bear that had bitten deep into the posts supporting the Nares tablet; Rasmussen could plainly see the marks of the animal's teeth in the wood. After Rasmussen's departure, forty years passed before Hall's grave was visited again. In 1958 an American team led by geologist William Davies and assisted by Danish explorer Count Eigel Knuth landed from the icebreaker *Atka,* the first ship to anchor in Thank God Harbor since the *Polaris.* The purpose of "Operation Groundhog" was to locate ice-free aircraft-landing sites as emergency alternatives to the bases at Alert and Thule. For a few weeks the sound of a Jeep was heard on Polaris Promontory. Then the area was returned to its accustomed silence. That silence was broken very briefly a few years later when British geologist Peter Dawes spent a few days in the area.

In August 1968 I arrived at Hall's Rest with three companions. Doctor Franklin Paddock, William Barrett, Thomas Gignoux, and I were flown from Resolute, far to the south in the Arctic Archipelago, by one of Canada's finest bush pilots, W. W. Phipps. The day we arrived was clear; as Weldy Phipps flew his Single Otter low across the hills that border

the plain of Polaris Promontory, we could see ahead the deep
blue of Hall Basin, the shoreline of Thank God Harbor, and,
as we lost altitude, the wreckage of Bessels's observatory close
to the beach. We circled, looking for the grave. We could
not see it, but knew that it was near the observatory, so Weldy
landed on a smooth stretch of plain a mile south of the
wreckage. After we had unloaded our equipment, Weldy took
off immediately, leaving us standing alone on the plain,
dazed in sudden awareness of how isolated we were. He was
due to return in two weeks, after he fulfilled some other contracts.

In the course of preparing this biography I had read the
government's book on the Polaris Expedition, the journals
of its men, the ship's log, the official dispatches, the transcript
of the Department of the Navy's inquiry, and masses of other
material. My conclusion was, not that Hall certainly had been
murdered, not even that he *probably* had been murdered,
but only that murder was at least possible and plausible. The
conclusion of the Board of Inquiry that he had died of
"natural causes, viz, apoplexy," also was possible and plausible, but it had been reached hastily and only by ignoring
much of the evidence that the Board itself had wheedled out
of witnesses. Secretary Robeson had been under considerable
pressure to end investigation; scandal was in the making.
That the government was eager to play down the ugly aspects
of the affair is indicated by the official book of the expedition,
Narrative of the North Polar Expedition, written by Rear
Admiral C. H. Davis a year after the inquiry. Davis gave the
impression that the expedition had been a Boy Scout Jam-
boree—a bit rough, of course, but enlivened by good cheer
and boyish high jinks. The original source materials that
Davis had used and distorted show how false that impression
was.

I had applied to Denmark's Ministry for Greenland for a
permit to travel to Polaris Promontory; arguing that if the
case were recent, a court presented with the evidence would

order an autopsy, I requested permission to disinter Hall's body and have Frank Paddock perform an autopsy on it. Given the high latitude of its burial, there was a good chance that the body would be well preserved. Approval of my application came only after many letters and finally a trip to Copenhagen, where I met Count Eigel Knuth. An archeologist and old-time sledge traveler, Knuth was one of the last men to have seen the grave. He also was an adviser to the Ministry on proposed projects in Greenland, and without his agreement I would have no chance of receiving permission. At first it appeared that he would not agree. Hall's grave, he said, was a hallowed place; its remoteness intensified the sense of mystery and beauty associated with any lone grave. The idea of having it disturbed repelled him. After I assured him that I would leave the grave in the condition in which I found it, however, he finally approved.

On the day we arrived at Polaris Promontory we set up camp near the place where Weldy had landed us, about a mile south of the observatory and the grave. We decided not to begin the exhumation until the next day, but after the camp was completed we walked to the gravesite. We could see the Nares tablet first, some distance away across the stony flats. As we approached it, we could see the shape of the mound, covered with large rocks; then a crowbar strangely jutting from the head of the grave; then, finally, Chester's headboard lying face down in the dirt. Change is slow in the cold dry air of the High Arctic; the tablet shone as if it had just been taken from a furnace, and the willow still grew on the mound. Under the benign blue of the sky that day, the place was peaceful—and profoundly still.

We wandered on to the observatory. Here was the litter of man, which is widely strewn throughout the Arctic, all the more noticeable because of the vast inhuman spaces around it. The building no longer stood; its siding lay broken, scattered around its floor as if it had burst from within. Rusted cans, brass nails, iron stoves, a huge davit, an ice saw, shattered glass, and pieces of sailcloth spread out from the observatory like a cancerous growth. Throughout the area were the bowling-ball shapes of ice grenades, packed with black powder that still could explode. While poking through the rubble Tom Gignoux turned over a board, and there was Sergeant Cross's name, carved more than seventy years before when *he* had been doing the poking. Bill Barrett found a broken blue bottle on which the word POISON still could be seen molded into the glass. After momentary, laughing excitement, we realized that it was of little significance: bottles marked POISON could, after all, be contained in a scientific observatory without ominous implications. On the beach I found a Danish shotgun shell, perhaps discharged by Eigel Knuth in 1958. Such sites in the Arctic usually contain layers of history: a hundred yards away were the graves of the two Nares sailors, and not far from them was a paleolithic Eskimo tent-ring.

During the night, under the unsetting sun, the weather changed. When we set out early in the morning to do the job for which we had come, the sky was suitably lowering, the land suitably bleak. The day before had been too bright for such a morbid piece of work.

For a year I had wondered how I would feel when the coffin was opened. Hall might well have become a skeleton— but in the Arctic air, lying on the permanent frost that had prevented his grave diggers from digging deep, he might have been perfectly preserved. It was impossible to know what was in the coffin, and much as I dreaded finding only a skeleton from which nothing could be proved, I also dreaded finding the man himself, just as he had been. Having spent three years violating his mind by reading his private journals, now I was going to violate his body. I had been haunted by a vision of a rather offended face peering out of the coffin, a face asking, "Is there no limit to what a biographer will do?"

While Frank Paddock, Bill Barrett, and I stood nervously by, Tom Gignoux, not long back from a tour of duty in

Vietnam as a Marine, did most of the digging. All of us wanted to be properly solemn, but our nerves short-circuited our sense of awe, and we found ourselves making absurd jokes. As Tom scraped earth off the long coffin lid, revealing pine that was still pale and fresh, Frank looked down at it and said cheerfully, "They didn't build it for the short Hall, did they?" We laughed immoderately. We stopped laughing a minute later when we caught a whiff of decay from within the coffin. During the next ten minutes, while Tom pried carefully at the lid, we stood silent. A piece of the lid broke off, and inside we could see a flag—part of the field of stars—and ice.

I removed the lid after Tom had done all the work, and we stood by the edge of the grave looking down. The body was completely shrouded in a flag. From the waist down, it was covered by opaque ice, but at the base of the coffin a pair of stockinged feet stuck abruptly through it. The front of the torso was clear of the ice, but we could see that its back was frozen into the coffin.

Frank carefully peeled the flag back from the face. It was not the face of an individual, but neither was it yet a skull. There were still flesh, a beard, hair on the head, but the eye sockets were empty, the nose was almost gone, and the mouth was pulled into a smile that a few years hence will become the grin of a death's head. The skin, tanned by time and stained by the flag, was tightening on the skull. He was in a strangely beautiful phase in the process of dust returning to dust. The brown skin, mottled by blue stain and textured by the flag that had pressed against it for almost a hundred years, made him somehow abstract—an icon, or a Rouault portrait.

The autopsy took about three hours. We decided not to try to remove the coffin from the grave or the body from the coffin, embedded as they were in ice. Frank Paddock had to straddle the coffin and lean over to do his work, an agonizing posture to hold for that length of time.

It was very discouraging. At first we thought that the

body, still well fleshed, was perfectly preserved, but Frank's scalpel revealed that the internal organs were almost entirely gone, melded into the surrounding flesh. Frank persisted in a meticulous search, but found little that held any hope for analysis. A fingernail and some hair, to be tested for arsenic, were the best samples we had. At last, exhausted, Frank gave up. We put the lid back onto the coffin, and Tom Gignoux shoveled earth back into the grave. After we had piled the rocks back onto the mound, I shoved the strange crowbar into the earth where it had been; later I was to be thankful that I remembered to do it. When we left, Hall's Rest appeared the same as it had been, with only one change that disturbed me: the ground willow planted by the men of the *Polaris* was no longer rooted amid the rocks.

We had almost two weeks to wait before Weldy was to return. We whiled away the time roaming Polaris Promontory, realizing only later that most of our roaming was to the south—the grave lay to the north, and we tended to avoid it. The beach made the best walking. Inland, the shale plain stretched out forty miles deep, depressing in its lifelessness, but along the beach there were life, movement, and sound. Sanderlings, sandpipers, and plovers picked at the waterline; fulmars flew offshore. Occasionally we would disturb nesting Arctic terns, to be delighted by their wheeling and darting attacks on us, their excited and exciting screams. One day when a high wind was blowing on the plain, I found a group of clucking ptarmigans strutting down the protected beach, ridiculous birds having a ladies' club meeting. Our rations were meat bars and dried potatoes; the Danes had forbidden us to live off the land, and only great self-discipline prevented mayhem on the beach that day. Every morning we found the tracks of a fox along the edge of the water, challenging us to catch a glimpse of him. Day after day the little creature eluded us; then one evening while I was sitting quietly, hoping to see him on his nightly route, out of the corner of my eye I saw something move behind me. Foolishly,

I jumped up to look. The fox had been stalking me while I was waiting for him. He moved away, not running or even trotting, but keeping his dignity in a stately pace, pretending not to be frightened by what must have been the only human being he had ever seen.

The sky and the light constantly change in the Arctic, because weather systems move rapidly there. Leaden clouds would settle, wind would blow, snow would fall; in a few hours the sky would clear to a deep blue and the wind would calm; then there would be a show of mare's tails and mackerel skies, forecasting another storm; and the cycle would begin again. Local fogs inexplicably would blow in, blow out; we would be walking down the beach in clear air, able to see the mountains of Ellesmere Island thirty miles across Hall Basin, when suddenly we would be plunged into clammy murk, able to see only the ghostly shapes of nearby icebergs.

Hall Basin was clear of ice the day we arrived, but two days later a south wind drove ice up from Kennedy Channel —both floe ice and bergs that had been spawned from glaciers to the south, especially the great Humboldt. Looking at and listening to ice was one of our best diversions. If we stood still and stared out across the basin, we could see it move with the currents, very slowly, very steadily. Many of the small bergs along the beach had eroded into fantastic shapes that changed as we saw them from different angles; some were so smooth that they appeared machine-tooled, others rough-textured; some were in strange animal and birdlike forms, others almost geometrically round, square, trapezoidal. As delightful as the sights of the ice were its sounds. Along the beach, we could hear many: the one that the wind makes when it blows uninterrupted by trees or grass, the lapping of the water on the sand, the cry of birds. But the sounds I remember best were of water steadily dripping from thawing icebergs, and the occasional crack and rumble of big ice breaking out in the bay.

Our two weeks of roaming were well spent. They were

lifegiving, images of the beach helping to purge images of the grave from our minds. After those two weeks, I also better understood the man who lay in the grave, and others like him who have felt impelled to travel to the Arctic, yearning for its cold beauty.

Weldy picked us up on schedule, and a few days later we were back in the United States. After consultation with specialists in pathology and toxicology, Frank Paddock sent the fingernail and the hair to Toronto's Centre of Forensic Sciences, where they were given a neutron-activation test, a highly sophisticated method of analyzing tiny amounts of material. For some reason I was not optimistic about our chances of receiving any significant information from the tests, so it came as a surprise when the Centre reported that they had revealed "an intake of considerable amounts of arsenic by C. F. Hall in the last two weeks of his life."

The fingernail had provided the best evidence. Doctor A. K. Perkons of the Centre had sliced it into small segments, working from tip to base, then submitted the segments to the neutron-activation test. The "read-back" from the neutron bombardment indicated increasing amounts of arsenic in the base segments. At the tip, the fingernail contained 24.6 parts per million of arsenic—at the base it contained 76.7 ppm. Assuming a normal growth rate of 0.7 mm a week, Doctor Perkons concluded that the large jump in Hall's body burden of arsenic occurred in the last two weeks of his life. The fact that his arsenic content was high even before the jump could be explained in several ways. Arsenic was often used medicinally in the nineteenth century, and it also was used in hairdressings, so many persons then had a relatively high content. The normal content today is only 1.5–6.0 ppm. Also, the soil near the grave contained fairly large amounts of arsenic (22.0 ppm); according to Perkons, some could have "migrated" from the soil to the body. "However," Perkons went on in the report, "such migration would not explain the differentially increased arsenic in the sections of both hair and nails toward the root end."

We checked with other authorities, all of whom accepted the accuracy of the Centre's report and agreed with its conclusion: Charles Francis Hall had received toxic amounts of arsenic during the last two weeks of his life.

What conclusions can be drawn? Excited by the report, after I received it I studied my material on the Polaris Expedition in light of the new information, testing various explanations for the arsenic contained in Hall's body. The trouble, as I soon discovered, was that several explanations were possible.

The following list of symptoms of acute arsenic poisoning is quoted from Gleason, Gosselin, Hodge, and Smith, *Clinical Toxicology of Commercial Products* (Baltimore, 1969):

1. Symptoms usually appear ½ to 1 hour after ingestion.
2. Sweetish metallic taste; garlicky odor of breath and stools.
3. Constriction in the throat and difficulty in swallowing. Burning and colicky pains in esophagus, stomach and bowel.
4. Vomiting and profuse painful diarrhea.
5. Dehydration with intense thirst and muscular cramps.
6. Cyanosis, feeble pulse, and cold extremities.
7. Vertigo, frontal headache. In some cases ("cerebral type") vertigo, stupor, delirium, and even mania develop.
8. Syncope, coma, occasionally convulsions, general paralysis, and death.
9. Various skin eruptions, more often as a late manifestation.

As one looks down the list, one sees many of Hall's symptoms: the initial gastro-intestinal troubles, the difficulty in swallowing, the dehydration, the stupor, delirium, and mania—even the day before Hall died. Given the results of the neutron-the late manifestations of skin eruption noticed by Chester activation test, this should be no surprise. There is no doubt

that Hall received a large amount of arsenic during the period
that he showed these symptoms. The question is, How did he
receive it?

Arsenic would have been available aboard the ship; in the
form of arsenious acid, it was commonly used as a medicine
in the nineteenth century. "Arsenious acid," comments the
Dispensatory of the United States of 1875 in one of its longest
entries, "has been exhibited in a great variety of diseases." It
was used in the treatment of headaches, ulcers, cancer, gout,
chorea, syphilis, even snakebite. In the form of "Fowler's
Solution," it was a very popular remedy for fever and for
various skin diseases. It was a standard part of any sizable
medical kit, and obviously the Polaris Expedition had a large
medical kit.

Hall may have dosed himself with it. With such a man,
suicide is almost inconceivable, but it would not have to have
been suicide; he might have died a victim of the capacity for
suspicion that had so often erupted in his life. Platt Evens
of the percussion-seal-press lawsuit, William Pomeroy, William Parker Snow, Isaac Hayes, Sidney Budington, Patrick
Coleman, and nameless others had aroused his fear of jeo-
pardy and his wrathful self-righteousness. From the beginning,
he did not like or trust Emil Bessels. In his sickness, which
may indeed have been a stroke, might not he have treated
himself rather than put his faith in the "little German dancing master"? Even during the period when he allowed Bessels
to treat him, he may have been taking medicine on his own.
Bessels testified that Hall had a personal medical kit, containing among other things "patent medicines." Some nineteenth-
century patent medicines contained arsenic; although its
quantity was not great in any of the medicines that have been
tested, Hall might have dosed himself heavily. Or perhaps
he gained access to Bessels's kit and took arsenious acid from
it. Tookoolito would have helped him do such a thing, and,
quiet Eskimo woman that she was, would not have said a
word about it later.

But murder also is possible. The coffee that Hall drank when he boarded the ship after his sledge journey could have been poisoned. Although arsenic is usually tasteless, it can leave a "sweetish metallic taste." Hall complained to Tookoolito about the coffee. "He said the coffee made him sick," she testified. "Too sweet for him." About one half hour after he drank it, he felt pains in his stomach and vomited, symptoms that suggest poisoning.

But the pain and the vomiting could have been caused by a stroke, as could many of the other symptoms listed in *Clinical Toxicology*. If Bessels was telling the truth when he said that Hall also suffered partial paralysis, then a stroke is as satisfactory an explanation of many of them as arsenic poisoning. There is also a possibility that Hall suffered both a stroke and arsenic poisoning. The initial attack could have been a stroke, then the arsenic could have been administered later, during the two weeks of his illness. It should be repeated: there is no doubt that the arsenic was administered. The question remains, How was it administered—and by whom?

The persons who had the most access to Hall during his illness were Sidney Budington, Tookoolito, Ebierbing, Hubbard Chester, William Morton, and Emil Bessels. Others could see him, especially those who shared the cabin with him, but these are the persons who were often with him, treating him or feeding him.

Budington, undergoing a psychological ordeal, drinking heavily, apparently afraid of being so far north, is a suspect, but he actually had less access to Hall than the others. Apparently he seldom approached the sick man or did anything for him. Tookoolito, Ebierbing, Chester, and Morton frequently attended, nursed and fed him, but there is no indication of any possible motive for their doing him injury. Like Budington, they cannot be entirely dismissed as suspects, but they are highly unlikely ones.

If Hall was murdered, Emil Bessels is the prime suspect. A

trained scientist, he had the knowledge, and, as ship's surgeon, the material needed to administer arsenic. He had access to Hall much of the time—and when Hall refused Bessels access, his condition improved. Joseph Mauch made a note in his journal on November 1, several days after Hall first refused treatment by Bessels: "Capt. Hall is much better this morning—for the last 2 days he has taken no medicine & today his health is greatly improved, although yet very weak."

When Bessels treated Hall, he gave him some medicines orally, especially cathartics; arsenic could have been mixed with such medicines. He also gave him injections of what he said was quinine; arsenic also could have been injected, as it sometimes was in the treatment of cancers. When Bryan saw Bessels prepare the injections, the process involved the heating of "little white crystals," precisely the way that quinine was usually prepared. But arsenic could be in the form of a white powder, easily mistaken for crystals or mixed with them, and it, too, can be prepared by such heating.

When one considers Bessels as a possible murderer, one notes little things in the transcript of the inquiry that are subject to various interpretations. There is the uncertainty about whether he was in the observatory while Hall was drinking the coffee, as he said he was, or aboard the ship, as Morton and Mauch believed that he might have been. There is his refusal to administer an emetic when Hall was first taken ill; if indeed Hall had suffered a stroke, an emetic would have been dangerous—but an emetic also might have emptied his stomach of poison. There is the persistence of his quinine treatment when Hall's fever had been allayed. And one night, according to Budington's testimony, Bessels came to him complaining that Hall was refusing to take any medicine. Budington volunteered to take the medicine first in front of Hall, like a parent with a child. Bessels refused to let him do so. Small things, straws in the wind.

Bessels had the opportunity, the skill, and probably the material, but why would he do it? He had no apparent rational motive; he would gain nothing concrete by Hall's death. Unlike Budington, for example, he was not afraid of their situation and did not want to retreat south, and therefore Hall's passion to go north was not a threat to him. In fact, Joseph Mauch and Henry Hobby testified that when the *Polaris* was run aground at Etah, Bessels secretively tried to bribe some of the men to return north with him—an ambitious act, and perhaps ambition could be motive enough. With Hall's death, the command actually fell to Budington, but Bessels had more power and independence because Budington was a far weaker man.

But ambition for what? To make major scientific and geographical discoveries and be given full, sole credit for them? This does not seem motive enough for murder. Here we enter the underground streams of mind, the darkness that the Board would not probe. When one of its members asked George Tyson if he thought that "there was any difficulty between Captain Hall and any of the scientific party that would be an inducement for them to do anything toward injuring him," Tyson replied firmly, "No sir." Then he paused and said, "Unless a man were a monster, he could not do any such thing as that." The Board, not wanting to consider the possibility of monstrosity, moved on to other matters, but perhaps the truth lay precisely in monstrosity.

Joseph Henry had warned Hall that Bessels was "a sensitive man." He must have been very sensitive to justify Henry's making such a comment in a letter that is remarkable for its dry, official tone, and Bessels's behavior on the *Polaris* Expedition, his quarrels with both Hall and Budington, indeed suggest that he was at least difficult to deal with. Little is known about his later career, but enough is known to indicate that he remained difficult, perhaps abnormally so. For more than ten years he maintained a connection with the Smithsonian. Part of that time was spent compiling the scientific results of the expedition, and he sometimes received needling letters from Baird suggesting that he hasten his work. There is evidence that the Smithsonian was eager to get rid of him.

One reason was his involvement in a controversy in 1880. An International Polar Year was planned for 1882–3, and in 1880 the scientific community in the United States was much concerned with what the country should do about it. Among those who spoke out was Captain Henry Howgate, who had some rather far-fetched ideas about colonizing the Arctic. On February 16, 1880, an interview on the subject with Emil Bessels appeared in the *New York Herald,* an interview that reveals much about the man. The reporter devoted some time to the difficulty of finding Bessels's office in the Smithsonian: "To discover this apartment without a guide would be almost as great an act as reaching the North Pole itself." Then he commented: "When the portals are entered, passing under the heavy folds of green drapery which nearly hide the entrance, the visitor would suppose he had been suddenly translated into the retreat of Faustus." As Bessels was interviewed, he indeed acted like Faustus in his worst manifestations—self-assured to the point of arrogance, scornful of others, convinced that all knowledge was his. He laid down for the reporter what the United States should and should not do during the Polar Year. That much of what he said was correct does not mitigate his irritating condescension:

> "What do you think of the plan originated by Captain Howgate?"
>
> "Howgate's plan? Why, Captain Howgate did not originate any plan whatever. He merely appropriated the ideas of Dr. Hayes and probably those of Lieutenant Weyprecht. As far as these are concerned Captain Howgate is all right; but with regard to the rest—well, I would prefer to talk about something more rational."

Bessels read aloud a passage of Howgate's writing about the possibility that a superior Eskimo culture already existed somewhere near the Pole; then he made passing reference to the Polaris Expedition: "This even beats Dr. Newman, who wrote for the Polaris Expedition a prayer to be read at the North Pole, consecrating the Pole to liberty, education and religion. I am only astonished that Captain Howgate did not quote him as an Arctic authority." Bessels was hardly being tactful, as Newman was still Chaplain of the Senate.

When the reporter asked him another question, he said: "Let me light a fresh cigar before I answer this question." One can see him, small, natty, his eyes bright with self-assurance, lighting the cigar and leaning back to say, "It amused me to find that a man writing such bombast [Howgate] should have the insolence to point out what caused other expeditions to fail in reaching the Pole, and in what manner they were mismanaged."

When Bessels was asked about an Arctic expedition that Howgate had organized not long before, he snapped, "The sole aim of the thing was to gain cheap reputation and to lay a snare for Congress to appropriate the means for a *real* Arctic expedition." The interviewer asked Bessels why he thought Howgate's expedition had been a failure. The doctor referred to the scientists who had accompanied the expedition without pay "for the mere love of science." Possibly he was thinking of his relationship with Hall when he said, "They had to submit to the orders of an incompetent, harsh skipper, who most seriously interfered with their duties." It should be noted that Howgate was not the skipper—by a wild coincidence, the skipper was George Tyson.

Bessels was right to distrust Captain Howgate. Some years later it was proved that he had taken advantage of his position in the Signal Corps to swindle large sums of money. But the intemperance of Bessels's attack might be explained by something other than his belief that Howgate was a fraud. Henry Howgate had been a member of the Board of Inquiry that investigated the Polaris Expedition. There is no indication that he said or did anything during the inquiry to earn Bessels's enmity, but there is at least a possibility that the

doctor held a deep-seated grudge against him for his membership on the Board.

Whatever the cause of Bessels's intemperance, it brought
the wrath of Spencer Baird down on his head. Baird wrote
him an icy letter, castigating him for his loose mouth. Bessels
remained at the Smithsonian for a few more years, but apparently under a cloud. Past trouble obviously lies behind
the terse note that he received from Baird's secretary in 1883:

> Dear Doctor:
> We need immediate possession of the room now occupied by
> you near the north entrance, as we find it necessary to make
> improved toilet arrangements for visitors. Please therefore
> remove your property and greatly oblige.
> Yours truly,
> WM. J. RHEES

The tone indicates that this was not the first attempt to dislodge him, but it apparently was the last; his Smithsonian
salary soon was stopped, and, presumably, the "retreat of
Faustus" became a toilet. Bessels soon after returned to Germany. He died there in 1888—ironically, of apoplexy.

A difficult man—but a monster? Bessels did not seem a
monster in the ordinary course of his life, but perhaps he had
monstrosity latent within him. The close atmosphere of a
wintered-in ship was a test of anyone's mind. Ambitions, dis-
likes, abnormalities of any kind could be unbearably magni-
fied and intensified, as the whole history of Arctic exploration
reveals. On the Polaris Expedition, Budington and others
drank, Tyson brooded, the carpenter went insane, young
Joseph Mauch, Noah Hayes, and probably most of the men
aboard drifted miserably toward paranoia. Hayes's assertion
at the conclusion of his journal rings of hard experience and
honest self-awareness: "I believe that no man can retain the
use of his faculties during one long night to such a degree
as to be morally responsible." Bessels scorned Hall, as he
apparently scorned many men. Hall was an uneducated boor,

but he, Emil Bessels of Heidelberg and Jena, had to serve under him and take his orders. Their relations had been strained at the outset, and Bessels faced at least another year, probably another two years, on that tiny ship, suffering the humiliation of an arrogant man in a subservient position.

Perhaps Bessels murdered Hall. Perhaps. The only certain truth that can be found in this case is a knowledge of the inevitable and final elusiveness of the past. What happened aboard the USS *Polaris* between October 24 and November 8, 1871, can never be entirely known. What went on in the minds of Hall, Bessels, and the others aboard that ship, and what they did furtively on their own, is done, gone, past. The questions that the Board of Inquiry did not ask can be asked today, but many of them cannot be answered.

One way or the other, Charles Francis Hall died, as his friend Penn Clarke said he would, a victim of his own zeal. If a stroke was the primary cause, then he drove himself into it, trying to reach the North Pole at the age of fifty. If Bessels murdered him, then his zeal, which made him strong, also made him an unbearable threat to the doctor's ambitions or a hateful object of the doctor's fears. If he poisoned himself, then it was because the zeal that had made him fiercely independent had also made him fiercely suspicious. The dark side of his independence was his distrust of anyone who seemed in any way to threaten him, his integrity, his desires. Independence is often loneliness, and Hall was a lonely man. Treating himself rather than trusting someone else for treatment would have been a characteristic, almost a symbolic, act.

Will power, energy, and independence are the qualities that made him and perhaps broke him. Nineteenth-century America was filled with the rhetoric of will power, energy, and independence but, as scholars, beginning with Frederick Jackson Turner, have shown, it was an age that increasingly controlled energy and individual will, channeling them into the communal and the cooperative. For better or worse, Hall was the real thing. Pious and patriotic as he was, he had

something of the mountain man in him. When he drifted
west from New Hampshire, he was looking for wilderness,
though he may not have known it. When Cincinnati did not
give him what he wanted, then he went north instead of west
—not drifting then, but driving with relentless energy and
concentrated purpose. In the North, too, he found that full
independence was not possible, not among the Eskimos, not
aboard the *Polaris*. Hall's voyages to the Arctic were not
merely geographical explorations. They were a quest for
the kind of independence that was gone from American life
—or, closer to the truth, the kind of independence that never
existed except in the minds of dreamers like Hall.

    Just before we left Polaris Promontory after the exhuma-
tion, I returned alone to the grave. I had to fulfill Arctic
ritual and bury a cannister there with an account of what we
had done. After doing the job, I took a last look at the grave,
hoping to feel some of the things that I believed I should
feel and had not felt during the day of the autopsy. The
biographer and the detective still dominated; in spite of
myself, all I did was puzzle about the crowbar at the head of
the grave—the crowbar that we had carefully put back in
place. After we returned home, while rereading Noah Hayes's
journal, I noticed something I had not noticed before; the
Indiana farmboy solved at least one mystery and deserves
the last word about his hero. The night they buried Hall, he
wrote, was too cold, too miserable for them to mount a headboard, so they jammed the crowbar into the mound. "A fit
type of his will," wrote Hayes, "an iron monument marks
his tomb."

notes
bibliography
and index

notes

prologue

1. Quoted in R. J. Cyriax: *Sir John Franklin's Last Arctic Expedition* (London: Methuen & Co.; 1939), p. 19.
2. Ibid., p. 22.
3. "Arctic Adventure," *Blackwood's Edinburgh Magazine* (March 1857), pp. 366, 367, 379.
4. Quoted in Walter Houghton: *The Victorian Frame of Mind 1830–1870* (New Haven, 1957), p. 34.
5. "The Navigator of the Antipodes," *Blackwood's Edinburgh Magazine* (November 1847), p. 516.
6. Quoted in Francis Leopold McClintock: *The Voyage of the "Fox" in Arctic Seas* (London: John Murray; 1869), p. xlv.
7. Quoted in Cyriax: *Sir John Franklin's Last Arctic Expedition*, p. 27.
8. Quoted in Frances J. Woodward: *Portrait of Jane* (London: Hodder and Stoughton; 1951), p. 264.
9. Ibid., p. 267.
10. *The Daily Telegraph* (May 2, 1857), p. 2.
11. *Doctor John Rae's Correspondence with the Hudson's Bay Company on Arctic Exploration 1844–1855*, ed. E. E. Rich, Hudson's Bay Record Society XVI (London, 1953), p. 267.
12. *The Times*, April 15, 1857, p. 2.
13. "Official Patriotism," *Household Words* (April 25, 1857), p. 390.
14. "Traveller's Tales," *Blackwood's Edinburgh Magazine* (November 1855), p. 589.
15. Vilhjalmur Stefansson: *Unsolved Mysteries of the Arctic* (New York, 1956), p. 36.

chapter one

Cincinnati, New London, and New York

1. E. Vale Blake: *Arctic Experiences: Containing Capt. George E. Tyson's Wonderful Drift on the Ice-Floe* (London: Sampson Low, Marston, Low, & Searle; 1874), p. 113.

2. Ibid., p. 114.
3. Quoted in Alvin F. Harlow: *The Serene Cincinnatians* (New York: E. P. Dutton & Co.; 1950), p. 159.
4. Ibid., p. 80.
5. The correspondence concerning this patent (#10,554) is on file in the Patent Division of the National Archives.
6. *Cincinnati Occasional,* August 1, 1851. The Cincinnati Historical Society holds a complete file of Hall's newspapers.
7. Ibid., October 23, 1858.
8. Ibid., October 4, 1858.
9. *The Daily Press,* February 22, 1859.
10. For a full discussion of Ericsson and his caloric engines, see Eugene Ferguson: *John Ericsson and The Age of the Caloric,* Smithsonian Institution Bulletin #228 (Washington, D.C., 1961).
11. Charles Francis Hall: *Arctic Researches and Life Among the Esquimaux* (New York: Harper & Bros.; 1865), XIX.
12. Ibid., XX.

chapter two

Baffin Island—Initiation

1. Hall: *Arctic Researches . . .* , xxvii.
2. Ibid., p. 41.
3. Ibid., p. 49.
4. Gontran de Poncins: *Kabloona* (New York: Reynal & Hitchcock; 1941), pp. 93–4.

chapter three

Frobisher Bay—Exploration

1. Vilhjalmur Stefansson, ed.: *The Three Voyages of Martin Frobisher* (London: Argonaut Press; 1938), Vol. I, p. 48.
2. Ibid., p. 48.
3. Ibid., p. 49.
4. Ibid., p. 49.
5. Ibid., cxi.
6. Ibid., II, 105.

7. Ibid., I, 61.
8. Ibid., p. 57.
9. Ibid., p. 65.
10. Ibid., pp. 59–60.
11. Ibid., p. 68.
12. Ibid., p. 61.
13. Ibid., p. 89.
14. Ibid., p. 116.
15. Ibid., p. 58.
16. Hall: *Arctic Researches . . .* , p. 404.
17. Stefansson, *The Three Voyages of Martin Frobisher,* p. 116.

chapter four

Interim

1. *New York Herald,* November 7, 1862. Henry Grinnell kept a large scrapbook of newspaper clippings concerned with Arctic matters. It is now among the Grinnell papers at the American Geographical Society. At one time or another, Hall was shown this scrapbook—beside some of the clippings are comments written in his unmistakable hand.
2. In 1965 I purchased Snow's own copy of Hall's book from an English bookseller (see p. 177). Jammed into the book were the various contracts made between Hall and Snow, now in my possession.
3. *New York Herald,* April 30, 1863.
4. Ibid., May 8, 1863.
5. Quoted in J. E. Nourse, ed., *Narrative of the Second Arctic Expedition Commanded by Charles F. Hall* (Washington, D.C.: Government Printing Office; 1879), pp. 40 41.
6. *The World,* June 10, 1864.
7. *Morning Post,* December 8, 1865.

chapter five

Roe's Welcome, Repulse Bay, Igloolik, King William Island

1. *New York Herald,* July 4, 1880.

2. R. J. Cyriax, "Captain Hall and the So-Called Survivors of the Franklin Expedition," *Polar Record* (July 1944), p. 176.
3. C. H. Davis, *Narrative of the North Polar Expedition . . .* (Washington, D.C.: Government Printing Office; 1876) pp. 359–61.
4. *Lewiston* (Maine) *Journal,* March 17, 1923.
5. Bayne is quoted at length in L. T. Burwash, *Canada's Western Arctic* (Ottawa, 1931), pp. 112–16.

chapter six

Interim

1. Scott Polar Research Institute, MS 248/207.
2. Quoted in Woodward, *Portrait of Jane,* p. 354.
3. Cincinnati *Daily Gazette,* July 25, 1870.
4. Ibid.
5. A copy of Walker's letter is contained in the Smithsonian Institution Archives, along with most of Hall's correspondence with Baird and Joseph Henry.
6. Clarke's letter, accompanying an original print of the photograph, which I purchased in 1967, is in my possession.
7. A copy of this letter is in the Spencer Baird Papers at the Smithsonian Institution Archives.
8. Copies of the Hall–Henry correspondence are in the Joseph Henry Papers at the Smithsonian Institution Archives.
9. Although most of the papers that Nourse and Davis used in their narratives are in the Hall Collection at the Smithsonian Institution, some, including this letter, RG 45, are in the Naval Records Collection at the National Archives, OC-Special Cruises, *Polaris,* 1871–3.
10. The *Journal of the American Geographical Society,* III (1870–1), 401–15, contains a transcript of this meeting.

chapter seven

Greenland—the Expedition

1. Blake, *Arctic Experiences . . . ,* p. 145.

2. Ibid., pp. 139–40.
3. Ibid., p. 147.
4. Ibid., p. 340.
5. Ibid., p. 331–2.
6. Ibid., p. 155.
7. Ibid., p. 186.
8. I am grateful to Sir Leonard Outerbridge of St. John's for this revelation. Tyson's auditor was Sir Leonard's father.

bibliography

In large part this book was prepared from manuscript and archival sources rather than from published works. In the vault of the Smithsonian Institution's Division of Naval History is a collection of manuscripts and objects known simply as the "Hall Collection" (catalogue numbers 58909–44–N). Most of this material was purchased by the government from Charles Francis Hall's widow not long after his death. The collection contains journals, notebooks, letters, telegraph wires, calling cards, photographs, newspaper clippings, railroad tickets, posters, ships' logs, maps, and such objects as medical kits, sewing kits, parkas, boots, gun-chests, empty bottles, rocks, and telescopes. It is a collection worthy of the Smithsonian in its role as "the nation's attic."

In the 1870's the collection was used in the preparation of two books published by the United States Naval Observatory, Davis's *Narrative of the North Polar Expedition* and Nourse's *Narrative of the Second Arctic Expedition,* both listed below.

In writing this biography, I have drawn heavily from the Hall Collection, and most of my quotation is from its manuscripts. Unfortunately, specific reference to this material is made difficult by the condition of the collection. When I found it, only part of it had been catalogued, and even that part was in considerable disorder, presumably left that way by Davis and Nourse. In the course of my work, I had to reorder the collection, and soon it will be recatalogued according to my recommendations. At present it is divided into three main sections, covering the First, Second, and Third expeditions. Each section contains material associated with the preparations for a given expedition, the expedition itself, and its aftermath. The materials are further divided into labeled folders: journals, notebooks, letters, miscellaneous materials, etc. The folders are dated as well as labeled, and the collection is now in a rough and tentative chronological order.

Because the order is only tentative, footnoting this material would be difficult and possibly futile, but the reader who wishes to track down a quotation or a fact should be able to do so by locating the proper folder; in most cases, the context of a quotation should be sufficient guidance for anyone using the collection.

Through Chapter Six of this book, it may be assumed that unfootnoted quotations are drawn from the Hall Collection. When writing of the Polaris Expedition, I drew on two other sources that I did not footnote. Noah Hayes's journal is in the National Archives (RG 45, Naval Records Collection), for some unknown reason separated from the other manuscript materials on the expedition, which are in the Hall Collection. The fullest source of information about the Polaris Expedition is contained in the *Annual Report of the Secretary of the Navy on the Operations of the Department for the Year 1873* (Washington, 1873), in which is printed the full transcript of the Navy's inquiry into the expedition. In the report, each testimony is separate and none is so long that a reader would have difficulty finding any statement that I have quoted.

Several other bibliographical notes are in order. Hall's own book of the Frobisher Bay Expedition first appeared in England in 1864 under the title *Life with the Esquimaux,* published by Sampson Low, Son, and Marston; in 1865 the American edition, by Harper & Brothers, appeared under the title *Arctic Researches and Life Among the Esquimaux.* In 1970 the book was reissued under its British title by Charles Tuttle Company.

The transcription of Eskimo words and names presents a problem, whether in manuscript or in print. Hall had no Eskimo dictionary, so he simply recorded what he heard, and it is impossible to know whether or not he heard accurately. Now that we have Eskimo dictionaries, the transcription of many Eskimo words has become standardized; for example, the Eskimo word for *shaman* is usually recorded *angakok.* Hall recorded the word as *angeko,* and I have accepted his transcription for this word and for all others, although I have not divided the syllables of words with hyphens, as he usually did.

Finally, a note about the illustrations of the Polaris Expedition. In 1967 I found a large collection of crude drawings and professional oil paintings in the basement of the United States Naval Observatory and immediately recognized some of them as sources for the illustrations in Davis's *Narrative.* The crude drawings were done mainly by Emil Bessels, whose efforts at photography during the expedition had failed. On the basis of drawings by Bessels and by Emil Schumann, the oil paintings were done, and then woodcuts were made of the paintings for use in Davis's book. At my suggestion, this fine graphic record was transferred from the Navy Observatory to the Center for Polar Archives at the National Archives.

Below is a list of books that I found useful in the preparation of this biography:

Bessels, Emil: *Die Amerikanische Nordpol-Expedition.* Leipzig: Wilhelm Englemann; 1879.

Blake, E. Vale, ed.: *Arctic Experiences, Containing Capt. George E. Tyson's Wonderful Drift on the Ice-Floe.* London: Sampson Low, Marston, Low, & Searle; 1874.

Burwash, L. T.: *Canada's Western Arctic.* Ottawa, 1931.

Cooper, P. F.: *Island of the Lost.* New York: Putnam; 1961.

Cyrinx, R. J.: "Captain Hall and the So-Called Survivors of the Franklin Expedition." *Polar Record,* July 1944.

———: *Sir John Franklin's Last Arctic Expedition.* London: Methuen & Co.; 1939.

Davis, C. H.: *Narrative of the North Polar Expedition, U.S. Ship Polaris, Captain Charles Francis Hall Commanding.* Washington, D.C.: Government Printing Office; 1876.

Ferguson, Eugene: *John Ericsson and the Age of the Caloric.* Washington, D.C.: Smithsonian Institution, Bulletin #228; 1961.

Greely, A. W.: *Three Years of Arctic Service.* 2 vols. New York, 1886.

Harlow, Alvin F.: *The Serene Cincinnatians.* New York: E. P. Dutton & Co.; 1950.

Hayes, I. I.: *The Open Polar Sea.* New York: Hurd & Houghton; 1867.

———: *An Arctic Boat Journey.* Boston, 1860.

Kane, Elisha Kent: *Arctic Explorations in the Years 1853, '54, '55.* 2 vols. Philadelphia: Childs & Peterson; 1856.

———: *The United States Grinnell Expedition in Search of Sir John Franklin.* Philadelphia: Childs & Peterson; 1856.

Kirwan, L. P.: *The White Road.* London: Hollis & Carter; 1959.

Markham, A. H.: *A Whaling Cruise to Baffin's Bay and the Gulf of Boothia.* London: Sampson Low, Marston, Low and Searle; 1874.

McClintock, Francis Leopold: *The Voyage of the "Fox" in the Arctic Seas: A Narrative of the Discovery of the Fate of Sir John Franklin and His Companions.* London: John Murray; 1869.

Mirsky, Jeannette: *Elisha Kent Kane and the Seafaring Frontier.* Boston: Little, Brown and Co.; 1954.

Mowat, Farley: *Ordeal by Ice.* Boston: Atlantic Little Brown; 1960.

Nares, G. S.: *Narrative of a Voyage to the Polar Sea.* London: Sampson Low, Marston, Searle & Rivington; 1878.

Neatby, L. H.: *Conquest of the Last Frontier.* Athens, Ohio: Ohio University Press; 1966.

———: *In Quest of the Northwest Passage.* Toronto: Longmans, Green & Co.; 1958.

Nourse, J. E., ed.: *Narrative of the Second Arctic Expedition Commanded by Charles F. Hall.* Washington, D.C.: Government Printing Office; 1879.

Peary, R. E.: *The North Pole, Its Discovery in 1909* . . . New York, 1910.

———: *Nearest the Pole.* London, 1907.

Poncins, Gontran de: *Kabloona.* New York: Reynal & Hitchcock; 1941.

Rae, John (E. E. Rich, ed.): *John Rae's Correspondence with the Hudson's Bay Company on Arctic Exploration 1844–1855.* London: Hudson's Bay Record Society, XVI; 1953.

Rasmussen, Knud: *Greenland by the Polar Sea.* London: William Heinemann; 1921.

Ross, John: *Narrative of a Second Voyage in Search of a North-West Passage.* London, 1835.

Stefansson, Viljhalmur: *Unsolved Mysteries of the Arctic.* New York, 1939.

———, ed.: *The Three Voyages of Martin Frobisher.* 2 vols. London: Argonaut Press; 1938.

Todd, A. L.: *Abandoned.* New York: McGraw-Hill; 1961.

Victor, Paul-Emile: *Man and the Conquest of the Poles.* New York: Simon & Schuster; 1963.

Williams, Glyndwr: *The British Search for the Northwest Passage in the Eighteenth Century.* London: Longmans; 1962.

Wood, George B., and Bache, Franklin: *The Dispensatory of the United States.* 12th edition. Philadelphia: J. B. Lippincott & Co.; 1866.

Woodward, Frances J.: *Portrait of Jane.* London: Hodder and Stoughton; 1951.

Wright, Noel: *Quest for Franklin.* London: Heinemann; 1959.

index

about the author

Chauncey C. Loomis, Jr., was born in New York in *1930*. He studied at Phillips Exeter Academy, Princeton University (A.B., *1952*), Columbia University (A.M., *1956*), and again at Princeton (Ph.D., *1963*). He served in the U.S. Army in the Far East in *1953–4*, and taught English at the University of Vermont in *1956–8*. Since *1960* he has been a member of the Department of English at Dartmouth College, where he is an Associate Professor. He held a Smithsonian Postdoctoral Research Fellowship in *1967–8*, and has published scholarly articles on Thackeray, Mark Twain, Stephen Crane, and James Joyce. An enthusiastic photographer, he came to exploration by way of that hobby, and has been a member of three expeditions in the Peruvian Andes and five to the Arctic, the latter including one in *1969* during which an autopsy was performed upon Charles Francis Hall's body ninety-seven years after his death. His motion picture on the capture of wild musk ox on Nunivak Island in the Bering Sea appeared as a part of a CBS National Special Television show, Wild River, Wild Beasts.

a note on the type

The text of this book has been set on the Linotype in a type-face called "Baskerville." The face is a facsimile reproduction of types cast from molds made for John Baskerville (1706–75) from his designs. The punches for the revived Linotype Baskerville were cut under the supervision of the English printer George W. Jones. John Baskerville's original face was one of the forerunners of the type style known as "modern face" to printers—a "modern" of the period A.D. 1800.

Composed, printed & bound by
The Haddon Craftsmen, Inc. Scranton, Pennsylvania.
Typography and binding design by
Bonnie Spiegel